FRANÇOISE HÉRITIER

Anthropology's Ancestors

Edited by Aleksandar Bošković, University of Belgrade; Institute of Archaeology, Belgrade; Max Planck Institute for Social Anthropology, Halle/Saale

As anthropology developed across geographical, historical and social boundaries, it was always influenced by works of exceptional scholars who pushed research topics in new and original directions and who can be regarded as important ancestors of the discipline. The aim of this series is to offer introductions to these major figures, whose works constitute landmarks and are essential reading for students of anthropology, but who are also of interest for scholars in the humanities and social sciences more generally. In doing so, it offers important insights into some of the basic questions facing humanity.

Volume 3
Françoise Héritier
Gérald Gaillard

Volume 2
William Robertson Smith
Aleksandar Bošković

Volume 1
Margaret Mead
Paul Shankman

FRANÇOISE
HÉRITIER

• • •

Gérald Gaillard

Translated by Andrew Wilson

berghahn
NEW YORK • OXFORD
www.berghahnbooks.com

First published in 2022 by
Berghahn Books
www.berghahnbooks.com

Library of Congress Cataloging-in-Publication Data

Names: Gaillard, Gérald, author.
Title: Françoise Héritier / Gérald Gaillard ; translated by Andrew Wilson.
Description: First Edition. | New York ; Oxford : Berghahn Books, 2022. |
    Series: Anthropology's ancestors; 3 | Includes bibliographical
    references and index. |
Identifiers: LCCN 2021042042 (print) | LCCN 2021042043 (ebook) | ISBN
    9781800733329 (Hardback) | ISBN 9781800733343 (Paperback) | ISBN
    9781800733336 (eBook)
Subjects: LCSH: Héritier, Françoise. | Women anthropologists--France--Biography. |
    Anthropologists--France--Biography. | Feminists--France--Biography. |
    Anthropology. | Ethnology. | Kinship. | Sex role.
Classification: LCC GN21.H46 G35 2022 (print) | LCC GN21.H46 (ebook) |
    DDC 301.092 [B]--dc23/eng/20211201
LC record available at https://lccn.loc.gov/2021042042
LC ebook record available at https://lccn.loc.gov/2021042043

British Library Cataloguing in Publication Data

A catalogue record for this book is available from the British Library

ISBN 978-1-80073-332-9 hardback
ISBN 978-1-80073-334-3 paperback
ISBN 978-1-80073-333-6 ebook

To my sister, Dominique

CONTENTS

•   •   •

FOREWORD
THE GAZE OF FRANÇOISE HÉRITIER
Michelle Perrot

● ● ●

Françoise Héritierwas a great scholar, and this book payshomage to her work. However, her influence reaches far beyond her field. She was an 'anthropologist of the city', the public place, as one of the titles of her seminars at the Collège de France suggested.[1] It is this civic role that I wish to evoke.

I came to know her at the National Council for HIV, which she chaired from 1989 to 1994 and to which I was appointed by the Prime Minister, Michel Rocard. Our meeting led to enduring companionship and unwavering friendship. She had been appointed by the president, François Mitterrand, in recognition of her professional competence, which she had demonstrated in her work for the High Council for Population; her knowledge of Africa (from where the disease spread); and her expertise in the 'anthropology of body', a branch of the discipline that she pioneered and that would be central to debates about procreation and filiation. Her theoretical concerns were also crucial to the understanding of pandemics, but we did not then realise that HIV/AIDS was a precursor and a warning of pandemics to come. She grasped the importance of conceptions of bodily 'humours' – blood, semen, milk – which seemed to play a role in the horrific spread of an epidemic of which we knew nothing, except that it resulted in an appalling mortality rate, particularly among young men. The 'scandal' of contaminated blood had shaken French public opinion and led directly to the establishment of the Council. It had twenty-two members: doctors; members of civil society, like Daniel Defert, founder of France's first AIDS advocacy group, AIDES; and representatives of Catholicism, Protestantism, Judaism and Islam, since sexuality still posed moral issues at the time. After she completed her term as president of the Council, Françoise Héritier asked to remain a member in order to represent a secular perspective. Although she was struggling with an ailment that she had contracted in Africa, which required regular hospitalisation, she was a remarkable chair, concerned to share her insights into the illness and to anchor – necessary – interventions within a framework that would be respectful of human rights.

Guided by Françoise Héritier, the Council was centrally concerned with four issues: insurance, prisons, addiction and the ethics of communication. Since they considered HIV a lethal illness, insurers obstinately refused to give coverage to 'suspects', who they tried to exclude by asking loaded questions, sometimes going so far as to demand tests. The Council strongly opposed what was considered invasions of privacy and insisted that the right to confidentiality should also apply in prisons. The medical care of inmates was managed by the prison administration, in poor conditions and without respect for confidentiality. On files that were widely accessible, HIV-positive inmates were identified by coloured dots! On the advice of the Council, responsibility for the health of inmates was transferred from the Ministry of the Interior to the Ministry of Health: a notable reform. Françoise Héritier herself played a major part, requesting a special audience with the President.

In the course of visits and enquiries in prisons, she came to realise the extent to which infections were transmitted through the sharing of needles. The Council addressed these risks, encouraging the provision of substitute drugs and instituting needle exchange schemes, modelled on the Dutch approach. 'The authorities' priority must be prevention and the protection of public health and not the repression of simple drug use' (1994). Later, the possibility of decriminalisation began to be considered.

The issue of media representations was particularly sensitive. 'How are we to evaluate the effects of a communication?' the chair would demand. She generally preferred case by case responses to a particularly abusive advertisement campaign, or serious longer-term studies, focused, for example, on 'the treatment of HIV in the popular press', or 'the media's handling of the "scandal" of contaminated blood'. She detested hasty press releases and clamorous interventions. She later summed up her views on the 'Evolution of perceptions and representations of HIV', drawing attention to refinements of language, emphasising the weight of words. A scientific approach was for her the indispensable foundation for policy.

At their meetings, the Council heard testimony from activists, experts or witnesses, and debated policy proposals. The sessions became multidisciplinary seminars, though always grounded in anthropology. They were unforgettable for participants in those stressful times, which would fortunately come to an end with the discovery of proteases inhibitors and triple therapies. The question then became how to allocate these new drugs, given initial shortages. The proposal that lots should be drawn at random, a measure recommended by the Council following a proposal by its chair, created a scandal. Françoise Héritier regarded this only as a temporary measure, thankfully soon rendered unnecessary by increased production. However, she continued to draw attention to the inequality of access to treatment, notably in Africa, and especially for women. Unable to enforce condom use, many women would become infected and yet were excluded from hospitals: 'places for men.' 'African women are the great forgotten of the HIV story.'

Françoise Héritier's other major policy concern had to do with differences between the sexes.[2] She herself had to rebel against a family, much loved but conventional, to study what she wished: initially 'history-geography', then ethnology, the structural ethnology of Claude Lévi-Strauss. But she had to battle to be sent to Africa to do fieldwork, which was then considered inappropriate for a young woman. Later, as the second woman elected to a chair at the Collège de France (following Jacqueline de Romilly),[3] she sensed the invisibility that Simone Veil evoked when in 1974 she presented to a National Assembly, 'almost exclusively composed of men', a draft bill on the voluntary interruption of pregnancy.

Nothing was easy for women of that generation, in practice or in thought. However, Françoise Héritier did not confront gender hierarchy head-on. She was not a follower of Simone de Beauvoir, repudiating her famous saying, 'one is not born a woman; one becomes one'. In a way, she was not a 'feminist', at least not during the 1970s. (At the time of the 'events' of 1968, she was engaged in fieldwork in Upper Volta.) She did things differently, and better. She gave feminism an intellectual dimension that it had lacked, namely an understanding of male domination, often denounced but barely analysed. This is the subject of *Masculin/ Féminin, la somme indépassable*, published in two volumes, in 1996 and 2002.

In the first volume, *La pensée de la différence*, she shows how the 'differential valence of genders', her great discovery,[4]establishes a universal hierarchy, the origin of which is lost in the mists of time. Everywhere and always, men have power over women. Lévi-Strauss situated this fundamental structure in kinship systems – 'exchange of goods, exchange of women' – but treated it as a 'self-evident fact' that did not warrant further investigation. Françoise Héritier identified it as a particular feature of Western thought (evident in Greek philosophy). She relates it to a male desire to appropriate for themselves the bodies of women, which are capable of generating both sameness (other women) and difference (men).

In the second volume, *Dissoudre la hiérarchie*, she discusses the consequences of women's access to birth control, which she describes as 'a true evolution' in gender relations. Published six years after volume one, this text marks a notable evolution in her thought ('thought in motion' was the title she gave to her autobiography). Convinced of the determinism of 'invariants', so central to the structuralist paradigm, she was not especially sensitive to change, an obsession of historians. In order to overcome the 'dominating archaic model', female action was insufficient, notwithstanding the crucial importance of the contraceptive revolution. All women, of all backgrounds, had to benefit from access to contraception. And ancient conceptions, stubborn 'roadblocks to thinking', had to be challenged. Such a 'Copernican revolution' would take a long time and encounter predictable reversals. 'History exists, changes do happen, but it should not be doubted that advances may be reversed.' She nevertheless recognised that one of those roadblocks was giving way. With control of contraception, women achieved a new sense of self. In the last years of her life, she was increasingly attentive to the demands of feminists, who, conscious of the strength of her analyses, frequently urged her to intervene. She influenced the programme of the Socialist Party, which she supported, in the direction of sexual equality. She expressed sympathy for the 'Neither whore nor submissive' movement; defended parity of treatment for men and women, although without illusions; and campaigned against the rapes committed in the former Yugoslavia, pointing, as an anthropologist, to its ethnic character. Shortly before her death, the *#MeToo* movement made her happy. It was a just and effective revolt: 'shame switched sides.'

To change the gender hierarchy requires nothing less than 'changing our entire understanding of the world'. Françoise Héritier contributed more than anyone to this project.

Michelle Perrot
Historian, Professor Emerita, University of Paris-Diderot
(translated by Adam Gaillard-Starzmann)

NOTES

1. Françoise Héritier, *Une pensée en mouvement*, Paris, Odile Jacob, 2009, ch.4, L'anthropologue dans la Cité.
2. There were many others: the Council for Francophonie, the UN's scientific council, the National Council for Ethics, and others that I am not introducing here, limiting myself to what I know.
3. And the arrival of Nicole Le Douarin, a famous biologist and contender for the Nobel prize, who contributed to the discovery of DNA.
4. To which she devotes an important chapter in *Une pensée en mouvement*, pp. 85–171.

PREFACE

●　　●　　●

This book follows Françoise Héritier in both the national context and the more confined world of the emerging discipline of
anthropology. Initially, her principal concern – the world of research and more particularly that of an Africanist – was gradually
eclipsed as national concerns became increasingly important. My
starting point were circumstances in which Héritier found herself in the early stages of her career, and later when her situation
changed with her election to a Chair in the Collège de France.
My goal is to give context to her words. To that end, I drew on all
the interviews (notably those with Caroline Broué, 2006a). *Retour aux sources* (2010a) also provides some basics, *Une pensée en
mouvement* (2009d) looks back at the central themes of her work,
and in 'Un parcours de vie et de recherche' (2009a and 2010h)
she gives the most comprehensive account of her life and work.
The same examples and references crop up again and again, so I
decided to weave together my text by referring to the material
without burdening the reader with copious references, indicat-
ing only those where an event or statement occurs for the first
and only time.

I also present an outline of the ethnography of Samo society, as some readers will be unfamiliar with African studies.
The central section of the book deals with Héritier's theoretical
contribution and political commitments. To give a clear and un-
complicated account of an intellect grappling with some of the
theoretical questions specific to a particular discipline was one of
the main aims of the book. It will be for readers to judge whether
or not I have succeeded. Finally, it is not for having solved the
'Crow-Omaha problem' that Françoise Héritier is known to the
wider public or has educational establishments named after her;

rather it is for her sustained political commitment, which had to be properly evaluated.

It seemed to me that it was my duty, as a historian of the discipline, to scrupulously report the list of professors or the number of researchers in anthropology, as well as other sometimes very minor facts.

And I thank my friends without whom it would be difficult to live. This book was inspired by Petr Skalník, who asked me to write an obituary of Héritier for the journal *Modern Africa*. Following that, Aleksandar Boskovic asked me to write the present volume for this series.

The translation of the French manuscript was made possible by grants from the MESHS in 2018 and funding for the translation from the University of Lille, which were generously supplemented by a contribution from the CNRS research institute Centre lillois d'études et de recherches sociologiques et économiques. The translation was done by Andrew Wilson, whom I thank.

CHAPTER 1

THE YOUNG WOMAN AND THE YOUNG PEOPLE IN HER CIRCLE

●　●　●

Françoise Héritier was born on 15 November 1933 in Veauche, near Lyon. Her grandparents were farmers deeply rooted in the age-old France of Burgundy and the Auvergne. Her father, who had left high school with the *baccalauréat*, worked for the Paris-Lyon-Mediterranean railway company and transferred to the SNCF when it was founded in 1938. Her mother, who held the *certificate d'études*, which was awarded at the end of elementary primary education, worked for the postal service and later became a postmistress. Héritier was exaggerating when she described her parents as 'minor civil servants': only 7% of any one age cohort obtained the *baccalauréat* at that time, and very few women worked outside the home. She further declared them to be: 'Catholic and authoritarian' with 'no intellectual curiosity whatsoever'. This was not unusual in this region, where small farmers, clergy and mining companies colluded against the teachers in the secular state school system and the manual workers' federations with their leanings towards anarchism. There were three children in the family: an older brother, a younger sister and Françoise in the middle. She remembered that her father used to hum the antimilitarist song 'Gloire au 17ème', suggesting that, like Claude Lévi-Strauss (1908–2009), he was a pacifist. On 3 September 1939, England and France declared war on

Germany. The Wehrmacht invaded Northern Europe and then, in May 1940, the Western offensive began. The French army was put to rout, Paris was declared an open city and Marshall Pétain signed an armistice on 22 June. Françoise's father was posted to Saint-Étienne; her grandmother, mother and the children travelled from Montargis to join him, a distance of 350 kilometres. Some Italian aeroplanes 'fired on the refugees', and Françoise, only seven years old, 'caught a glimpse of death' (Héritier 2017a). The demarcation line having come into force on 25 June, Germans left the region, economic activity resumed, and Françoise was enrolled in a convent school. 'Our parents wanted their two daughters to have the same opportunities as their boy ... so we all went on to higher education. My sister trained as a dentist, my brother went to one of the elite *grandes écoles* and I went to university' (Héritier 2009a, 2010g). This upward social mobility across three generations (small farmer, 'minor' civil servant, academic) reflected a broad trend.

Following the Allies' invasion of Africa, Germans entered the southern zone on 11 November 1942, and the town was the centre of operations for the steel levy for the German army. Françoise's parents did not openly declare their beliefs apart from the day when Françoise came home with some cakes a soldier had given her. 'You're not to accept anything from our enemies,' her father ordered. The children went to live with their grandparents. Françoise learnt to milk goats, to feed pigs and to yoke oxen. She also witnessed some barbaric customs: her female cousin served everyone their food and then had to eat her meal standing up while her husband remained seated. An Epinal print on the stairs revolted her. It was a chromolithograph depicting the good life: the woman was pictured alone bowling a hoop at the age of ten and then with her sweetheart, her husband, her children and her grandchildren, while the man, alone, successfully pursued his career. And to add insult to injury, her brother rode around the countryside on his bicycle while she and her sister knitted or peeled vegetables at their grandmothers' feet while chatting 'about the daughter of Martine's niece's son who married the third son of Gaston's sister to whom Martine is a cousin through André'. This gossiping was to help Héritier develop the mental gymnastics required for the anthropology of kinship. On 26 May 1944, American aircraft bombed the valley, destroying the military-industrial complex: 'each explosion shook all the walls of our school, including those in the cellar where we were sheltering, distraught' (Héritier 2006, 2017a). In 1946, the family reached Paris, and Françoise, aged thirteen, attended the public Lycée Jean Racine in the 8th arrondissement and then a preparatory class at the Lycée Fénelon in the 6th arrondissement. In 1953, she enrolled for the university degree in history and geography.

A number of students with communist leanings, who read the journal *Temps Modernes*, entered the philosophy section of the French national union of students at the Sorbonne, at the time the only university in Paris. Among them were Michel Cartry (1931–2008), the son of a Calvinist bourgeois family, and Alfred Adler (b.1934), a young Jewish man who had survived his family's murder; they had known each other since their days at the Lycée Condorcet. Cartry introduced Adler to Michel Izard (1931–2012), another Calvinist and the son of a famous lawyer. After failing the entrance examination for a *grande école*, Izard opted for philosophy and became friends with Félix Guattari (1930–1992), a card-carrying member of the Communist Party since the age of fifteen, who lured him into the Party. The group was joined by Lucien Sebag (1934–1965) and then Jeanne Favret-Saada (b.1934), who arrived from the Lycée Carnot in Tunis. Other members of the group included Hélène and Pierre Clastres (1934–1977), Philippe Girard, Marc Piault (1933–2020), Colette Benveniste (b.1933, soon to become Mme Piault) and then Olivier Herrenschmidt (b.1934), who had known M. Izard since their days at the Lycée Pasteur in Neuilly. It was as Joan Vincent described it '*a group of men and women with shared life experience*' (Vincent 1990: 9).

Neither a communist nor a philosopher, Françoise Héritier was outside the group and met 'the boys' at the library. A 'studious' young woman, she dreamed of being an Egyptologist and would have chosen to study for a degree in history, but being 'by nature insufficiently equipped intellectually to devote themselves specifically to one of the disciplines' young women were admitted only for a joint degree in history and geography. Sociology was taught for the 'moral and sociology' certificate, part of the philosophy degree, by the sociologist Georges Gurvitch (1894–1965) and Raymond Aron (1905–1983). Aron had just succeeded the Durkheim scholar Georges Davy (1883–1976), who had chaired the committee that examined C. Lévi-Strauss's PhD thesis. Having known Lenin and Trotsky, Gurvitch had taken refuge at the University of Strasbourg before taking up a post at the New School for Social Research in New York when the Germans occupied France. On his return to France, he obtained a post at the Sorbonne. Memories of his teaching varied. Daniel Defert (b.1937) spoke affectionately of him (Defert 2014), M. Piault[1] and Etienne Balibar (b.1942) said some fairly good things,[2] while M. Izard conjured up an image of 'the dreadful lead weight that he cast over sociology'.[3] Héritier attended the lectures given by Henri-Irénée Marrou (1904–1977), who held the chair of the History of Christianity and was to denounce the use of torture during the Algerian war), as well as those given by the communist geographer Jean Dresch (1905–1994), who was heavily involved in the anticolonial movement), by André Aymard (1900–1964), a specialist in the Hellenist period, and by Victor-Lucien Tapié (1900–1974), who was professor of modern history, although she did not mention these names until 2017 (Héritier 2017b: 109).

These young people were unfamiliar with the teaching of the Africanist Marcel Griaule (1898–1956), who died in February 1956. When André Leroi-Gourhan (1911–1986) succeeded him, they had already completed a degree made up of four certificates and, as philosophy students, had an obligation to obtain one from the Faculty of Sciences. The move by Paul Rivet (1876–1958) to add to the Institute of Ethnology's certificate in ethnological sciences a science faculty certificate was a stroke of genius (Gaillard 1989). While students were motivated by a great desire to depart (Adler 2014: 232), this certificate was said to be 'easy to obtain', according to Jacques Soustelle (1912–1990)[4] and to M. Piault[5] and J. Favret-Saada (Favret-Saada 2008). Holder of a diploma in advanced mathematics, M. Izard was exempt from this obligation and enrolled in November 1955 in the 'Ethnology and literature' course. O. Herrenschmidt was on the same course, and Françoise Héritier accompanied them. Talking 'of inequality', she reported that her parents 'kept a close watch on her' (Héritier 2009a). M. Izard, who was single, had a studio apartment, (where she joined him before she rented a room in the Rue Gay-Lussac (Héritier 2017b: 106; Dosse 1991: 177). It should be noted that on the occasion of dinner with friends it was she who arrived 'early' in order to get the meal ready for the 'guests' (Héritier 2017b: 104). She later wrote:

> Lévi-Strauss is a man of his time. He considers this a good distribution of tasks .... On this point, he has not been pushed intellectually to conduct the analysis as I have done. It might be said that this is because I'm a woman, but I think it's more reasonable to think that it's because I'm from a different generation. (Héritier 2008a: 10)

At the Institute, the trio met up with Claude François Baudez (1932–2013) and Françoise Flis (b.1935, soon Françoise Zonabend). Baudez enrolled in American studies, and Herrenschmidt studied Sanskrit and attended the seminars of Louis Dumont (1911–1998), Director of Studies since 1955. They all frequented the library in the Musée de l'Homme and were critical of the Institute. 'Mediocrity' was the word used by Izard.[6] Not having paid secretarial services at his disposal, Paul Rivet had enlisted his two sisters to help him; the young people nicknamed them 'the moth and cockroach' (Pairault 2001: 37).

The second doctors' plot against Stalin disturbed them, the Khrushchev report following Stalin's death crushed them, the kiss to the 'traitor' Tito (Yugoslav president Josip Broz Tito, 1892–1980) mortified them, and the bloody suppression of the Hungarian uprising in November 1956 did not go down well at all. Sebag, Izard, Adler, Cartry and Clastres left the Communist Party. Maurice Merleau-Ponty (1908–1961), invited by the philosophy section in 1955, spoke to them about a new way of thinking. After Marxism was rejected, the publication of *Tristes*

Tropiques (1955) came just at the right moment, after 'Des Indiens et leur ethnographe' (Levi-Strauss 1955: 1–50) had 'dazzled' them (Adler 2010: 485).

After a short stint as the cultural attaché to the French embassy in Washington, C. Lévi-Strauss had returned to Paris in February 1948. He was a Senior Research Fellow at the Centre national de la recherche scientifique (CNRS) and Assistant Deputy Director at the Musée de l'Homme when, in June 1948, he submitted the two theses required for his doctorate: 'The Family and Social Life of the Nambikwara Indians' and 'Elementary Structures of Kinship'. In December 1950, he succeeded Maurice Leenhardt (1878–1954) as the Director of Studies of the Religions of Non-Civilised Peoples[7] in the Religious Sciences section of the Ecole pratique des hautes études (EPHE).

The year M. Izard spent studying for the *Diplôme d'études supérieures*, which preceded the preparation for the *agrégation*, was a fairly easy one, and he took advantage of it to attend the seminars of Georges Balandier (1920–2016), who held a professorship in the Sociology of Black Africa from 1955 onwards, and with Herrenschmidt of C. Lévi-Strauss. Françoise Héritier accompanied the two young men. About Lévi-Strauss, she wrote: 'It was the revelation of my life. I discovered things that were totally alien to my field of perception. I was unaware of the nature of the phenomena he was talking about. I was unaware that they even existed. And then his way of speaking and explaining was so interesting.' And:

> The subjects he was addressing never failed not only to surprise me but also to disconcert me, such was the havoc they played with all my mental habits. The first year I attended his lectures, he was looking at the joking relations in Fiji that are established between brothers-in-law when one is the husband of the other's youngest sister, whereas the relationship is marred by respect and avoidance when one is the husband of the other's older sister. (Héritier 2011a: 149)

She described the professor: 'His was a voice one didn't forget. Once you'd heard it, you simply couldn't get it out of your mind. A low-pitched voice, slightly quavering, relatively neutral, almost silent' (Héritier 2009d), 'and his speech, taut as a bow, sparing in its use of effects, had the knack of always falling impeccably on its feet, despite the complex sentence construction' (Héritier 2010b: 19). Finally, she described his appearance: 'He was young, already austere in appearance behind his large spectacles. By way of a necktie he wore a knotted shoestring, and later he had a definite taste for Hollington clothes, corduroy jackets with a Nehru collar and lots of pockets.' 'Those were wonderful years. I was suffused with freedom, friendship and intellectual adventures' (Héritier 2017b: 111–13). She 'was crazy about West Coast jazz', listened to Miles Davis and 'strolled to Maspero's bookshop' (Héritier 2012a: 70).

Françoise Héritier and her friends went three or four times a week to the legendary picture palaces: le Champollion, le Studio Christine, le Mac Mahon and la Pagode and read *Les Cahiers du cinéma*. Their taste in films was different from that of the third generation of Africanists like G. Balandier or Jacques Lombard (1926–2017) (Gaillard 2018), and the list of films that Héritier mentioned as 'having left their mark on her', and which ranged from *Gone with the Wind* (1939) to *Out of Africa* (1985), included only Hollywood productions, with the exception of Truffaut's *Tirez sur le pianiste* (1960). In her interview for *Télérama* (Héritier 2009b), the only films she mentioned were American *films noirs*. Héritier admitted: 'I like the cinema but the cinema of a certain period and particularly American cinema, Westerns and war films' (Héritier 2017e). It is hardly surprising that she said she was still a fan of 'Singin' in the Rain' and 'Quo Vadis' having read, at age fourteen, the novel on which the latter film was based. In the field of literature, she was still mentioning Robert Graves (1895–1985) and *Jane Eyre* (1847), for which she repeated her passion, 'as opposed, for example' to the novels of Michel Houellebecq (b.1956). On two other occasions, she cited *The Woodlanders* (1887) by Thomas Hardy (1840–1928) and *Le sang noir* (1935) by Louis Guilloux (1899–1980), which she had read at the age of twenty and whose 1955 reprint made it one of the novels of her generation (Héritier 2017c: 9–13). To this list, let us add Simone de Beauvoir (1908–1986) and Jean-Paul Sartre (1905–1980) and note that most of the references stop at around the age of thirty, as if Héritier's tastes had remained more or less unchanged since her formative years.

C. Lévi-Strauss's seminars began with a 45-minutes lecture, followed by an hour devoted to presentations on fieldwork or texts suggested to students. It was in the absence of Herren-schmidt that Izard 'registered us both for two presentations on the "componential analysis of Floyd Lounsbury and Ward Goodenough"' (Herrenschmidt 2014: 227). It was America that attracted M. Izard. He had spoken to J. Soustelle, who despite being a member of parliament taught him before becoming Governor-General of Algeria in February 1955.[8] As in the previous year, Piault and Colette Benveniste (Mme Piault) left for Mexico, while M. Izard and Françoise Héritier (intending from that time on to study the Aztecs) (Héritier, 2017b: 120) attended the seminars of Guy Stresser-Péan (1913–2009), where they, with Baudez, were almost the only ones present – 'almost', since the mother of the Professor of the Religions of America attended every session. Baudez and Izard both obtained the Institute of Ethnology Certificate. In September of the same year, Baudez went to Costa Rica. Izard headed for Africa. Michel Leiris (1901–1990) and Aimé Césaire (1913–2008) introduced the continent from the perspective of the anticolonial struggle, and in academic terms Africa belonged to the successors of Griaule, to the Institut français d'Afrique noire and to the Office de recherche scientifique et technique d'Outre-mer (Orstom). Claude Tardits (1921–2007) and then Éric de Dampierre (1928–1998) spent time at Orstom, and Robert Jaulin (1928–1996) and Jean Pouil-lon (1916–2002) were welcomed to Chad by Griaule's disciple, Jean-Paul Lebeuf (1907–1994).

NOTES

1. Marc Piault, interview with the author, Paris, 22 May 1989.
2. Etienne Balibar, interview with the author, Paris, 20 September 1989.
3. Michel Izard, interview with the author, Paris, 3 February 1988.
4. Jacques Soustelle and Georgette Soustelle, interview with the author, Paris, 4 April 1989.
5. Marc Piault, interview with the author, Paris, 22 May 1989.
6. Michel Izard, interview with the author, Paris, 3 February 1988.
7. Later changed to Comparative Religions of Non-Literate Peoples.
8. Michel Izard, interview with the author, Paris, 3 February 1988.

CHAPTER 2

THE IZARDS' AFRICA
AND THE LABORATORY
FOR SOCIAL ANTHROPOLOGY

• • •

C. Lévi-Strauss introduced M. Izard to Georges-Henri Rivière (1897–1985), who was setting up the Khartoum museum. The application having been rejected, he offered him an alternative. The Institute of Applied Human Sciences at the University of Bordeaux, commissioned by the colonial administration, was looking for a geographer and an ethno-sociologist to assess a region to which people displaced by the construction of a dam were to be moved. M. Izard was to be the ethno-sociologist, and his first letter to Herrenschmidt, dated 22 July 1957, is striking: 'I've spent a week in the bush . . . the colonial town of Ouagadougou is depressing' and 'my colleagues all appalling . . . . One has to be really careful not to lapse, but to remain oneself in the midst of people who are horrifyingly stupid, vulgar and sceptical' (Herrenschmidt 2014: 228). Aged twenty-five, he should be forgiven: he had not yet experienced life outside the academy.

Françoise Héritier said that it was during his seminar that Lévi-Strauss informed his students of this opportunity. She applied for the post even though she was studying for a postgraduate degree in history, her first degree included only one geography certificate, and she knew nothing at all about demographics. Having not found anyone by August, the Bordeaux Institute hired her, and the Orstom geographer Jean Hurault (1917–2005) taught her how to carry out land surveys. In September, she discovered 'the intensity of the smell of the African earth, hot, humid and peppery' and was repeatedly to declare that she had only been recruited because no man had applied (Héritier 2017b: 131).

The researchers were based at the Centrifan in Ouagadougou, inaugurated by Guy Le Moal (1924–2010) in 1949. Offices and a library were accommodated in a colonial building behind which there was a park designed as a botanical garden. In the middle, there were four detached houses, one of which was for visitors. At the end of 1957, Jean Rouch (1917–2004) came to film the funeral ceremonies of the Moro-Naba king of the Mossi ethnic group and the enthronement of his successor. Le Moal and Rouch were members of the third generation of French Africanists, while the Izard-Héritiers belonged to the fourth. They were invited to dinner, and Rouch was later to recall a young man 'swamping him with Lévi-Strauss'.[1] Rouch was looking for someone to do research on migration, and M. Izard informed Piault, who had seen *Les maîtres-fous* (1953). This was an extraordinary ethnographic film (by J. Rouch) that had been screened at the premier of Bergman's *The Seventh Seal*. Once they had been recruited, Piault and his wife Colette supervised teams counting lorries and met migrants across an area from Ghana to Niger.

Working symbiotically, the Izard-Héritiers returned to France in June 1958. She remarked: 'I remember getting married in 1958 in Touganin in the presence of a commander of a *cercle*' (Héritier 2017b: 84).[2] She had read *The Second Sex* (1949): 'freedom for women, freedom of choice, which it had never been possible to exercise' (Héritier 2009b) and added: 'at the same time, my sister got married in white. That was exactly what I didn't want' (Faure and Daumas 2017). The couple set up home in Antony, a Paris suburb, and spent the summer writing two reports: 'Human Aspects of the Hydro-agriculture Scheme in the Sourou Valley' (Héritier as Izard 1958a) and 'Bouna: A Case Study of a Pana Village in the Sourou Valley in Upper Volta' (1958b). A third report: 'The Mossi of the Yatenga: A Study of Economic and Social Life' (1959a) was mimeographed again in 1960 and 1961. It was under the heading of 'demography' that they were to be found

collaborating again in *l'Année sociologique*, with four reviews by
Michel and three pages by Françoise, about a *Handbook of De-
mographic Research in Underdeveloped Countries* (1959). Authors
of the chapter on 'Ethno-demographic Surveys' (Héritier 1968a)
in *Ethnologie générale*, then an essential book (J. Poirier editor),
the Izard-Héritiers were categorised as 'ethno-demographers';
an approach that C. Lévi-Strauss described as the future of the
discipline (Lévi-Strauss 1958: 303–53).

The referendum of 28 September 1958 led to the constitution
of the French Fifth Republic. The peoples of the French Union
approved it, with the exception of Guinea. An electoral college
elected Charles de Gaulle (1890–1970) to the presidency of both
the French Republic and the French Community, and elections
based on direct universal suffrage were to be held in 1965. Since
the Algerian National Liberation Front had rejected the 'peace
of the brave', the war dragged on for another four years. M.
Piault noted: 'Our debates on the call-up were dramatic. . . . and
it's something none of us has ever spoken about.'[3] He was conscripted at the end of 1958 and sent to Algeria after three months.
M. Izard was conscripted on 1 November 1958. He served 27
months and 27 days, first in Germany and then with the *batterie
géographique* in Oran. Soon, O. Herrenschmidt was following.
On 14 October 1960, Izard wrote to Herrenschmidt: 'I intend to
devote myself as soon as possible to studies in theoretical social
anthropology and epistemology' (Herrenschmidt 2014: 225).

Françoise Héritier attended Lévi-Strauss's seminar on 'the ritual hunting of eagles'. The second session took the form of presentations by students. Herrenschmidt presented a study of the
mythology of the Gond people of India and Héritier her research
in Upper Volta. This was her first presentation: 'What Lévi-
Strauss liked was the seminars . . . . He had the ability to bring
into the open questions that the presenters themselves had been
unable to formulate' (Héritier 2006). Having been awarded the
certificate of the Institut d'ethnologie in June 1958, she applied
for a position with the CNRS. 'I went to see him [Lévi-Strauss].
He started to list the members of the CNRS committee that I had
to meet. I didn't know anybody.' So she waited but was starting

to enter the profession. On 10 October 1958, she was elected a member of the Société des Africanistes;she was proposed by Raoul Hartweg, teaching the Institute's physical anthropology course, and Germaine Dieterlen (1903–1999), who had been appointed *Directeur d'études* of the Religions of Black Africa at the EPHE in 1956 and supervised the PhD students of Griaule.

The accounts given by Françoise Héritier make no mention of the Algerian War, Marxism and of G. Balandier. Nevertheless, she was sitting in on his lectures while becoming a contract researcher at the Institut national d'études démographiques.

Among those presenting at Lévi-Strauss's seminar series was Clemens Heller (1917–2002), who was in charge of awarding Rockefeller Foundation grants. Lévi-Strauss had a plan to set up a centre for comparative ethnology that would oversee the regional ethnographic centres, while Heller was developing an area studies programme with Fernand Braudel (1902–1985), chair of the economic and social sciences section at the EPHE. From this emerged the Centre for African Studies (The Centre d'études africaines), where Denise Paulme (1909–1999), Paul Mercier (1922–1976), Gilles Sautter (1920–1998) and Ariane Deluz (1931–2010) joined G. Balandier. In 1957, the publication of *Ambiguous Africa* by Balandier, the third title in the *Terre Humaine* series, was a major event (Gaillard 2017). Since 1952, G. Balandier had been director of an international research department on the social implications of technical progress, an offshoot of UNESCO's International Social Science Council, of which Lévi-Strauss was the secretary-general. Balandier employed Claude Meillassoux (1925–2005) to write summaries of articles and other documents in English. There were a number of black African deputies in the French Parliament, among them Félix Houphouët-Boigny (1905–1993). His country, Ivory Coast, was on the way to becoming the world's leading producer of coffee and cocoa. In 1958, Balandier sent Meillassoux and Deluz to investigate the economic and social consequences of this, and Françoise Héritier temporarily took over Deluz's position as 'technician-researcher'.

Lévi-Strauss *Anthropologie structurale* was published in February 1958 and, at the Collège de France, M. Merleau-Ponty obtained agreement for the establishment of a Chair in social anthropology to which Lévi-Strauss was elected and then appointed on 29 June 1959.

The decree of 19 April 1958 shook the education world by introducing a doctorate situated between the first postgraduate degree (*diplôme d'études supérieures*, the equivalent of a master's today) and the *doctorat d'État*, thereby constituting a third level of higher education around which teaching was to be organised. The Centre d'études africaines launched a course entitled 'Introduction to Africanism', in which Meillassoux lectured on 'socio-economic systems' while Balandier devoted his lectures to an examination of African societies in which political authority was centralised (1959–1962), part of a plan to produce the French equivalent of *African Political Systems* (E.E. Evans-Pritchard and M. Fortes 1940). Among those attending these lectures were Izard and Cartry.

However, we have to go back to 1950. In that year, the CNRS allocated the French Archaeological Institute in Beirut funds for the creation of a mecanographic file. Its designer, Jean-Claude Gardin (1925–2013), attended Lévi-Strauss's seminars, where he presented a paper on 'the notion of model in archaeological documentation' (Gardin 1955). At the same time, describing his method for interpreting myths, Lévi-Strauss declared that it was necessary to make use of mecanographics. In December 1957, Gardin's mission for Archaeological Documentation became the CNRS Mecanographic Centre. The Centre then embarked on a semantic analysis of the Quran and an interpretation of Zuni mythology. The analysis of the Quran gave rise to an inventory of the material culture, institutions, concepts and entities encountered, but while Gardin was to write later that 'under no circumstances [should this work be taken] for scientific knowledge' (Gardin 1974: 75), it was actually as early as 1963 that the file was described as a simple 'data collection machine' because of concerns about semantic leaps (Allard 1963: 7). This 'machine' was based on the principle of a polarity introduced into syntactic agreements between concepts that are first mentioned singly and then coupled together. Thus we have: 'god assisting men' and, conversely, 'men aiding the divinity'. The first is coded positively, the second negatively (remaining a potentiality). This is in fact the principles developed by Lévi-Strauss, who worked for a whole year with Gardin on the interpretation of Zuni myths. Furthermore, 'the years 1959–1962 were largely devoted [in the seminar] to discussing the use of analytical codes and punch cards' (Lévi-Strauss 1973a: 79).

The earliest of the CNRS *Reports* simply mentioned 'groups' directed by 'a supervisor', since the organisation was originally conceived as a means of putting PhD students on a salary and placing them under the supervision of a professor. Ethnology was confined to the group led by Dieterlen, although the 1959 report on the current state of research in France indicated that the CNRS had on its books 11 researchers in physical anthropology, 23 in prehistory and 63 in ethnology. On 5 January 1960, Lévi-Strauss gave his inaugural lecture and the Laboratory for Social Anthropology (LAS), which came under the authority of the Collège de France, moved into the former bathroom of Emile Guimet (1836–1918), who had established the eponymous museum and bequeathed his residence to the religious sciences section at the EPHE.

It was on her return to Ivory Coast that Deluz sent a report (1959) to Heller in which she called for 'the use of M. Gardin's methods for collecting scientific information, under the latter's exclusive supervision', before leaving her post for the CNRS. After Lévi-Strauss's recommendation, Françoise Héritier succeeded her in September 1960, and it was under the aegis of Gardin that she was given the task of compiling a punched card file of African ethnographic documents, around a thousand items in all. Herrenschmidt cites a letter from M. Izard dated 14 October 1960, in which he mentions this work with enthusiasm (2014: 224).

Thus Balandier's Centre for Africanist Documentation was reduced to a library at a time when the EPHE yearbook listed sixty-one students as registered for his seminar (1960–1961). He was also teaching at the National Foundation for Political Sciences and at the Ecole normale supérieure, where he recruited

Pierre (1932–1974) and Mona Etienne, Marc Augé (b.1935) and
Emmanuel Terray (b.1935). It was *The Elementary Structures
of Kinship*, 'loaned' from his pal Alain Badiou (b.1937), that attracted Terray to the discipline. However, Badiou and Terray
were above all political animals who joined the adventure of the
Unified Socialist Party (PSU), founded in April 1960. In that year
of Patrice Lumumba's death, Terray had opted for dynamism
rather than structuralism. Balandier appointed him at the Sciences Po research centre. Among the newcomers registered to
attend Balandier's lectures were Pierre Smith (1939–2001) and
A. Adler. The former, from Belgium, was abandoning psychol-
ogy in favour of anthropology, while the latter was teaching in
a lycée and in May and June 1961 did a placement at Gardin's
centre, which was expanding following the agreement obtained
by Gaston Berger (director general of higher education) that the
copy of the *Human Relations Area Files* that the American government was making available to Europe should be handed over
to the 6th section of the EPHE. Established by George Murdock
(1897–1985) at Yale University in 1937, this was the codified com-
pilation of data contained on 1,300,000 cards pertaining to 170
populations, to which new ones were being added. The copy was
entrusted by the EPHE to the burgeoning LAS, which was also
allocated two new members of staff for what was called the Documentary Centre for Comparative Ethnology. Françoise Héritier
went to the USA in 1961 for training in how to process the files.
On her return, the Centre for Documentary Analysis and Research on Black Africa (CARDAN) was established, of which she
was appointed director (1962). Herrenschmidt was appointed to
the position of senior researcher (1962). For his part, M. Izard,
after the end of his military service, joined the multidisciplinary
study of the isolated Breton village of Plozévet, which was the
major French social science research project of the early 1960s.

In 1958, the Gaullists took up the idea that there was a need for
research planning and established an inter-ministerial committee
on scientific research. This marked the beginning of a period that
has been described as a 'golden age' of scientific research; between the 1959 financial year and that of 1962, the CNRS budget

doubled. In 1959, this committee proposed ten priority research themes. Robert Gessain (1907–1986), the new assistant director of the Musée de l'Homme, wanted research on 'human adaptation' and proposed a multidisciplinary study of three isolated populations: Ammassalik (Greenland), Kédougou (Senegal) and Plozévet-Goulien in Bretagne. Since demography was for him the bridging discipline between biology and the social sciences, he took the decision to base the entire edifice on the quantitative foundations laid down by demography and the rates of intermarriage. Thus Lévi-Strauss signed a contract in the name of LAS for Georges Kutukdjian and M. Izard, who submitted a report on the marriages in 1963. At the same time, Françoise Héritier was directing CARDAN and dealing with Africanist documentation. Consequently, she managed to escape the mythical undertaking of analysing myths, directed by C. Lévi-Strauss.

Having initially espoused reflection theory, Lévi-Strauss argued that, since they were 'free to abandon themselves to spontaneous creativity', the structure of myths was the mediating factor that would reveal the structure of the cortex. After a few sessions given over to an examination of Sartre's *Critique of Dialectical Reason*, he dedicated his lectures between 1962 and 1971 to the enterprise. The research pointed to major themes of American mythology and, more specifically, the representations of the transition from nature to culture; the meta-theoretical framework that Lévi-Strauss put forward in justification of his undertaking then gradually became the very subject of the whole project. The Documentary Centre for Comparative Ethnology was very quickly pressed into assisting with the enterprise, and the funds managed by Heller were used to set up, within the LAS and in conjunction with the CNRS Centre for Automatic Analysis, a research group engaged in the semantic analysis of the oral literature directed by L. Sebag. He had moved from the Communist Party to the teaching of Jacques Lacan (1901–1981) and then to Lévi-Strauss. In an unedited foreword to *L'invention du monde chez les Indiens pueblos*, the latter writes that 'the studies by Gardin and Lévi-Strauss will be the subjects of future publications', while a letter in the archives of the 6th section mentions the imminent publication of three books: *Totemism Today* (C. Lévi-Strauss), *Les exercices d'analyse mythologique* and *L'Analyse structurale de la mythologie des indiens Zuni du Nouveau Mexique* by C. Lévi-Strauss and J.-C. Gardin. And yet Gardin was declaring that the social sciences were only humanities, an opinion with which Lévi-Strauss did not agree. In 1961, 'the permanent staff' of the LAS increased in number from six to nine, including M. Izard; the permanent staff was supplemented by temporary employees paid by the Ford Foundation.

NOTES

1. J. Rouch, interview with the author, Paris, 15, 18, 29 April and 7, 14 May 1987.
2. A *cercle* (circle) was the smallest unit of political administration in French colonial Africa.
3. Marc Piault, interview with the author, Paris, 22 May 1989.

CHAPTER 3

KINSHIP AND SAMO ETHNOGRAPHY

●　●　●

During his military service, Michel Izard had 'decided to do absolutely nothing other than ethnology'. However, he further explained that 'if everything goes as I would wish it to, Africa will sooner or later be reduced to a source of work that pays the rent' (Herrenschmidt 2014). Thus the young man essentially remained more of a philosopher than an Africanist but still managed to produce eleven reviews of books for the demography and human geography columns for journals *L'Année sociologique*, *L'Homme* and *Etudes rurales*. Demobilised in February 1961, he researched marriage in Plozévet under the terms of a contract between Lévi-Strauss's institute and the Directorate-General of Scientific and Technical Research. When that contract came to an end, he was recruited as 'chef de travaux' (senior technician) by the 6th section of the Ecole Pratique des Hautes Etudes, where Françoise Izard-Héritier was still director of CARDAN. Along with their review of *Tribes without Rulers* for *L'Homme*, the young man wrote 'Tradition historique des villages du Yatenga' (Paris, LAS, roneo, 1961). The Yatenga region of Upper Volta (subsequently, Burkina Faso), far from being only 'a source of work that pays the rent', was to keep him occupied for more than a quarter of a century. Working together, the couple produced a *General Bibliography of the Mossi* (1962) and in October 1963 returned for six months to the newly independent Upper Volta. Having assumed the presidency on 5 August 1960, Maurice Yaméogo (1921–1993) refused to enter into any of the military agreements proposed by France but did accept technical assistance and signed an agreement with the CNRS in 1961.

M. Izard was appointed research assistant at the CNRS from 1 October 1963. For her part, Françoise Héritier had the status of research technician seconded by the EPHE to the CNRS Africanist team (the Rcp.11) led by G. Dieterlen while at the same time being registered as a PhD student under the supervision of D. Paulme. Her PhD thesis was never to be submitted, but she was to write Paulme's obituary (Héritier 1999g), and the preface to the posthumously published *Cendrillon en Afrique* (Héritier 2007a). D. Paulme was to be one of the four Africanists to whom her *Retour aux sources* (Héritier 2010a) is dedicated. She wrote that she had been 'a very close friend of hers, particularly after the death of her husband', the ethnomusicologist André Schaeffner (1895–1980). They were friends, meaning they shared a 'passion for the cinema, walks and good wine' but 'little in the way of scholarly conversation'. And indeed: 'Kinship and marriage among the Matya-speaking Samo people', the title of Héritier's PhD thesis, was a long way from the functionalism of Paulme. Héritier relates: 'When [in 1957] we were travelling across the region . . . , I had become aware of something strange in their kin naming system' (Héritier 2000a: 10) and

> I did not know that there actually existed a kinship system that differed in structure from our own. . . . Neither the certificate in ethnography nor Claude Lévi-Strauss's seminar had had much to do with kinship. So what I'm saying is that I was absolutely bewildered by what, to me, was an utterly absurd order of terminology that I had noted firstly among the Mossi and then among the Samo. And I was always coming across these same 'absurdities'. (Héritier 2006)

And indeed, one of their 1958 reports includes sixteen 'Pana kinship' terms, classified simply as 'descriptive and classificatory terminology', while the 1959 report excludes any typology of Mossi kinship.

Héritier writes: 'My first mission was given over to a general ethnographic study of the society, about which there was virtually nothing in writing, apart from Tauxier' (a colonial administrator). Having settled in two successive waves of Mandé migration between the fifteenth and sixteenth centuries, the 120,000 Samo people remained a segmentary lineage society, despite a number of attempts at establishing political federations. Once a lineage reached a certain size, it divided, and the original community was gradually forgotten. Given the name Samo by neighbouring groups, they were made up of Maya, Maka and Matyr peoples, to whom Héritier attached herself and who were themselves divided into three mutually unintelligible dialect groups. Their clay brick houses were rectangular in shape and had flat roofs that served as drying platforms for crops. A group of dwellings linked by a defensive wall formed a concession. Several concessions constituted the patrilineage quarter headed by an elder, in which all the men bore the same 'praise name'. These quarters were divided into two moieties adjoining a wide empty square in which the market and traditional combats were held (Héritier 2010a: 80). The actors reasoned that two camps were necessary for a combat.

> I told him [Lévi-Strauss] of my astonishment at having found a society in which each village was divided into two moieties: the earth moiety and the rain moiety. Lévi-Strauss had theorized about moiety societies, and I asked him if he thought that this could be the same type of organization .... His response in essence was: 'My dear Françoise, what it is important to do in the field is not to try to find what you've been taught or what you may have read about but rather to let yourself be carried away by what unfolds before your eyes'. (Héritier 2008a)

Few ethnographers have described the conditions under which they carried out their field work; Héritier is one of the few to have done so:

The times required almost complete immersion, which was impossible to achieve. Water filters, mosquito nets, folding beds, oil lamps, portable stoves . . . . And even though I wanted to live as they did and eat like them, I always set up an enclosed space shut in by a fence of plaited straw . . . I always had at least some instant coffee, some rusks and jam for breakfast. I certainly couldn't stomach cold millet porridge. And I could leave whenever I wanted, that was obvious. (Héritier 2010a: 16)

She was no longer the young woman whose parents had feared for her safety in Africa; she now knew that all the viable space was generally occupied in sub-Saharan Africa. She asked for a piece of land, and the young people's association built a group of two houses separated by a shed. She was doubtless entrusted to the care of a young girl who would do her washing, fetch her water, do the housework and cook her meals; of all this, however, readers were to be told nothing. What we do know is that the inhabitants accepted her even during the performance of rituals that women did not attend, since her knowledge of the genealogies dispelled any misgivings. She was to declare herself 'captivated by the land', and when a journalist asked her 'what is the most beautiful light in the world?' her answer was: 'the morning light on the African bush' (Héritier 2017e). And the most moving moment? 'That was when I was cleaning a little girl's leg that was crawling with maggots.' Emphasising the patient's stoicism, she used the anecdote on several occasions to illustrate people's resignation, but here she was also talking about the ethnologist's status as nurse, which opened doors. On two occasions, children whose mothers had died in childbirth were entrusted to her, since no woman was willing to breastfeed them for fear of the witches. The aim here was to make it known that Rousseauism, very fashionable at the time, was not acceptable.

Héritier wrote: 'the expressions: "at the time", "in my day", "in the past", ring out like the declarations of identity that they are in the face-off between the generations' (Héritier 2017b: 76). After six months of research, the couple returned to France in

April 1964. Maoism was in fashion, especially among students at the Ecole Normale Supérieure, who, cossetted by Louis Althusser (1918–1980), were editing the *Cahiers marxiste-léniniste* and shortly thereafter *Les Cahiers pour l'Analyse*. Probably unaware of this, the Izard-Héritiers, at barely thirty years of age, were already members of a generation left behind by the style of the next.

In 1963, Guy le Moal left his post as director of the centre in Ouagadougou, which, under the name of the Voltaic Scientific Research Centre (Centre Voltaïque de Recherche Scientifique (CVRS)), was no longer attached to the Presidency but to the Ministry of Education and Literacy. After five months in France, the Izard-Héritier couple left again for six months between October 1964 and April 1965 (Izard 1966). Françoise Héritier devoted this second mission 'to a study of kinship and the regulation of marriage'.

Earlier travellers had highlighted the 'absurdity' of the kinship-naming system among many populations outside Europe, some of whom use the term 'mum' to denote a whole group of women and 'dad' to denote their female cousin's baby, although neither the encyclopaedists nor the Indo-Europeanists saw fit to investigate this phenomenon. This is why Lewis Henri Morgan (1818–1881) is regarded as having inaugurated the study of kinship terminologies with his *Systems of Consanguinity and Affinity of the Human Family* (1871). In 1909, Alfred Kroeber (1876–1960) made it an appropriate object of scientific study by identifying the logical principles underlying such terminologies, such as the sex of the speaker or of the person being named, whether that person was alive or dead, etc., and in 1910 William H.R. Rivers (1864–1922) borrowed small signs and diagrams from biologists that indicated Ego's level position relative to all his or her relatives and vice versa. In 1949, G. Murdock produced a stable typology of terminologies, and it is this one that will be expounded here. In the so-called Eskimo terminology, Ego's siblings, who have a common father or mother, are brothers (or half-brothers) and sisters. In the generation + 1, both parents have parallel siblings: the mother's sister(s) and the father's brother(s). In French or English, Ego calls them aunt and uncle, as he does his parents' so-called cross siblings (i.e. individuals of the opposite sex: the father's sisters and the mother's brothers). Here, the designations are merged (MB=FB). Ego's uncles and aunts give Ego cousins, and his brothers and sisters give him nephews and nieces. While this terminology is that used in Western societies, others exist, including the Iroquois terminologies. As in the Eskimo termi-nologies, Ego's siblings are brothers and sisters. Similarly, in the generation + 1, those who are of the opposite sex to the reference parent – that is, the father's sister and the mother's brother – are called 'uncle' and 'aunt' (with the use of a local term). But the parent's parallel siblings that are of the same sex as the reference parent are called by the same term as that denoting the 'fathers' and 'mothers'. The designations are merged so that FB=F and MS=M. Ego's uncles and aunts give Ego cousins when all the 'fa-thers' and 'mothers' (father, father's brother, mother, mother's sister) give Ego brothers and sisters. The parents' cross siblings are gendered and, taking this logic further, the Sudanese termi-nology retains this pattern but uses specific terms to distinguish the daughters and sons of the mother's brother from those of the father's sister. The so-called Hawaiian terminologies are genera-tional: all relatives of the same sex and same generation are de-noted by the same term: the mother's brothers and the father's brothers and the mother's sisters and the father's sisters are fa-thers and mothers, and all their children are brothers and sisters. In practice, Iroquois systems are found in generation zero and Hawaiian systems in generation + 1, while Ego's sex or a chronol-ogy of births can be used as a classificatory principle – and of course terminologies evolve.

The systems described hitherto are commonly both symmet-rical (the same things happen on the mother's and father's sides) and use the generational principle as a classification tool (a cousin is not a grandfather). On the contrary, there are Crow-Omaha oblique terminologies that are both asymmetrical and non-gen-erational and, as Héritier emphasised, 'they are not uncommon' (Héritier 2000a: 24). At Ego's level, siblings are brothers and sisters. In an Omaha terminology, at the generation +1 level,

Ego finds his mother's sisters placed in the same category as his mother, which gives him brothers and sisters similar to his own siblings; as in an Iroquois terminology, there is a term signifying 'maternal uncle' that denotes his mother's brother. However, the children of this 'mother's brother' (the maternal uncle) are not denoted by Ego by a word that is the equivalent of 'cousin' but by the same (local) term used to denote 'maternal uncle' in the case of boys and 'mother' in the case of girls. Subsequently, regardless of the genealogical level, any man called 'maternal uncle' always produces for Ego 'maternal uncles' and 'mothers'. On Ego's father's side, the term 'father' is used to denote the father's brothers, but for the father's sister, this changes. She is sometimes an aunt (with her own separate designation) and, as such, gives Ego cousins (both male and female). However, as in the case of the Samo people, she may also be designated by the same term as Ego's female sibling – that is, by the term 'sister'. Since all 'maternal uncles' always, from Ego's perspective, produce 'maternal uncles' and 'mothers', the children that these 'mothers' bring into the world are known to Ego as 'brothers' and 'sisters' regardless of their generation relative to him. Still at the generation -1 level, if Ego is male, the children of those he calls 'brothers' are his children, and the children of the women he calls 'sisters' are designated by terms signifying 'nephews' and 'nieces'. Like Ego's own children, those of his brothers, nephews and nieces are his children as well. Although there is no perfect symmetry, we can say that, to make things simple, in order to establish a Crow relationship, one simply reverses the entire statement (the cross cousins on the father's side are raised up a generation and called 'father' and 'father's sister').

Morgan assumed that there was a connection between types of marriage and kinship terminologies and inferred, in the case of an Iroquois system, that women were exchanged between groups of brothers. Similarly, he reduced the existence of the Omaha and Crow systems to archaic group marriage. At the end of the 1920s, Robert H. Lowie (1883–1957) interpreted the Crow-Omaha terminologies as the result of exogamous patrilineal clans. This explanatory logic was continued by Alfred R. Radcliffe-Brown

(1881–1955), with the principle of clan unity leading to the terms 'father' and 'mother' being translated as 'man' or 'woman' of the 'lineage whom my father or my sister married'. Following on from Henri Alexandre Junod (1863–1934), the same Radcliffe-Brown used 'joking relationships' to establish an 'attitudinal sphere' to add to those of terminological designations, descent and residence. The ethnographic data were piling up, and Fred Eggan (1806–1991), E.E. Evans-Pritchard (1902–1973), Meyer Fortes (1900–1983) and others were exploring these spheres as entities with the aim of identifying the connections between them. In regard to marriage, they viewed it not as an object of investigation in its own right but rather through the prism of arrangements of descent. In 1949, G. Murdock sought to bring evolutionary order to the enormous mass of ethnographic data at a time when Lévi-Strauss, in *The Elementary Structures of Kinship* ([1948] 1967), was embarking on a 'radically new' enterprise by proposing 'to organise all the recognised social facts relating to kinship' around the autonomous sphere not of marriage but of alliance (Héritier 1999a).

Thus kinship was divided into five domains: terminologies, descent, residence, relationships and alliance. For Lévi-Strauss, alliance was the way in which groups of men exchanged (or put into circulation) their women as a liminal way of creating a society among human beings, since the prohibition on incest was less a negative proscriptive rule than a positive rule governing the gifting and exchange of women. Since it was universal in its form and specific in its implementation, it formed the interface between nature and culture. Having posited this idea, he identified three types of exchange: elementary, semi-complex and complex. In the first type, the terminology of kinship sets out positively the categories within which Ego was to seek his wife. *The Elementary Structures* is given over to an examination of this type of exchange, and Lévi-Strauss further subdivides it into symmetrical 'restricted exchange', in which group A gives its wives to group B, which in turn provides group A with its wives, and asymmetrical 'generalised exchange', in which group A gives its wives to group B, which in turn gives them to group C, which then provides group A with its wives. Although he defines them, Lévi-Strauss does not deal with the complex and semi-complex structures, which are governed by prohibitions (rather than prescriptions). In the case of complex structures, the classifications set out a number of prohibitions corresponding to various degrees of proximity to Ego, who appears to be free to marry whomsoever he wishes otherwise. Semi-complex structures amalgamate positions belonging to several generations from which it is forbidden to choose a marriage partner, thereby imposing on Ego lists of prohibited positions, since every time Ego chooses a spouse from a particular lineage, all its members find themselves excluded from the number of marriage possibilities for his lineage. But in such a case, does Ego choose a marriage partner 'at random'?

Three years after having submitted the thesis that founded alliance theory, Lévi-Strauss wrote to Roman Jakobson (1896– 1996) on 15 March 1951:

> I have realized that, in order to move from elementary to complex structures, one has to envisage intermediate systems that fall within each other's province, that is to say that function at one and the same time on a structural basis and on a statistical basis .... Now, I haven't succeeded in developing a theory of these systems because each of them allows for too large a number of solutions for one to be able to study them intuitively. For some weeks now, a mathematician has been working with me voluntarily in his spare moments, but we're having difficulty establishing a common language. (Lévi-Strauss 2018a: 137)

Following his election to the religious sciences section at the EPHE (1950), Lévi-Strauss turned to the study of mythologies. Inspired by remarks made by the British anthropologists Rodney Needham (Needham 1962) and Edmund Leach (Leach 1961a), he returned to kinship in 1954–55 and in 1961–62 but without making any further headway with the problem. And since exchange theory was often refuted because people's behaviour did not correspond to the description of it in *The Elementary Struc-*

tures, he came to a decision in 1962; namely, that he had only described representations and not practices. If the field was reduced in this way to the superstructures (Lévi-Strauss 1962), then its formal structures could be analysed, and mathematicians were called in in order 'to express . . . the Crow-Omaha systems in terms of elementary structures' (in other words, to attempt to find some closures) but came up against the fact, stated in 1965, that with two prohibitions and seven clans, an individual had, in theory, 23,436 possible alliances; with 15 clans, that number would increase to no fewer than 3,766,140 (Lévi-Strauss 1965). And while semi-complex systems were not to be reduced to elementary exchange structures in this way, M. Izard's empirical investigation in Bretagne produced no results either.

Six years had passed between 1957–1958 and the first six-month stay in October 1963, and then another year before the second stay in 1964–1965. This was a long time, and the first chapter of *L'Exercice de la parenté* (Héritier 1981b) reveals a familiarity with the literature that Françoise Héritier had only been able to acquire over a considerable length of time. She had first discovered that the 'absurd terminologies' she had encountered in 1956–1957 were of the Omaha type and that, probably to her astonishment, their presence in Africa had remained 'hitherto unknown'.[1] Moreover, the discovery provided her with a challenge; namely, to take up the alliance problem again at the point at which Lévi-Strauss had stopped. Her plan was to identify the actual prohibitions on marriage among the Samo people. Before leaving for Africa, she drew diagrams representing 'all the possible (kinship) combinations'. In the field, the people she spoke to found the diagrams incomprehensible, largely because many of the individuals represented did not exist, having not yet been born, while others had died. So she resorted to the method all ethnologists use almost instinctively, replacing the diagrams with matches or sticks linking small pebbles (representing men) and cowry shells (representing women). 'Thus equipped, and with her daughter on her back swaddled in a wrapper or *pagne* in the African style, she listed the prohibitions based on all the possible cousinhood situations.'[2]

In January 1965, she was assigned temporarily by the EPHE to the Laboratoire d'anthropologie sociale rather than to the Rcp.11. The sole objective she set herself was to continue the genealogical survey, the ultimate aim of which was

> to establish the statistical model of marriage alongside the theoretical model, to investigate in detail the choice of spouse and to verify the starting hypothesis, based on our initial contacts, concerning endogamy in Samo village communities and to understand and demonstrate the mechanisms by means of which a small community is able, given the burgeoning number of matrimonial prohibitions, to form itself into a matrimonial isolate. (Héritier 1975a)

Since Samo villages could have up to 3,000 inhabitants, far too high a number for an exhaustive genealogical survey, she selected three small neighbouring villages and set up a base in Dalo, as described above. The village was said to have 370 inhabitants distributed among six lineages, five of which were Samo and the other Fula captives. The two other villages were located approximately one kilometre away. In December 1965, she announced:

> I've conducted an intensive genealogical survey in three villages that form a sort of matrimonial isolate ... , separated by a sort of vast no man's land from the nearest villages. These three villages currently have a total population of some 1,300 people. The genealogical survey lists about ten times more and each individual of adult age has given a list of his or her spouses, with an individual history for each one, as well as a list of all the children born to each woman. This survey of marriage ties is situated in a space spanning three to seven generations, depending on the individual case.

And she emphasised that 'at the time [1963], terminologies were recorded up to the second ascending and the second descending generations and one stopped there.' Recording 'five and nine (extreme case) generations on the agnatic side and up to twelve on the uterine side' (Héritier 1974, 1975a) was undeniably new.

At the same time, M. Izard was trying – somewhat idealistically – to find a pristine (original and first) state; since he encountered only kingdoms already in existence, he began to reconstitute the Mossi migration to the country, lineage by lineage. On his return, he presented 'the political organisation of the Mossi people' at Lévi-Strauss's seminar, and Mossi circumcision and funerals were the subjects of eight lectures given under the umbrella of G. Dieterlen's seminar.

THE FIRST INTERNATIONAL COLLOQUIUM ON VOLTAIC CULTURES (DECEMBER 1965)

Since December 1960, Dieterlen, Rouch and Meyer Fortes (1906–1983) had wanted to organise a meeting in order to compare British and French research. Mary Douglas (1921–2007) had not yet published 'If the Dogon' (Douglas 1967), but Fortes was already asking: 'if the Dogon had such an elaborate cosmology, why not the Tallensi?' (Drucker-Brown 2000). Finally, a seminar was held from the 6th to the 8th of December 1965 at G. Dieterlen's country house. Those present were G. Dieterlen; J. Rouch; M. Fortes; Susan Drucker-Brown (b.1936); Marie Schweiger-Hefel (1916–1991), from the Völkerkunde Museumin Vienna; Dominique Zahan (1915–1991), professor at Strasbourg; Robert Pageard (1927–2020), magistrate in Ouagadougou; G. le Moal; W. Staude; M. Cartry; M. Piault; M. Izard; and F. Héritier, 'senior technician at the EPHE' and 'secretary for the series'*Recherches voltaïques*. The 'grown-ups' were put up in the house, while the youngsters stayed in a hotel. The debates took place in a living room, and 'It had been decided . . . that each participant should simply give an account of their work', wrote Le Moal, and Drucker-Brown added: 'when it so happens that you meet a colleague who has worked in the same region as you, you get carried away and . . . your impassioned conversation becomes extremely tiresome for all the others. Thus . . . , this desire for a "chat" can seldom be fulfilled. The Sonchamp conference was one long conversation of this type' (Drucker-Brown 2000). The time came for Héritier's presentation, the transcript of which fills five pages followed by seven others of questions and answers. She located her ethnic group and, in an aspect that drew on Dieterlen's approach, related its origin myth. As is the case 'throughout the Sudanese region, the clan names have mottos bestowed upon them'(in the sense that France's motto is Liberty, Equality, Fraternity), which are set forth in the form of esoteric litanies repeated several times as part of a chanted myth. Thus the motto of the Drabo clan (the gravediggers' clan) is celebrated by reciting the Samo origin myth. It relates that in days gone by, men lived in the sky but that the chief's wife was unable to feed them since there were now too many of them. So the chief left in search of a solution. He soon met an old woman, who advised him to follow a 'red thing'. This turned out to be 'the old woman's inordinately extended tongue, resting on the blacksmith's shoulder', to whom the chief 'promised unknown things'. The blacksmith forged a chain, to the end of which he attached a hammer that tumbled down to the earth,which was covered with water and thus 'boiled on impact' to reveal the soil beneath. The chief's brothers descended: 'when you are down on the ground, you will be called gravedigger', then *Tyiri*, griot, Muslim, Fula and Mossi followed. The blacksmith claimed of the earth: 'unknown thing, it belongs to me, you promised me that'. But the chief of the gravediggers (the Drabo clan), having earlier placed his young brother in a hole covered with lopped-off branches, demanded that the earth be consulted as to its owner. The earth was silent but when asked if it belonged to the blacksmith replied that it did not. Having climbed out of the hole, the young brother refused to live with his older brother; he set up home some distance away and declared that he did not wish to be buried after his death because 'the earth is too warm' (Héritier as Izard [1965]1967a).

Even in this abbreviated version, I hesitated to reproduce this myth, analysis of which could fill an entire book. Nevertheless, apart from the fact that it reveals a neglected aspect of Françoise Héritier's work, the descent presents the gravediggers' clan named Drabo (engaged in burying the dead), the *Tyiri* clan (in whose hands the legal power rests) and the blacksmiths' clan (to whom G. Dieterlen had just devoted her seminar). These were the first lineages (the *Tyiri* and Drabo clans) to occupy this land, and they clashed with the lineages that arrived subsequently and who finally conducted the market altars, hunting and rituals wrestling. This dualism intersects with another, since, as already noted above, the villages are divided into two moieties, reflecting 'a dichotomy between *Tyiri* and grave diggers' that manifested itself in Dalo in a sort of furrow dividing the village and, on occasions, in vengeance and fights. It was the *Tudana*, chief of the gravediggers' lineage (the Drabos) and master of the earth, who fixed the dates of the traditional hunts, presided over the earth altar ritual, decided on the sitting of tombs and, most importantly of all, designated – at one and the same time – the woman from the lineage who would give birth to the rain master, the *Tyiri* and the woman from his own lineage whose child would marry him. The *Tyiri* was forbidden to leave the village, to take part in any wars, to cut his hair and to wash except for once a year on the occasion of the day of the dead and the council of patriarchs, over which he presided. He delivered judgments, but there were also justice altars (pieces of pottery hung from trees) from which a ball of earth was removed in the event of abductions of women, robberies or murders. Deposited in the guilty party's courtyard, they were intended to kill him or someone of his family.

There 'were three sorts of unions' or rather three possible statuses for women among the Samo. The word *Furi* denotes a 'married woman', a 'girl promised at birth' and the marriage bond itself. However, when she reaches puberty and after the appropriate ceremony, the girl whose hand has been promised in marriage enters into a sexual relationship for one to two years with a boy she has chosen for herself; a union of this kind is denoted by the term *sandana*. When she gives birth to a child, the *zinifuri* (the legitimate spouse) offers a final gift to the family and the girl is handed over to him with a child regarded as the couple's firstborn. Surprised readers should be aware that this is a social fact that is by no means exclusive to the Samo but is widespread, particularly in the Voltaic cultural region to which the Samo belong. Besides the *Sandana* and *Furi* unions, there is a third one, known as *lo sana*, which is based on a mutual choice by the two spouses (Héritier 1974: 201). Any widow or divorcee who then remarries enters into this *lo sana* union, which also denotes her status, which is also that of the girl who refuses to join her legitimate husband. In a later book, Françoise Héritier added the status of 'wild [women] ... because they have no husband to subjugate them. Having been widowed or separated, they find themselves free and therefore wild. They earn their own living and are also unrestrained in their sexuality' (Héritier 2011b).

Since descent is patrilineal, a Samo man does not take either *furi*, *sandana* or *lo sana* into his own lineage nor, incidentally, into that of his mother, his father's mother or his mother's mother. The presenter explained that the working of the marriage system 'will not be known until the genealogical data have been processed'. This, in brief, is the exotic world portrayed in Françoise Héritier's first written paper (1967a). It is interesting to note just how young African study was at that time, since the questions asked reveal participants' lack of knowledge outside of their own fields. Thus Fortes asked if the Samo paid a bride-price, Le Moal if there were any masks, and G. Dieterlen enquired into the allocation of land.

In 1965, Michel Izard, who was reviewing books on the Mossi, submitted pages devoted to Breton kinship to the important special issue of the journal *L'Homme* (vol.5, no.3–4) devoted to kinship. In the same year, Héritier, who did not contribute to the special issue, gave a presentation on the Centre d'Analyse et de Recherche Documentaires pour l'Afrique Noire in collaboration with her successor, René Bureau (Héritier 1966a). The following year, she gave papers on 'the social organisation of the Samo' and 'marriage among the Samo of Upper Volta' at Lévi-Strauss's seminar. While this was undoubtedly an ordeal for her, the main story was that Lévi-Strauss invited her to attend the 'Conference on resources for research in comparative cultural anthropology' held in September 1966 by the Laboratoire d'anthropologie sociale, the 6th section of the EPHE and UNESCO's International

Social Science Council. Entitled 'Units for Comparing and Sampling Cultures', Héritier's paper (Héritier 1966b) was a text of thirty-four pages in which she evaluated the attempt to use the Human Relations Area Files in order to uncover some of the constants around which societies are organised. After six years of computer processing, she no longer believed in this approach, and her paper set out the insurmountable epistemological obstacles and critiques, which, although written in a scholarly manner, are based on common sense and, for many, echoed those already expressed by André Köbben (1925–2019) and Raoul Naroll (1920–1985). Among the difficulties described was the problem of the unit of comparison and the existence of subcultures, the construction of a representative sample, the division into and validity of the categories used and the mediocrity and, especially, heterogeneity of ethnography. Describing herself as from 'another planet', Héritier nevertheless apologised for her harshness, since 'comparison is one way of bringing the enormous volume of ethnographic material we have at our disposal under control' and concluded, ahead of her time: 'ethnographers are *authors*' (Héritier 1966b), anticipating Clifford Geertz's famous book's title to come (Geertz 1989).

Adapting his Huxley Memorial Lecture (1965) into a preface to the second edition of the *Structures élémentaires de la Parenté*, Lévi-Strauss wrote: 'in 1957–1958, I contemplated approaching the study of complex kinship structures in a second volume to which several allusions have been made but which doubtless I shall never write' (Lévi-Strauss 1967: xxiv). Although it was included in the Huxley lecture, the reference to M. Izard's Breton survey has disappeared and, as in 1965, Lévi-Strauss makes no mention of Héritier's work.

In 1965, in Algeria, the overthrow of Ahmed Ben Bella (1916–2012) put an end to any lingering illusions of socialism, while for several countries in sub-Saharan Africa a long period of instability was beginning. Che Guevara (1928–1967), seeing these countries as a 'weak link', met all the revolutionary leaders, including Kwame Nkrumah (1909–1972), who chaired a summit meeting of the Organisation of African Unity that was boycotted by eight

Francophone countries. Once his tour had finished, Guevara tried to spark a revolution in South Kivu in the Democratic Republic of Congo, but he departed with his Cuban comrades as early as 21 November 1965. Three days later, lieutenant-general Joseph-Désiré Mobutu (1930–1997), the Americans' placeman, consolidated his position in Leopoldville (present-day Kinshasa) and while he was establishing his 'peace' began the first of the three civil wars in Chad (1965–1979). Dahomey suffered its second coup d'état, Rhodesia declared unilateral independence in order to maintain apartheid, and 1966 came to an end with the seizing of power in the Central African Republic by colonel, and future emperor, Jean-Bedel Bokassa (1921–1996).

The Ouagadougou centre published the journal *Recherches voltaïques*, of which G. le Moal was the editor and Héritier the editorial secretary. It is here that Héritier published with Michèle Huart and Philippe Bonnefond a *Bibliographie générale de la Haute-Volta, 1956–1965* (Héritier 1967b). In 1967, the *Notes et documents voltaïques* series was added. Up to this point, Françoise Héritier had been simply seconded to the Centre national de la recherche scientifiquebut remained an employee of the EPHE; in 1967, however, she was formally recruited on the dual recommendation of C. Lévi-Strauss and G. Dieterlen. At the Laboratory for Social Anthropology of CNRS, she joined a small group of overseas ethnologists that was surpassed in numbers by a rural ethnology section that had expanded under the leadership of Isaac Chiva (1925–2012) and, above all, by a large semiolinguistics group (R. Barthes, J. Kristeva, J. Greimas, G. Genette, etc.) that was soon to have its own research centre.

Between October 1966 and April 1967, the Izard-Héritiers were on a third mission in Upper Volta, and M. Cartry was in Ouagadougou when Gilbert Rouget (1916–2017) landed there in February 1967. He had come to record the Dogon Sigui ceremony (Rouget 2011). On returning in June, M. Izard submitted two volumes of a PhD thesis entitled 'Introduction to the History of the Mossi Kingdoms' (Izard 1970), and six months later, having come home for Christmas, Françoise Héritier gave a paper entitled 'The Problem of Samo Kinship Terminology'. Although there is no published abstract for it, the title suggests that it was intended as a sort of foretaste of the article that was published in *L'Homme* in 1968 and that constitutes the first step in a brilliant and distinct body of work.

MICHEL IZARD, DIRECTOR OF THE CENTRE VOLTAÏQUE DE RECHERCHE SCIENTIFIQUE (CVRS)

M. Yaméogo, the first president of the Republic of Upper Volta, was the first African head of state to be welcomed to Washington D.C., from where he returned with financing for his legislative and presidential campaigns. Re-elected in October 1965, he then married Miss Ivory Coast, made fun of the marabouts sorcerers and introduced modernising measures (including a prohibition on promising girls in marriage at birth), thereby alienating at one fell swoop the Catholic church, Muslim imams and traditional dignitaries. A fathomless budget deficit, which forced him to cut civil servants' pay by 20%, and the demonstration of 3 January brought to power Lieutenant-Colonel Aboubacar Sangoulé Lamizana (1916–2005), from Sourou province, where Michel Izard and Françoise Héritier had carried out their first survey. M. Izard reported enthusiastically on the Second International Congress of Africanists, held in Dakar from 11 to 20 December 1967, which closed with a recommendation that research should be Africanised (Izard 1968). And yet the Upper Volta citizen Marcel Poussi (b.1937, former librarian at Centrifan) turned down an invitation to become director of the Voltaic Centre, and so M. Izard and M. Cartry were appointed director and deputy-director respectively (Kabore 1992). In this new centre, which was very similar to its predecessor, M. Cartry, his wife and their son lived in one of the villas, the Izards and their daughter occupied a second one and Suzanne Platier, an ethnolinguist, and her husband, an engraver, made their home in a third. Ouétian Bongnounou, who was not yet the famous botanist he later became, lived with his family in the fourth villa. Françoise Héritier, who continued to be the managing editor for the *Recherches voltaïques* and *Notes et documents voltaïques* series, collected a herbarium of 300 plants for him, the Samo names for which she had noted down. M. Cartry visited F. Héritier's territory, while she accompanied G. Dieterlen into hers. As in Niamey and Abidjan, where other Africanists were working alongside each other, the exchanges between researchers were intense. Cartry thanked Suzy Platier for 'her transcription work' (Cartry 1968: 189), and he discussed 'point by point' an article on 'the enunciation of marriage prohibitions' with its author, Françoise Héritier. The article was published in the third 1968 issue of the journal *L'Homme* (Héritier 1968b). This marked the beginning of Héritier's original work. She was 35 years old. The genealogical survey of the three villages was not finished, but it was probably by comparing the prohibited degrees of kinship with actual practices that Héritier discovered two essential facts. We said above that, according to the explicit rules, a Samo male Ego cannot marry within his own lineage nor within that of his mother, his father's mother or his mother's mother (nor can he take a second wife from the four fundamental lineages of his first wife). However, with the aid of her pebbles and cowry shells, she noticed that the forbidden degrees of kinship actually went beyond these prohibitions. Not only did the Samo seem to comply with their prohibitions but there were others that were not made explicit; 'it appears that one cannot, in addition, marry a relative with whom one shares the same maternal lineage, the same grand maternal lineage or whose maternal lineage is one of your two grand maternal lineages or vice versa.' The fact that the formal rules do not cover the totality of prohibitions perhaps encouraged her to ascertain whether or not the unformulated prohibitions of a male Ego are derived from the female alter when she is in the Ego position.

In 1958, the Izard-Héritiers had pointed out that 'the kinship ties defined below are referred to a person labelled Ego of undetermined sex' (Héritier 1958b). Ten years later, she asked: 'is there symmetry between the case of a male Ego and that of a female Ego?' Thus the article goes through all the possible cases of cousinhood in the fourth degree for Egos of both sexes by examining the prohibitions and their opposites and

whether a male Ego could not marry MBsd or FFSd because of a prohibition due to this potential spouse's affili-
ation to one of Ego's four prohibited lineages; by this very
fact, this potential spouse could not marry Ego even if, from
her point of view, Ego was not a member of one of her four
prohibited lineages. . . . Consequently, the prohibition that
applies to male Ego such that E cannot marry MBD applies
symmetrically to female Ego (Ego cannot marry MBS), although in this latter case the prohibition is not formulated.

Among fourth degree relatives, there is concomitant symmetry
between the situations of the man and the woman in the case of
the marriage of male bilateral cross cousins or female parallel
cousins but not if only one of the cross cousins is a permitted
marriage partner for a male Ego. Since the male and female positions alternate and are in opposition to each other, symmetry
continues to exist only through disjunction and alternation. Thus
in semi-complex systems, the prohibitions do not depend on the
descent system but are extracted from a group of descendants
considered bilaterally; 'the extension of lineage exogamy to a
third order of consanguineous kinship' proceeds 'independently
of the strategy defined by the type of descent'. But does this in-
volve greater dispersion of the matrimonial alliances?

MAY 1968

The typescript of this article had already been sent to *L'Homme*
when in March 1968 Héritier was staying in the north of Samo
country on the border with Mali, and then in April in her village
of Dalo (Héritier 1978: 259), and it was while listening to a radio
brought back from the Ivory Coast by migrants that she learnt
that the 'Latin Quarter is on fire' (Héritier 2006).

Built gradually on a former military site at the beginning of the
1960s, the campus of a second Paris university known as Nanterre opened in 1964 close to an enormous public housing estate.
Leftist groups politicised the university, notably in opposition to

the Vietnam War. And then, there was a dispute around a women's hall of residence, which some students wanted open at all times. A number of arrests sparked demonstrations and then an occupation of the university. Then, on 4 May, the first street skirmishes broke out, and anthropology students were among the first to join the demonstrations.

The youngest ones had organised themselves by age group in 1965 with the founding of a young anthropologists' circle strictly for the under-40s. The group's mouthpiece was a publication called *L'Echange*, which contained reading recommendations, news of members, abstracts of lectures and political opinion pieces, including some acerbic critiques of 'the anthropology of development'. The comments about the need to change teaching are instructive: 'imprisoned in their posts, professors cannot hope that a dialogue will develop with their students,'[3] and there are repeated references to the need to create more posts in the CNRS, the French state research agency. The circle gave way in 1967 to a trade union liaison committee, which complained about inadequate funding and the same 'lack of jobs'. The Africanist generation of G. Balandier, P. Mercier and J. Lombard had begun their careers with a bachelor's degree and a job at age twenty-three. M. Izard and E. Terray had begun theirs with the *agrégation* or a postgraduate degree at about age twenty-five. What could this generation expect?

The night of 6 May was violent, but the Africanists' Society held a meeting on 8 May during which the Egyptologist Jean Leclant (1920–2011) spoke of Meroe. J. Rouch, one of the Society's mainstays, who was not there because he 'was taking part in a new ritual. We went to fight with the police on the barricades every day at the same time'.[4] Every day from now on meetings were held every afternoon in the cinema of the Musée de l'Homme at which researchers, museum staff and students greeted each other as 'comrade'. On 13 May, the day that strikes replaced the barricades, C. Lévi-Strauss was chairing a meeting of the Société des Américanistes, which had invited Ettore Biocca (1912–2001) to give a talk on 'endocannibalism among the Yanoama Indians'. C. Lévi-Strauss was severe in his judgement: 'May 68 disgusted

me ... trees were cut down to make barricades ... university
buildings were left in a filthy state and intellectual work was par-
alysed by sheer verbiage.' His observations probably applied to
many of the mass movements, but he went further: 'on a more
theoretical level, these events seemed to me to be a further indication of the disintegration of a civilisation that is no longer
able [unlike primitive societies] to integrate its young generations' (Gaudemar 2009). On the same day, the action committee
of the 'Ethnology, prehistory and anthropology' section of the
CNRS, together with, to coin a phrase, 'the students concerned',
occupied the Centre's offices. On 16 May, those present elected
a 'provisional action committee', which included a female student and M. Leiris, who was enjoying a second youth. On 17
May, four committees were given the task of thinking about how
a new Musée de l'Homme might operate. A motion that the
CNRS must 'create new jobs' was passed with a vote. Chaired by
J. Rouch, M. Leiris, H. Balfet and G. Rouget, a 'research workers'
assembly' met on 18 and 19 May, disbanded the CNRS's electoral
commission and the committee that managed the ethnology
section and passed a motion calling for the Musée de l'Homme
to be administratively and financially independent. On 23 May,
this same assembly decided to reclaim the top floor apartment
designed by P. Rivet, the museum's founder, which had become
the official residence of the Minister of the Interior. A delegation
scaled the railings that separated off the terrace and got the minister to agree to leave. At this same time, there were eight million
people on strike in France.

That same day, 23 May, saw enormous demonstrations, a
night on the barricades and the cancellation of the meeting of
the Société des Océanistes that was to have been held the next
day. And then everything changed. On 27 May, the government
of Georges Pompidou (1911–1974) signed the 'Grenelle agreements' with the trade unions. President De Gaulle, who had
remained in the background and even absented himself, reap-
peared on 30 May and went to the National Assembly; 800,000
people then marched down the Champs-Elysées. On 31 May, not
realising that the party was over, the anthropologists' general as-

sembly elected a provisional committee to run the museum. The Museum professors' assembly preferred to appoint R. Gessain to the directorship, a post he retained until he retired in 1972.

Nothing happened in Upper Volta, and in Dalo on 18 May Françoise Héritier was present at the village council and the rituals that 'open up the path for the rain' (Héritier 2010a: 113). In Ivory Coast and Senegal, however, students did demonstrate, and there were deaths. The Senegalese government closed down the Faculty of Humanities, and the French minister of education took advantage of the situation to repatriate the jobs the ministry was funding as part of its cooperation programme. Louis-Vincent Thomas (1922–1994), Paul Pélissier (1921–2010) and J. Lombard were invited to find themselves universities in France that would accommodate them, along with their tenured posts.

As part of its legacy, May 1968 brought certain themes and practices to the fore. This was the case, for example, for religious movements and alternative lifestyles. Young militants gained a foothold in factories while others set up communes in the countryside. Patients rushed to psychoanalysts, and the state granted this discipline a place at the University of Vincennes, which opened its doors on 7 December 1968. The sociology department at the same university recruited E. Terray, who had been expelled from Ivory Coast. Anthropology was taught there in a highly politicised way, with Sylvain Lazarus (b.1943), one of the founders of the Marxist-Leninist Communist Party of France, Pierre-Philippe Rey (b.1942), who published *Colonialisme, néo-colonialisme et transition au capitalisme* (1971), Gérard Leclerc (b.1943), who denounced the discipline's role in his *Anthropologie et colonialisme* (1972), and Catherine Quiminal, soon to be the author of *La politique extérieure de la Chine* (1975). Three male anthropologists and one female anthropologist. Although there were few women at the forefront, they did exist and in increasing numbers since the movements' campaigning for changes in women's position in society exploded in the aftermath of May '68. The calls for change had begun to emerge in the mid-1960s; contraception was legalised in 1967, and from then on the demands were focused on the right to free abortion, recognition of the value of domestic work and a sexuality that included 'the liberation of homosexuality'. In the spring of 1970, the University of Vincennes hosted the first meeting of the Women's Liberation Movement. In March 1971, activists from the Women's Liberation Movement took part in the emergence of the Homosexual Front for Revolutionary Action. Opinions had begun to change. In the theatre, *Pauvre France*, which portrayed a homosexual couple sympathetically, played to sold-out audiences, and two years later *La Cage aux folles* was a huge success. A new society was taking shape. On 5 April 1971, *Le Nouvel Observateur* circulated a petition launched by S. de Beauvoir, in which 343 women declared they had had an illegal abortion. In October 1972, G. Pompidou, who had succeeded De Gaulle as President of the Republic in 1969, declared the legislation punishing abortion to be 'outmoded'. The activists calling into question 'the patriarchal society' fell into two broad categories: on the one hand, radicals – many of them Marxists – who were seeking to destroy the system and, on the other, reformists, who were represented by the League for Women's Rights (Ligue du droit des femmes), which was chaired by S. de Beauvoir and had a presence in the political parties. Following the death of Pompidou, Valéry Giscard d'Estaing (1926–2020), who was elected President of the Republic on 27 May 1974 in a contest with François Mitterrand (1916–1996), set up the first secretariat of state for women. Four months later, Simone Veil (1927–2017), the Minister for Health, submitted a draft bill to the National Assembly that decriminalised the termination of pregnancy; the bill was passed by 284 votes to 189 and became law on 17 January 1975.

While it is likely that between 1966 and 1968 Françoise Héritier remained relatively isolated from the feminist movements, this was impossible in 1970. It was then, after several years, 'that she noticed' the differences in the ways Samo boy and girl babies were treated and that it was the little boys who were given something to drink (Héritier 2015a). This attention paid to an example on her part, often to be repeated, was undeniably a consequence of the social movements mentioned above.

THE CONCEPT OF PERSON IN BLACK AFRICA

The Izard-Héritiers were living in Ouagadougou when UNESCO held its first meeting on the urgency of collecting oral traditions in sub-Saharan Africa in Niamey; the second meeting was hosted by the Voltaic Centre between 29 July and 2 August 1968. M. Izard oversaw and reported on the meeting in the *Journal of Modern African Studies* and in *Notes et documents voltaïques*. These reports preceded a 'Note sur la situation de la documentation en Haute-Volta' by Françoise Héritier (1968c) and followed the review of the book that came out of the Sonchamp seminar.

Director of the Centre voltaïque de la recherché scientifiquein Ouagadougou since January 1968, M. Izard resigned at the end of September 1969 and interceded with the minister in order to ensure that he would urge M. Poussi to take over the directorship. France continued to pay 50% of the research centre's budget, and M. Izard became its 'scientific advisor'. He used his greater freedom to rewrite his PhD (1970).

Françoise Héritier did not re-emerge until October 1971 at the tremendous conference on 'the concept of person in black Africa'. It was held at CNRS headquarters in Paris. The researchers lunched in the 'staff canteen', where Françoise Héritier bumped into M. Augé, who had just left the Orstom to return to the 6th section of the Ecole Pratique des Hautes Etudes. The title of the paper Françoise Héritier presented at the conference was 'The female universe and individual destiny among the Samo' (Héritier 1973b). She noted, firstly, that the Samo recognised the presence of nine components in a person: the body, provided by the mother; blood, provided by the father; shadow; breath, flowing into the foetus as the mother breathes; life, given by god; sweat-warmth-presence of this life; thought or the ability to conceptualise and plan; an immortal double given by god to every being; individual destiny leading to responsibility although it is a function of the mother's destiny. In addition to these components, there were also attributes: names, genies and sorcerers that chose an individual as their medium. She also indicated that the

birth rituals used a combination of roots macerating in a 'medicine bowl', which both sexes worshipped annually by drinking
or washing themselves with the liquid. This 'imparting of fertility mediated by plants' belonged to the wife's mother, or in the
case of a man, to his own mother. It was said to be 'a strictly female universe . . . quite separate from the agnatic descent'. This
'non-lineal reproductive force generates a solidarity of another
type [than that of kinship] and underpins female cohesion' just as
'the existence, [which] I am trying to demonstrate statistically, of
a duplication of women's matrimonial destinies' (marriage in the
same place) is an indication of 'female solidarity'. Thus the paper
highlights the fact that a central element of the social world, the
notion of 'female solidarity', is transmitted matrilineally and that
persons are formed in part by the incorporation of fluid. The argument was developed further at C. Lévi-Strauss's seminar on
identity organised by Jean-Marie Benoist (1942–1990) in 1974,
which reviewed what had already been presented and drove the
point home: 'in this patrilineal society, very few components
come from the father': just the blood and, above all, the name.
And although the women 'do not have a subversive ideology',
their conscious search for a duplication of matrimonial destinies
is 'a subversive act'. Moreover, Françoise Héritier emphasises
that 'individual responsibility and feelings of guilt' are principles
'of individuation' that 'are absent from Samo morality' and that
'the collective rule is embodied in individuals and gives them an
identity by assigning them a place'. This was repeated during the
discussion with C. Lévi-Strauss, M. Izard, J.-M. Benoist, Jean Pe-
titot (b.1944). When C. Tardits asked: 'Is someone in possession
of the code?' she replied, 'No, it's a collective thought' (Héritier
1977: 75). It was during this same period that M. Augé conceptu-
alised the idea with the notion of 'ideo-logic', which he defined
as the inner logic of the representations symbolic and semantic
systems could offer.

    After the paper on the concept of person, Françoise Héri-
tier took part in the celebrated Meillassoux seminar on 'slavery
in pre-colonial Africa', which took place between September
1971 and June 1972. At that time, she was no longer calling her-

self Françoise Izard-Héritier but just Héritier. She met up again with M. Augé: 'We were sitting next to each other and continued our conversation in the café ... Subsequently, our lives followed their course together for 20 years' (Héritier 2008c: 45). She had to get a divorce, which was finalised in January 1973, before she could become Héritier-Augé. Although they worked side by side and no doubt with a passion that one cannot but envy, they specialised in very different fields. They were concerned with very different questions and were to produce only one joint publication (Héritier 1982).

NOTES

1. However, John Beattie (1915–1990) described it among the Nyoro people in 1960 (Beattie 1960: 48).
2. Confidence of Flora Petit at that time secretary of the Center for African Studies and linked to Françoise Héritier.
3. *L'Echange*, flyleaf of issue 4, November 1965 (author personal library).
4. J. Rouch, interview with the author, Paris, 15, 18, 29 April and 7, 14 May 1987.

CHAPTER 4

SAMO ETHNOGRAPHY AND WORKING OUT KINSHIP

●　●　●

POLITICAL-SOCIAL MORPHOLOGY OF THE SAMO SOCIETY (1972–1973)

The Sonchamp paper (1965) presented the first material collected, and the research on kinship led to consideration of women's contribution, from which emerged 'Univers féminin et destin individuel' (1973b), when the ethnographic part was supplemented with 'La paix et la pluie' (1973a) and 'Des cauris et des hommes' (1975b), a paper given formerly at the seminar on forms of dependence, led by C. Meillassoux. Meillassoux's seminar confirmed the establishment of a network and, with the exception of Bernus, of a general direction of inquiry characterised by use of the Marxist concepts, which even permeated Héritier's paper, in which she spoke of the 'production of slaves' and 'forces of production'. She soon abandoned this vocabulary, putting the emphasis on social contradictions, and rather used the expression 'common good', which better reflected her ideals.

At the Meillassoux seminar, Héritier presented her research on 'her ethnic group'. Although the Samo were not a society linked to the production of slaves and were in fact victims of the Fula and Mossi peoples, they did, nevertheless, 'collect' 'unattached objects without an owner': tools, animals and people, since 'any person crossing a village's territory could be seized'. These captives were handed over to the master of the rain (the *Tyiri*), which meant they were turned into 'instruments of agricultural production' or sold to Dioula traders. The matrimonial isolate (the three villages of Dalo) constituted a completely secure space, which, extended to include the dependent villages, created 'an area of relative peace': having been captured, their inhabitants were released in exchange for a ransom, and it was while 'seeking to calculate the numbers sold into slavery' that Françoise Héritier referred explicitly for the first time to her genealogical records. At the same time, the relationship between the social organisation of the Samo and their beliefs was the subject of the article 'La paix et la pluie' (1973a). When they were establishing their presence in the territory, the Samo 'set about distributing' the masterships of the rain, earth and blood, the latter responsible for collecting the fines imposed on both the guilty party and his victim, since all 'conflicts disturb the peace of the community'. Samo migration engulfed the indigenous clans, some of whom merged without becoming diluted and, in accordance with the duality mentioned above, one of them constituted a group that during the first wave of migration opposed the lineages that arrived subsequently. The fate of the master of the rain, guarantor of the 'common good', who, as we have seen, was chosen by the master of the earth from the gravediggers' lineage, is comparable to that of virtually all those in charge of climatic vagaries in other societies. Having been chosen against his will, the individual is regarded as sacred, and an impressive list of prohibitions make 'of him a personage whose head gives off the heat that attracts the rain'. He organises hunts, uncovers the misdeeds (fornication in the bush, burial of a zama) that 'prevent the rain from falling', carries out the sacrifices required to make the rain come and convenes the councils. In 1968, Françoise Héritier was present at one of these councils: it was 'essentially a question' of one sacrifice at a rain altar and a second at the sacred baobab tree in order to ward off an epidemic and a hot wind. In the discussions on the misdeeds that had precipitated these phenomena, the council noted 'the failure to organise the dolo cabarets', which was women's responsibility. This omission was contributing to the degradation of traditional structures, for while deploring that 'for the first time' the inhabitants of the two subsidiary villages had not taken part in the ritual combats, the council also 'observed' that each village was tending towards its own individual destiny. Even though the presidency of Burkina Faso had prohibited the wearing of insignia evoking chieftainship (1962) and then made it compulsory to elect chiefs (1964), Françoise Héritier made no mention of this but remarked that the ensuing peace had removed the need for alliances to protect against abductions.

Finally, the article observes that a short-lived Samo politico-religious federation, having been constituted, had subsequently endowed itself with a single master of the rain but that this centralisation had been accompanied by two changes: this master could not convene the council, and the responsibility was no longer handed down within the same lineage. Thus, just like Castres' Guarani Amerindians, the Samo had protected themselves against the advent of the State. Thirty years later, expressing her views on the Grand Paris project, Françoise Héritier emphasised the point once again: 'it is the notion of the common good that forges a community' (Héritier 2012d).

THE PROCESSING OF THE GENEALOGIES

'La paix et la pluie' emphasises the fact that the central factor in social cohesion, endogamy, was achieved in '75% of primary marriages'; since manual analysis of her genealogical records refuted the hypothesis that the norms were not respected, how could that be possible in an Omaha system with its proliferation of prohibitions? Since Lévi-Strauss's mathematicians had been unable to answer that question, Françoise Héritier examined the genealogies and acknowledged: 'although the whole corpus contained barely 3000 individuals, I would never have managed to deal with all the hypotheses without using computers' (Héritier 2007b: iii). G. Kutukdjian, and then Marion Selz-Laurière, was in charge of programming at the CNRS Computer Centre; this work comprises four documents, the oldest pages of which were not published until 1976 (Héritier 1976a). They were written for a handbook in which Françoise Héritier noted that the genealogies helped to improve understanding of land tenure, transfers and logics of all kinds (political, economic and religious). She then moved on to investigate the Samo 'regulation of marriage', which proceeded in three stages: collection of the genealogies, coding of the data and computer processing. The questionnaire used to collect the data included the respondent's family unit, his name, those of his father, of his father's father, etc. and, from the oldest known generation onwards, a list of brothers and sisters, wives and promised spouses who were not handed over, with name, neighbourhood, father, mother, type of marriage (primary, secondary, leviratic, separate), a list of living, deceased and stillborn children, and the same for each of the women (wives, mothers, sisters). The data collection process then moved on to the following generation, 'lineage by lineage' through the chain of agnatic descent. Those lineages that had disappeared were retraced from those that had received the wives, and as soon as the first one was identified, index cards were compiled with cross-references to the others. Once the survey had been completed, an index card was compiled for each individual, classified by lineage and line.

Lévi-Strauss had not written about kinship since the second edition of *Elementary Structures* in 1967. In 1973, the publication of a collection of articles by Luc de Heusch (1927–2012) offered him an opportunity to return to the subject in order to contradict some long-standing objections and reprimand young scholars for interpreting his work 'inaccurately' (Lévi-Strauss 1973b). His intervention was limited to a number of clarifications, and he made no mention of Françoise Héritier's work. And yet in 1974 she published: 'Systèmes omaha de parenté et d'alliance: Étude en ordinateur du fonctionnement matrimonial reel d'une société africaine' (Héritier 1974), which was republished later (Héritier 1976b), of which Lévi-Strauss must have been aware beforehand. This article, the second one dedicated exclusively to Samo kinship, set out the three possible statuses for women, the Omaha rules on prohibition and the unformulated prohibitions. Héritier concluded that, contrary to spur-of-the-moment judgements suggesting that the proliferation of marriage prohibitions implied that spouses were likely to be chosen from outside, the initial results from the computer analysis showed the three villages were 70% endogamous, with a mere 2.7% violating the prohibitions. The computer analysis also revealed endogamous alliances contracted in the fourth generation (with members of the FFM, FMM, MFM, MMM lineages), in the fifth generation (with members of the FFFM, FFMM, FMM, FMFM, FMMM, MFFM, MFMM, MMFM, MMMM lineages) and between individuals belonging to one or other of these lineages (e.g. EFMM x AMFM). A total of 174 marriages created a union of this last type; in 45 cases the lineage of the (male or female) Ego was MFM, MMM, FMMM, FFM for that of Alter and in 32 cases that of Ego's mother was one or other of these four lineages of Alter, and so on. Furthermore, there was an ideal marriage among the Samo in which Ego and Alter, having none of the four basic lineages in common, knew the same man Y, who has 'to do everything possible to marry them', as their maternal uncle. However, since this marriage never took place and the endogamous unions did not correspond to any formulated norm, Françoise Héritier concluded above all that the normative assertions of interested parties, who did not understand how the system worked, should not be taken into account.

It was the joint presence of polygamy and the extension of prohibitive rules (to the A, AM, AFM, AMM lineages) that enabled the marriage system to function in such a way as to link all the unions entered into by a man and his 'brothers' to those contracted by their daughters. In short, restricted exchanges between lineages took place in such a way that if a man had received a wife from lineage X and a wife from lineage Y, the daughter born of Y could be given to a man from lineage X since the two wives were not related in any way (other cases concerned the level of daughters of 'brothers' and the daughters of sons). An initial analysis found that the percentage of such cases was approximately 25%. In other words, 204 marriages were followed by a reciprocation of this type; in 38 of these, Ego had received two wives, and a daughter (or daughter of a son) born of these unions was given to a man belonging to the lineage that had provided

Ego with his other spouse. Thus there were regular exchanges between lineages that paid back the debts incurred in women by giving daughters. And if 'The results of the programs concerning compliance with the prohibition on Ego taking a wife from the lineage in which a brother or his father had already taken a wife have not yet been analysed', it could already be observed that the proportion of legitimate marriages leading to cycles of reciprocity was twenty times greater than that of secondary marriages, even though they were both subject to the same prohibitions. These unions 'bring cognates back into the realm of close kinship . . . , it is possible that this type of system is to be found in many societies of the Omaha type', and it might be thought 'that the former are following an implicit policy of generalised exchange (prestation)' (Héritier 1974: 211). It is 1974, but the main elements are already in place.

In 1975, another article entitled 'L'ordinateur et l'étude du fonctionnement matrimonial d'un système omaha' (Héritier 1975a) resumed the account of the procedures of 1971 and 1973. Readers learn that the lineage is the exchange unit and that there is never a child without a father. They learn about Omaha terminology and the three marital statuses and that the marriage prohibitions make it impossible for Ego to marry one of his sixteen female cousins up to the fourth degree. Héritier tells us that the three villages had a living population of 1,500 people, comprising 34 patrilineal lineages, divided into 93 lines, and 74 outlying villages that appeared in the genealogies, 26 of which had only one recorded marriage while another immediately adjacent village had more than 150. Thus again: since the genealogical survey indicated an endogamous marriage rate of 75%, how were the prohibitions observed?

The researcher concluded that 'it would seem that it is the profusion of prohibitive rules, combined with polygyny that enables a system that aims to combine the standard Omaha prohibitions and village-based endogamy to function.' Since a lineage consists of unconnected lines, if a women A is given in marriage B, the child B born of this union cannot enter into marriage with any of the constituent lines of his mother's lineage A, but in the next generation, only the grandmother's own line within lineage A is strictly forbidden to the grandson or granddaughter. Because of the prohibition on alliance, the two spouses' lineages have no kin relationship, and a man may give to one of these lineages a daughter that his wife will have borne him on condition that the line (and not the lineage in its entirety) is different, otherwise he will give the daughter that his brother's wife will have borne him.

This article was a contribution to *Domaines de la parenté*, the third title of the *Dossiers Africains* series, which, like the *Bibliothèque d'anthropologie*, disappeared when the Maspero publishing house closed down in 1978. However, the series was circulated among a very wide readership, and Françoise Héritier, who had hitherto been little known, became a researcher to be emulated by virtue of an article that was immediately translated into Italian and then into Spanish.

THE CHARIVARI AND THE ZAMA

From 25 to 27 February 1977, the historians Jacques Le Goff (1924–2014) and Jean-Claude Schmitt (b.1946) organised 'a round table on the theme of the charivari'. The assembly was a large one; among the sixty-seven participants were M. Augé, Nicole Belmont (b. 1931), I. Chiva, Maurice Godelier (b.1934), F. Zonabend, Yvonne Verdier (1941–1989), Daniel Fabre (1947–2016), Raymond Jamous (b.1939) and F. Héritier. Previously referred to in her writing simply as a 'pariah', a zama was defined here as a person having had a sexual relationship with a corpse or with animals; since no cases of necrophilia or zoophilia had been discovered in Dalo, the zama there were all second-degree relatives, since the status was transmitted by sexual contact or fathering or giving birth to a child.

The individuals thus labelled led a normal existence but neither they nor their spouse could be buried, since their burial would cause a drought. Lashed to a stretcher, the corpse was transported in a westerly direction accompanied by a large 'charivari' (drums, whistles, horns etc.) as far as the closest village, where it was abandoned in the branches of a tree. The men of that village, having been alerted, would take it down and, still accompanied by a large 'charivari', would cast it out, abandoning it in a tree once they had crossed the boundary of their territory. The peregrination continued as far as Turu, the most westerly of the Samo villages, where the corpse rotted in a grove set aside for that purpose. In order to explain this point of arrival, Héritier returned to the origin myth she had related to us previously. Men having descended to earth by means of a chain forged by a blacksmith 'to whom unknown things were to return', he was expelled when the gravedigger insisted that the earth should be asked for its opinion and, having been put in a hole in the ground, the gravedigger's young brother replied on the earth's behalf. Having climbed out of the ditch, the younger brother refused to be interred after his death and was 'the first man to be left to rot in the trees for having had an excessively carnal union with the earth'. He was said to have settled in Turu, where the bodies of zama ended up (Héritier [1977]1981a: 335).

When the rains did not come, the seers could decide that a zama who had been buried because of a lack of awareness of his status be disinterred. However, the rains could also be stopped by the burial of hunchbacks and albinos, who had been 'cooked for too long in their mother's belly' (sexual relations had given the foetus too much nourishment), or by couples, whether married or adulterous, copulating on the bare earth. The article extended the ethnographic space to other cases of interment causing drought: a woman of reproductive age suffering from amenorrhoea among the Bobo, hunchbacks and lepers among the Dogon and zoophiles and those they had contaminated among the Mossi.

Other transgressions that also caused illness (adultery with a brother's wife or a grandmother giving birth when her grandchildren were beginning to do so) obeyed the same logic, since it was the failure to conform to the norm that caused the misfortune. Now among the Samo the logic was based on the balance of opposites: 'everything in nature and the world falls into one or other of two opposing categories: hot and cold and their corollaries, dry and wet. The village is cold and the bush is hot, men are hot, women are cold' (Héritier [1977]1981a: 358). A blacksmith working his materials with fire is cold, while a griot, making the air vibrate with his drum, is hot. The figures of the master of the rain and the master of the earth clearly embody this polarity. The first, who is hot, is the guarantor of the rain, which is cold, and he cannot strike the ground either with his feet or with his staff, nor can he leave his village, run, dance, etc. The second, who is cold, handles the hot justice altars of the earth and can speak only in a low voice in order not to make the cold air vibrate, etc. There is a balance between the social, biological and climatic orders, which are linked in such a way that an imbalance causes a fracture in the opposite direction in another register because: 'what is important is the attraction that opposites exert: hot attracts cold and damp, while cold attracts hot and dry.' Thus the sex act, which is 'hot', performed within a marriage, which is 'cold', produces fertile flows.

In 1978, Héritier made a new contribution to Samo cosmology. G. Dieterlen was retiring, and the profession presented her with a Festschrift entitled 'Systèmes de signes: Textes réunis en hommage à Germaine Dieterlen', which included contributions from thirty-five students and colleagues, including Françoise Héritier, who produced an article for the occasion entitled: 'Comment la mort vint aux hommes: Récit étiologique samo' (Héritier 1978). Having used the term 'praise names' in 1972, 1973 and 1975, she explained: 'praise names take the form of narratives ... interspersed with sorts of litanies, charged with a condensed meaning and which very quickly become esoteric when the main reference text has disappeared .... Hearing them declaimed gives rise in the person addressed to a feeling of pride in their lineage.' They are recited by a griot, who declaims in free verse what he knows of the narrative associated with the lineage and 'the text [collected] here is but a fragment of the great "saga" of the Drabo'.

Thus the great 'saga' would be like a complete ancient version, and it is surprising that the student of Lévi-Strauss fell in here with this approach (Griaule/Dieterlen) rather than with that of the master, for whom no authentic version existed. As for the rest, the griot tells of 'the appearance of death': the Drabo, wishing to sample some lalsô, a funeral dish forbidden 'to those who do not die', go off in search of death, which they finish by buying for the cost of a cat in order to lift the dietary prohibition. Although Françoise Héritier divulges the recipe for the lalsô, she does not offer any interpretation of the content of the myth, but a lalsô is certainly worth a Christian apple.

In the spring of 1978, the CNRS awarded its silver medal for the human sciences to Françoise Héritier. This was all the more remarkable since there was just one medal for all the sections. She had produced neither a PhD thesis nor a book, and most of the members of the awards committee were probably incapable if not of understanding then at least of taking the time to read the four articles on kinship for which the medal was awarded. Was Lévi-Strauss the instigator of the award?

Unlike university professorships, the Collège de France offers the privilege of allowing holders of chairs to remain in post until the age of seventy-two and, age seventy, it was time for Lévi-Strauss to consider his succession. Had he already read a manuscript version of the magnificent 'Symbolique de l'inceste et de sa prohibition' (Héritier 1979a)?

In 1971, R. Needham, in his introduction and chapter in *Rethinking Kinship and Marriage*, and then, in 1976, David Schneider (1918–1994) both called into question the relevance of Lévi-Strauss's general theory of prohibitions on alliances, marriage and incest, which, in their view, dealt with phenomena that had different causalities. For Needham: 'There is no such thing as kinship' (Needham 1970: 5), and for Schneider, 'it had become clear to many anthropologists that the notion of the incest taboo or the prohibition of incest was not universal and that its definition as a comparative or analytical tool was not standardised' (Schneider 1976: 149).

In Héritier's contribution to *La Fonction symbolique*, a book dedicated to Lévi-Strauss, and edited by M. Izard and P. Smith (Izard 1979), she takes the opposing view by proposing to reconstruct the category of incest on the basis of a profound cause common to all actualisations of the prohibition. Lévi-Strauss's argument was that, as a result of the prohibition, women formed the basis of a society by circulating 'like words'; Héritier noted, discreetly, the 'finalistic aspect' of this argument and proposed to take representations as her starting point. Like thousands of French people, she had just read *Montaillou* (1975) by Emmanuel Le Roy Ladurie (b. 1929) and drew from it the case of a woman rejecting a suitor on the grounds that she was already the mistress of one of his cousins. She then identified beliefs, sanctions and situations, revealing the prohibition on having sexual relations with two sisters that Lévi-Strauss's theory does not take into account. This led her to conclude that the general category of incest prohibitions should be extended to include the prohibition on sexual relations with a person to whom Ego is already linked through the intermediary of another person. She explained that she owed this idea (soon called 'incest of the second type') to P. Etienne, who in 1972 and 1975 noted that Baoulé purification ceremonies were concerned not with a man who had had sexual relations with two sisters or first cousins, but rather with the two women who were 'stricken by a plurality of identities' (Etienne 1975). The incest, she argued, results from this excess of identity. If the Samo system prohibited Ego from taking a wife from several patrilineal lineages, his four fundamental lineages and three generations of cognate consanguine not stipulated by the exogamy rule and lifted after three generations, it was because 'there is something passing through the individuals that never disappears from the men's side and takes three generations to disappear from the women's side'. Having drawn this conclusion, she linked the facts of prohibition to beliefs and representations around bodily fluids (blood, sperm and milk). For Emile Durkheim, the incest prohibition arose from a fear of Ego coming into contact with the taboo blood of his own clan through menstrual blood that had endured (Durkheim 1898). Ethnography, however, decreed a broader principle, since the institution and prohibition arose from a rejection of combinations of the identical that extended beyond blood. Thus homosexual play with cross cousins, which was permitted among the Nambikwara (whom Lévi-Strauss had studied), was prohibited with parallel cousins, and the role of sperm donor (required for the growth of boys in New Guinea, either through fellatio or penetration) was forbidden to a parallel relative, as was the burial of a 'hot' zama in the hot earth (Héritier 1979a: 237). All this arose from the same prohibition on combining the identical and extended beyond the sexual sphere. Such combinations disrupted harmony by overloading the desirable balance between the identical and the different, which constituted a fundamental symbolisation that manifested itself through variable contents and objects. Françoise Héritier was here extending her argument so far as to contradict the functionalist explanation for the common prohibition of sexual relations during breastfeeding, namely the wish to space pregnancies, in order to come down in favour of a more symbolic explanation: like sperm, milk was hot, and the purpose of the prohibition was to avoid combining the identical.

A Samo man's bone marrow and joints produced hot blood and its concentrate, the sperm that engendered a child's blood. Women were cold because they lost blood regularly and hot when pre-pubescent or post-menopausal, and these conditions prohibited relations that combined hot with hot. Thus the cognate prohibitions could be explained by the fact that a baby's body and organs were made by the blood transmitted by the mother's fathers, and it was necessary to wait three generations for it to be diluted.

The rule did not need to be made explicit because it was part of 'a grand, generally implicit universal organisational design'. Héritier's article ended on a cautious note: 'to seek to explain the incest prohibition by drawing on the symbolic is not to contradict Lévi-Strauss's argument. By regulating exchanges of all kinds, the aim always is to construct society.' In putting forward a rationality extending beyond her mentor's conclusions, Héritier is as much the daughter of the *Structures* as the daughter of the second part of his work (*Mythologiques*).

In searching for a universal logic underlying all the prohibitions, she encountered the contrast between identical and different that manifested itself in the form of dyadic categories: left/

right, male/female, high/low, etc. The article also advanced the idea that 'the impossibility of negating the difference between the sexes, which is the fundamental indication of otherness, probably brings us close to the core of human groups' deliberations about themselves.' And she suspected that these deliberations 'perhaps involved, moreover, an organisation based on negative and positive poles' (Héritier 1979a: 223).

While Françoise Héritier showed in her contribution to a book edited by Evelyne Sullerot (1924–2017) that she was not hostile to one of the founders of Planning familial (an organisation that promoted freedom of birth control since 1960) but also supported the traditional family, the content of the twelve pages of 'Fécondité et stérilité' (Héritier 1979b) is not in any way moderate. This time 'ethnological experience demonstrates the existence . . . of a dualist language', which is one of the basic elements of any system of representation, 'qualitative series everywhere are marked positively or negatively', and expressed in them is 'always the supremacy of the masculine'. That said, the article expounds the Samo rationalisation of conception. A woman possesses a matrix containing a small ball, which has an orifice and rolls up on itself. Chance determines whether it makes its way towards the vagina during sexual relations, in which case the act gives rise to conception, provided that the woman's individual destiny desires it. The woman's 'waters' provide the child's organs, skeleton and body within the uterine blood clot, where 'it cooks'. Since the man produces blood that he does not lose (unless through ejaculation), he gives the child blood through his sperm. Because she menstruates, the woman lives in alternate states of hot and cold, since she is 'regularly heated up by sexual relations' (Héritier 1996: 82). During the pregnancy, the woman no longer loses this blood, which helps to produce the child whose growth is nurtured by the husband as he continues to engage in sexual relations with his wife until the sixth month. She in turn uses his heat to transform these waters into milk during the lactation period.

While male impotence was recognised, sterility was not, and 'all cases of infertility are attributed to women'. Later, 'Stérilité, aridité, sécheresse, quelques invariants de la pensée symbolique'

(Héritier 1984a) added, less radically, that in some cases the spouses' blood did not mix and in 'La cuisse de Jupiter' (Héritier 1985a) that supernatural beings or ancestors may be opposed to the union. It remained the case that while the woman was not always culpable the 1978 article stated that (while a woman did not have this option) a sterile man always had sons of brothers who would make the needed sacrificial after his death. It was through conception that a girl obtained the status of woman. Those who remained sterile were buried in the children's cemetery, and the kidneys of women who failed to menstruate were pierced in order to let out the accumulated heat. These pages end with the Jungmannen of Michel Tournier's novel *Le Roi des Aulnes* (1970) hymning inequality: 'We are the light and the warmth that banish darkness, cold and damp.'

In 1984, Héritier returned to the same theme, extending its ethnographic reach thanks to her vast knowledge of the literature acquired through prolonged acquaintance with the Human Relations Area Files. The article includes a sort of list systematising the interpretations of the causes of sterility and conception and diligently investigates 'the sterility of the adolescents' in the bachelors' houses of the Muria (Elwin 1947), Trobrianders, Maasai and Ifugao. An investigation into representations offered an opportunity to affirm that these societies all understood the necessary connection between copulation and procreation while being ignorant of its biochemical nature and that there was no connection between the type of descent (matrilineal, patrilineal, indifferential or bilineal) and representations of the role of blood, since 'if fertility is women's prerogative, it would follow logically that sterility could equally be attributed to a reluctance to conceive' (Héritier 2000a: 35). Once again, male sterility was 'insignificant' because there was disjunction between father-pater and father-genitor, as evidenced by the common West African custom of the prenuptial lover, and in the case of a sterile wife, the men are polygamous.

Besides 'reluctance', sterility sanctioned behaviours that deviated from the norm, such as the prohibited mixing of blood, and everywhere there was an order prohibiting the 'spanning' of the generations. Finally, the patrilineal Samo 'believe that a woman will not have children unless a spiritual element wishes it to be so', which leads us to that 'specifically female universe' (set forth in 1973), since 'a son-in-law must give himself a good chance of success by means of sacrifices, since the reproductive forces stem from his mother-in-law's uterine line, mediated by plants macerating in water. Drinking this water will make his wife fertile . . .' (1984a: 147–49).

THE *ENCICLOPEDIA EINAUDI* (1976)

At the same time, the Italian publishers of the *Enciclopedia Einaudi* had commissioned Héritier to write the entries on kinship. Seventy-five large format pages were published in 1979–1980, and 'Maschile/Femminile' offered an opportunity to consider the sexes in 'opposition' to each other (Héritier 1979c). The French translation of these pages opens with a declaration that was henceforth to recur frequently: 'Women's subordination is manifest in the political, economic and symbolic spheres.' But are we dealing here with determinism or immanent causation? In all societies, the differences between men and women are the object of 'a binary, hierarchised language' that symbolically subjugates women: 'the negative discourse present women as irrational and illogical creatures, hysterics,' who 'by their very nature need to be subjugated, overseen and controlled by a man'. Evidence for this was to be found in *De l'éducation* (Julien Virey, 1802) in which it is stated that a woman's docility is 'the necessary precondition for family harmony'. Although she surprisingly did not note that this manual was published at the same time as the Napoleonic Civil Code, why, nevertheless, are women everywhere diminished in this way?

Just as she was to do in 1996, 2010 and 2013, Héritier refuted both the argument that a primal matriarchy had existed and the assertion that the great patriarchal religions had caused this oppression (Héritier 1985a, 2010c . . .). The domination was primal, and the thirty or so hunter-gatherer societies that had been seriously studied at that time also systematically demonstrated its existence. The myths spoke of dispossession. According to the Dogon myth, for example, men had stolen from women the skirts of the masks that are necessary to communicate with spirits, while in Papou Baruya myth, women had invented the bow and the ceremonial flutes used for the same purpose, which were stolen from them by men, and both (Dogon and Baruya men) turned those tools to the correct direction for their functioning. Thus women were creative while men established order after an act of violence. It was also a man who married 'the daughter of the mother's brother' (MBD) rather than a woman who married 'the son of her father's sister' (FZS).

Nevertheless, ethnography showed older women marrying men younger than themselves (matriarchal Iroquois societies or, conversely, the patriarchal Piegan), and a sterile Nuer woman had a wife whom a slave could impregnate for her. What these examples and many others had in common was that 'it is not sex but fertility that makes the difference between the masculine and the feminine . . . . Marriage opens the way to an exchange of life since women give children. It is undoubtedly here that the fundamental link in male domination is situated, combined with the economic constraint occasioned by the division of labour' (Héritier [1979c]1996a: 232).

This notion that women ('producers of the reproduction of the labour force') are appropriated by men for their reproductive capabilities had already been put forward by C. Meillassoux in 1960. The elders kept younger men under control by means of a bride-price that enabled them to acquire a wife; Meillassoux's model, however, did not consider that wives were as much social objects as social subjects. While the rules of descent and alliance were always a particular way of appropriating the reproductive power of the women in a group, Héritier extended this argument in 1976 by suggesting that this control 'is made possible' by a disability that is the price of fertility; namely, a reduced capacity for mobility during pregnancy. The phrase 'is made possible' cautiously implies that domination is the result of this constraint.

DIRECTOR OF STUDIES AT THE
ECOLE DES HAUTES ETUDES AND
THE END OF THE FIELD MISSIONS (1980)

In 1975, the 6th section of the Ecole Pratique des Hautes Études became an independent institution under the name of the Ecole des Hautes Etudes en Sciences Sociales. The Centre d'Études Africaines was still in existence, and G. Balandier and M. Augé had posts there, the latter having been elected to serve on the School's board. Françoise Héritier joined them in 1980, having been appointed director of studies. The years of field missions were now ended, and although she described herself as 'haunted by her country' (Wehn-Damisch 2008), the territory in question was in an Upper Volta that no longer existed.

In 1966, the first president of Upper Volta had given way to a military government that established a second republic (1970). In 1980, a colonel who had been in power since 1974 was removed from power by a coup d'état launched by a Military Committee of Recovery for National Progress. On 4 August 1983, Thomas Sankara (1949–1987), a former prime minister who had been placed under arrest the day after a visit from F. Mitterrand's adviser, seized power with a National Revolutionary Committee. On the anniversary of this event, the country was renamed Burkina Faso ('land of the honest (or incorruptible) men'), but Sankara was assassinated in 1987. At this time, the Africa full of hope for the future following independence was no more. As if to put an end to such hopes, the 1970s had begun with four years of intense drought in the Sahel. The period was also marked by a succession of zany dictatorships, armed conflicts, bloody repression and coups d'états, as in Ghana (coups d'état in 1966, 1972, 1978, 1979 and 1981), Nigeria (coups in 1966, 1983, 1985, 1993 and 1995 and civil war from 1967 to 1970) or Mauritania (coup in 1964 and racial terror in 1978). In the Chad of J.-P. and Annie Lebeuf (1921–1995), J. Pouillon and A. Adler, a civil war lasting more than twenty years broke out. Having suffered a coup d'état every two years from 1963 onwards, Dahomey was renamed the People's Republic of Benin under the control of the Military

Council of the Revolution (1972), which destroyed the country. Liberia and Sierra Leone were soon to embark on the 'short sleeves/long sleeves' campaigns of terror against voting, with victims being asked whether they preferred amputation at the elbow ('short sleeves') or the wrist ('long sleeves'). In Rouch's Niger, Hamani Diori (1916–1989) was overthrown (1974), and a military regime characterised by violent intrigues was established. In Dieterlen's Mali, President Modibo Keïta (1915–1977) was overthrown in 1968 by the junta led by Moussa Traoré (1936–2020), who put in place a police state; he was to be overthrown after hundreds of people had died.

At the same time, the ideological monopoly of the former colonial powers was being demolished. There were demands for an 'African-style democracy'; the colonialists' ideology was replaced by Arabisation, Malgachisation and Zaïrianisation (also known as 'authenticity'), while the Sharia prevailed in Sudan, Mauritania and the north of Nigeria and was introduced into Niger and Mali. The colonial period was also coming to an end in the economic sphere. Japan was building bridges and conquering markets, and China established commercial relations with Guinea, Angola and Zaïre before extending across the entire continent.

All across Africa, the state had preceded nations, and it seemed that unity could be achieved only through veneration of a leader, through war or by attacking foreigners, as evidenced by the expulsion of immigrants from Nigeria and of Asians from Uganda and the violence perpetrated against foreigners in Zaïre, Gabon, Mauritania, Senegal . . . Behind all this, networks aspiring to the power of the state were competing with the emerging upper classes, whowere getting organised in the midst of this chaos. Nigeria and Gabon joined OPEC, and the first Lomé Conventions agreements were signed, as were the agreements establishing the Economic Community of West African States and the Economic Community of Central African States. Although the 1980s saw the imposition by the IMF of structural adjustment plans, the emergence of these upper classes on the national and international scenes was and is a stable and continuous historical phenomenon.

Although Françoise Héritier had little connection with this re-shaping of the continent, Africa was catching up with her through immigration.

CHAPTER 5

AT THE COLLÈGE DE FRANCE

• • •

L'EXERCICEDE LA PARENTÉ (1981)

Responding to the challenge of integrating semi-complex structures into alliance theory, *L'Exercice de la parenté* was published in December 1981. Its first chapter, which concerns 'the fundamental laws of kinship', provided an opportunity to dissect the works of a dozen authors, but its boldness lies primarily in its attempt to construct the very object of its area of inquiry. For Héritier, kinship is based on a biological substrate. There are only two sexes (male and female), procreation gives rise to a succession of generations, and births result in the coexistence of older and younger individuals within the same generation. The fundamental point is that this universal reality, which is material and biological in nature, stands in opposition to a vision based on cultural relativism, in which the words used in kinship terminologies cannot be compared with each other, since they refer only to themselves (the meaning of the word 'brother' differs depending on the society in question). By manipulating these three elements (two sexes, generation and order within the siblings), kinship systems transform the biological into the cultural. All the possible combinations of kinship designations can be observed, with the exception of that which places the father and the mother's brother in the same category in order to set them in opposition to the father's brother. The nomenclature used to denote Ego's full siblings and parallel and cross cousins has the same particularity; namely, that the combination that would place Ego and his cross cousins in the same category by separating them from his parallel cousins does not exist. Since this double absence is universal, Françoise Héritier elevates it into a 'law' of kinship, which she explains in two ways. On the one hand, given that the difference between the sexes within the group of full siblings is 'the fundamental mark of otherness', a cross relative is 'never an implicit medium for equivalence'. However, other pieces of implicit information such as 'generational assessment' are sometimes refuted, giving rise to a second, even more fundamental law; namely, that the two sexes are always unequal in status, which explains why the equivalence: MB=F≠FB (mother's brother = father different from father's brother) does not exist. And if it does not exist, it is because, according to Héritier, it would open up the possibility of female predominance.

The second chapter of the book concerns 'the functioning of semi-complex alliance systems' and gives an account of the fieldwork and analysis of the Samo system that was carried out after the list of marriages contracted in the genealogies of the three villages of the 'matrimonial isolate' had been compiled. It had already been noted that the 75% share of endogamous marriages thus observed were difficult to reconcile with adherence to the Omaha marriage prohibitions, and Robert H. Barnes (b.1946) challenged the Omaha categorisation 'because of the variations recorded'. Thus Héritier reaffirmed the existence of an Omaha-type kinship by extending the prohibition to four generations in the maternal lineage. This 'Omaha' characteristic had not been previously identified, she argued, because for informers it was an implicit rule. Moreover, it had been known since her 1968 article (Héritier 1968b) that if 'things are represented by conventions' and/or that the rules 'speak in a masculine voice' Ego's gender is not without its effect on the prohibition, since exchange does not imply symmetry. This is why the system permits a brother and a sister, forming an opposite-sex couple, to choose a spouse from the same group provided that they change line. It is true that the repeating of a marriage is prohibited when the two successive candidates constitute a parallel pair (brother/father's brother/sister's son/sister, father's sister/father's daughter), but it is recommended if they constitute a pair of cross relatives (father/brother's daughter/sister, father's sister/father's son). These matrimonial exchanges between alternate lines of different patrilineages enable the formation of relationships that are compatible with the prohibitions on the duplication of alliances and are therefore a fundamental mechanism in the functioning of semi-complex systems. Computer analysis shows that the choice of spouse has certain positive regularities with an exchange of sisters and that as soon as the prohibitions permit Ego marries a 'distant' relative. Cycles of exchanges analogous with those in elementary systems are created, with 'consanguineous loops'; the system, Héritier argues, functions like an Aranda super-system in accordance with the hypothesis already formulated by C. Lévi-Strauss (1965). Nevertheless, Lévi-Strauss had predicted in 1967 that Crow-Omaha systems would form 'a bridge between elementary kinship structures and complex kinship structures' (1967: xxix), enabling an elementary system to move gradually towards a complex system; however, Héritier concludes that an elementary structure evolves towards either a semi-complex or a complex system, which are alternative, as studies on Peru will demonstrate (Héritier 1986). Furthermore, it is in this book that the expression 'differential valence of the sexes' appears in print for the first time, conceptualising the places of the two sexes on a scale of values and the dominance of the masculine principle over the feminine principle, which Françoise Héritier was to say she had formulated in 1974 (Héritier 2013b: 36). However, she obviously did not hold on to it at the time, and even in *L'Exercice de la parenté* she mentions it only in passing. The 1982 review of the book by Alan Barnard (b.1949) makes no mention of it at all. On the other hand, the review by E. Terray published five years later makes this 'valence' another 'fundamental law of kinship' (Terray 1986) at a time when Françoise Héritier herself had returned to the notion. The absence of the terminological system ($MB=F \neq FB$) mentioned above is the indicator of this universal predominance of the masculine, the profound cause of which is not revealed in *L'Exercice*, whereas in 1976 it was diagnosed as resulting from pregnancy, which forced women constrained by their physical condition back into the domestic sphere. Françoise Héritier writes simply in *L'Exercice* that it is men who exchange women and not the other way round and that what is at stake in kinship systems is not so much exchange as the 'appropriation of women and their reproductive capacities by men'. *L'Exercice de la parenté* also brought 'on to the conceptual market' (to use Héritier's expression) the expression 'consanguineous loop', and historians and anthropologists were henceforth to speak of 130 or 199 loops out of a total of 236 marriages (Héritier 2001h). The book was a real bolt from the blue, but one that remained unsung: it was not until 1986 that a French periodical published a review of it.

A CUNNING PLOY AND AN INAUGURAL LECTURE

The year 1980 probably alternated between being comical and tiresome at the Laboratoire d'Anthropologie Sociale. Who would take over the directorship and the chair at the Collège de France when the boss stepped down? The leading candidates appeared to be Godelier and Izard. The former's prolific writings had been translated into numerous languages, but *The Making of Great Men: Male Domination and Power among the New Guinea Baruya* (1982) was published just a little too late. As for the latter, Lévi-Strauss noted in 1979 that: 'Monsieur Izard has finished writing his doctoral thesis.' It was entitled: 'The Oral Archives of an African Kingdom: Research on the Formation of the Yatenga' (Izard 1980), and Izard defended it in 1980 in front of an examining committee consisting of C. Tardits, L.-V. Thomas, J. Lombard and G. Balandier, Izard having obviously remained loyal to the last of these. Academics harbour lingering grudges, and Lévi-Strauss left the room when Balandier was getting ready to speak (Kawada 2017). The thesis set out to investigate 'history and structure', the fundamental theoretical question for young people born between 1930 and 1938. Having embarked on their thinking with a Sartrean subject, that is a subject aware of him/herself, they encountered this question with Lévi-Strauss then

Althusser and Lacan. For the discipline, it was the focus of the early works of Sebag and Godelier (1962), and it remained the central question for philosophers from Pierre Verstraeten (1933–2013) to A. Badiou. In Izard's work, the history took the form of the initial Mossi violence, and it was effaced by acceptance of a symbolic domination that found expression in the appropriation of a power over nature embodied in a king. Mediated through rituals, he was the locus of the junction between the worlds and hence between a forgotten history and a contemporary social structure. This leads one to suppose that it was the theme of a divine king embodying nature that led M. Izard to join N. Belmont in re-editing in French *The Golden Bough* (by J.G. Frazer 1854–1941), which was enriched with exemplary introductions (1981–1984).

In 1980, Lévi-Strauss opposed the election of Marguerite Yourcenar (1903–1987) to the Académie Française on the grounds that it was 'the house of men'. So Geneviève Delaisi De Parseval (b.1940) remarked that it was a splendid idea, therefore, to appoint a woman as his successor (Delaisi 2017). However, Héritier added: 'Lévi-Strauss had chosen me himself . . . and I was undoubtedly the one who was most in tune with his theoretical concerns.' While the two scholars did not have 'a special relationship' (Héritier 2008a: 10) and there was much that separated them, they had kept company with each other for thirty years, and Lévi-Strauss knew all the members of his research institute well. He also knew that once he had retired it would be easy to reverse the votes that had been more or less promised by the assembly of Collège de France professors, since the candidate he wished to dub his successor possessed only a bachelor's degree. Marcel Mauss (1872–1950), who had been elected in1936 after two failed attempts, did not have a PhD, but he had at least passed the *agrégation* (1895). Consequently, Lévi-Strauss adopted a strategy that has remained unique in the annals of the Collège. Before he retired in 1983, he managed to have a chair of 'Comparative study of African societies' created. He deliberated this coup, and particularly the title of the proposed chair, with his accomplice and found a solution by insisting that the proposed title should include the word 'comparison' (Héritier 2017g). It was impossible for there to be two chairs dedicated to comparative studies (i.e. to anthropology); one was required for the Collège's important Laboratoire d'Anthropologie Sociale and so Françoise Héritier was duly enthroned. Aged fifty, she was the second woman to be elected to the Collège since 1530, and the often reproduced photograph, in which she appears in the midst of some thirty men, is a remarkable ethnographic document.

Lévi-Strauss's retirement being planned for December 1983, the new professor gave her inaugural lecture on 25 February of the same year. She observed that, in electing her, the Collège had also elected Africa, study of which had not begun until the expedition led by D. Paulme and Deborah Lifchitz (1907–1942) because the continent was looked down on (Héritier 1984b: 13). In fact, she was mistaken because Africanism was established much earlier, and she also forgot to mention Negritude, Griaule and Dieterlen, who gave Africa the accolade of being 'civilised'. In her lecture, Héritier observed that, contrary to a widespread view, Africa had a history (cultivation of plants, large empires, etc.) and that its social structures were very diverse, ranging from semi-complex kinship structures to organisations based on age group ('as it is thought the Indo-European peoples might have had'). Having completed her eulogy, the professor outlined her ontology: the cultural is in the social, and the social is in the symbolic, whose 'raw material is the body', since the body is the 'locus for the observation of sensitive data'. Then she turned to structuralism: 'what I call a given social system's logic and inter-nal necessity is the possible logical combinations', and 'since it exists, any social system necessarily appears coherent. It seems that the content of its various parts has nothing arbitrary about it and that none of its constituent parts can be modified or re-moved.' However, this is an illusion, the facts are changed by ad-justment procedures and the apparent necessity merely updates a possible series of combinations whose 'flexibility' 'is the open door through which the changes that history brings are intro-duced'. In making these remarks, which were quite conventional at the time, Françoise Héritier referred by way of example to acculturation phenomena. This could have been an opportunity to mention Balandier, but she did not. On the other hand, in insisting that individuals have strategies that seek to 'circumvent the rules without infringing them' (a major lesson from Malinowski), she paid homage to M. Augé with the case of the Alladian of the Ivory Coast, whose ethnography he had compiled and among whom heads of family in a matrilineal kinship system have an interest in marrying captives or foreigners from a patrilineal system. There followed an explanation of her planned teaching programme, which repeated what had already been outlined earlier: 'I propose ... to connect societies' variable phenomenological givens with invariable underlying mechanisms, which are small in number and give order and meaning to those givens.' Using all the possible combinations to work on the 'biological given', humanity has produced all the kinship terminologies 'except one', which shows that there 'exist what Holton [Gerald Holton] calls ancient themes that act as organising schemas'. The existing combinations result in hierarchical relationships between men and women 'that could have been reversed in the event that the missing combination had been produced', since a merging 'of the maternal uncle and the father, together opposed to the paternal uncle, would require a different identity model' and 'the preeminence of the feminine'. And then the argument took a different turn: African thinking is rooted in dualistic oppositions (hot/cold) encompassing the three orders – meteorological, biological and social – and governed by the search for an equal balance, since an imbalance gives rise to catastrophes. Since women's fertile life is shorter than that of men, the age systems of East Africa constitute 'one of the most successful attempts to link together the three relationships between older and younger siblings, parents and children and men and women', since 'a son cannot become a father as long as his own father has not withdrawn from reproduction at a point in time that is acceptable to all his group' – that is at about the age of thirty, which reduces men's fertile life to a length very close to that of women. A strange eulogy for a social structure and concept of equality. The lecture concluded: 'It was thanks to ethnography' that De Gérando (1772–1842)

> saw ... the world thronged with happier, wiser, people' and 'this is the motivation for continuing our work' that 'aspires to go beyond differences without reducing them. ... There are many paths leading to knowledge ... they also pass through shared intimacy with the Other, that understanding in which C. Lévi-Strauss saw 'a supplementary form of proof' and which for me are 'the familiar faces and friends' of Voltaic territory. (Héritier 1984b: 42)

THE LABORATOIRE, LECTURES AND SEMINARS

Having submitted a report to the minister of research, M. Godelier was appointed director of the CNRS's department of humanities and social sciences (1982–1986). M. Izard, for his part, chaired the national committee of CNRS section 33 (Anthropology, ethnology and prehistory) between 1983 and 1986.

In the same year and in her first year of teaching, Françoise Héritier was hospitalised for two months with pericarditis. The doctors said she was suffering from relapsing polychondritis, a rare autoimmune disease characterised by recurrent inflammation of cartilage and other tissues throughout the body. The prognosis was that she had five years to live. Her response was to work all the more, directing the Laboratoire, giving lectures and writing. At the Collège, she had to give the so-called *Grand cours*, a lecture in which the obligation on the professor was always to produce a new lecture. There was also a seminar series led by the professor, which was easier, since the seminars consisted of papers given by participants. While the seminar series focused for a long time on the theme of matrimonial alliance, the theme of the lecture postponed from 1982 to 1983 was 'the symbolic anthropology of the body', with the subtitle: 'fertility, sterility'. It was to be given in 1983–1984 and was followed by 'the humours of the body' in 1984–1985. Héritier would explain that these themes represented a continuation of her earlier work, since the lifting of marriage prohibitions at the fourth cognatic generation stemmed from a 'concept relating to blood', the aim being to avoid relationships that bring identical substances into contact with each other (Héritier 1985f). Thus she set about examining this theme with some rigour in order to show that that 'a relationship that brings two identical substances into contact with each other . . . is forbidden, not only among the Samo but in all societies that function with a wide range of marriage prohibitions'. When it comes to style, Véronique Nahoum-Grappe (b.1949), speaking of 'an implacable display of demonstrative logic . . . to which nobody can say no', reported that it was in a 'soft voice' that Héritier 'delivers a dense text fairly quickly: for her audience, the essential thing is not to fall behind, since the argument progresses cumulatively and requires, at any one point in the lecture, that they have taken in not only what has just been said but also the logical mechanisms underlying the argument' (Nahoum-Grappe 2018).

Having joined the LAS after completing a PhD supervised by C. Tardits, Elisabeth Copet-Rougier (1949–1998) took over the management of the seminars and co-editing (34 papers on matrimonial alliances). Pierre Lamaison (1948–2001), to whom *L'Exercice de la parenté* refers, was the deputy director of the Laboratoire between 1983 and 1991 and took over its management. Thanks to these two, Françoise Héritier found the time she needed for other endeavours and when elected to the Collège entitled her EPHES seminar 'Anthropology in the City'; that is to say, a new and different field of inquiry.

THE NATIONAL CONSULTATIVE ETHICS COMMITTEE

Once elected to the Collège, Françoise Héritier assumed national responsibilities by chairing the National Health Institute's Human and Social Sciences Commission (1983–1987) and becoming a member of the Human Sciences and Society Commission of the National Advisory Committee on Ethics for Life Sciences – set up following the birth of the first French baby conceived by in vitro fertilisation in 1982.

Françoise Héritier, who chaired this committee between 1985 and 1988, educated herself in biology and law, and it was a long-established legal expert who was to co-edit *Questions autour du handicap* (Héritier 2010d). In the meantime, she was – among other things – vice-chair of the board of governors of the Médéric Alzheimer Foundation, a member of the National Council on Handicap from 2004, and one of the thirty public figures who made up the High Council of Francophonie. 1984 saw the publication of her inaugural lecture, two articles for the *Encyclopedia universalis* and 'Stérilité, aridité, sécheresse' (1984a) in a book edited by M. Augé. Having been a member of the board, M. Augé was elected president of the EHESS (1985–1995) and joined forces with the historian Jacques Revel (b. 1942) to set up the *Ordres sociaux* series (Editions des archives contemporaines), in which were to be published, notably, the papers presented at Françoise Héritier's seminar. Having also seen the publication of the Italian translation of *L'exercice de la parenté*, Françoise Héritier visited the University of Palermo from the 3rd to the 5th of December 1984 to attend the Di studi antropologici conference; she was accompanied by M. Augé, Jean-Pierre Vernant (1914–2007), Jean-Louis Flandrin (1931–2001) and Julian Pitt-Rivers (1919–2001). There, she presented a paper entitled 'La logique des humeurs comme sanction sociale' (The logic of the humours as social sanction) and met Salvatore D'Onofrio (b.1951) (D'Onofrio 2018a). She was to return to Palermo in 1989, 1990 and 2000, but in 1984 she had to return promptly to Paris because the first 'Annual Ethics Seminar' was held on the 6th and 7th of December in preparation for the 'Genetics, procreation and the law conference' organised by the three ministries of justice, social affairs and research.

Inaugurated by a message from President Mitterrand, who 'expects much from it' thanks to the 'clash of different varieties of knowledge', and launched by Robert Badinter, Keeper of the Seals, a.k.a. Minister of Justice, the conference (18 and 19 January 1985) was to give rise to the regulations that were to be put before parliament. The minister gave the short inaugural speech, Jean Hamburger of the Academy of Sciences was in the chair, and biological scientists repeatedly declared that 'new moral problems' were emerging as the science advanced. Facing them were the philosopher Michel Serres, five legal experts, two sociologists (François-André Isambert and Bruno Latour) and an anthropologist. This was Françoise Héritier-Augé, whose paper ('The Donation and Use of Sperm and Ovocytes: A Point of View Based on Social Anthropology') was to form the basis for three publications. There was of course the oral presentation published in the conference proceedings (1985b) and a reprint for the generalist journal *Le Débat* under the title 'The Individual, the Biological and the Social' (1985c) and finally 'Jupiter's Thigh, Reflections on the New Modes of Procreation' (1985a), which extended the deliberations for readers of *L'Homme*. Since the legal norms were being drawn up, Françoise Héritier's paper was a response to the minister, whose generosity she highlighted while at the same time lecturing him. She cited a passage from Mitterrand's introductory message: 'as soon as we have control over reproduction, humanity itself has to choose some rules' before delivering an ironic précis of the minister's statements, which she summarised thus: 'through the use of a mode of procreation dissociated from sexuality our centuries-old concept of filiation would [according to the minister] be radically transformed. . . . The traditional legal order would be left reeling since a child would no longer necessarily be conceived or carried in the mother's belly and there may be more than two parents' (1985c: 27). And then came the first lecture: 'there is a major ambiguity here, namely that which likens the begetting of a child to filiation.' When the conference proceedings were published in September 1985, 'Jupiter's Thigh' had already appeared in *L'Homme*, and although politicians would not have read it, she did refer to it:

> I have shown elsewhere that all the substitutes for natural procreation that we are discovering today have or have had, to a greater or lesser degree, institutional equivalents in var-

ious societies . . . . Posthumous descent is practised in societies regarded as primitive . . . so let us reject all novelty in
the history of humanity . . . . There is no society that does
not distinguish filiation from the begetting of a child. The
fact that there may henceforth be single-parent families
does not fundamentally change the concept of filiation as
social integration into a line, . . . Moreover, it is difficult to
see what radical changes might be implemented, unless we
go down the road to cloning or Plato's Republic.

After these remarks, delivered in a professorial tone, the speaker
turned to France, where the rule whereby the mother's husband
was the father of the children born or conceived within the marriage already sanctioned recognition of the social world. In other
words, the minister should have known that it had long been en-
shrined in law that filiation and begetting were not linked. This
having been established, Françoise Héritier raised the question
of 'the rights of the child' in the form of a second lecture. When
the minister called on his audience to imagine the 'full realisation'
of human rights, he was alluding to the European Convention on
Human Rights, which enables each individual to have access to
'the paths to fulfilment by the means that best suit him or her'.
Now this vision of human rights was, she argued, invalid in other
civilisations and would be more accurately defined the 'rights of
the individual'. However, pure individuality does not exist, either mentally or socially (Héritier 1985c: 29). Since the question
being posed ultimately concerned the possibility of creating a
child oneself, even doing so alone (as we hear from the news),
Françoise Héritier gave her opinion: 'the right to life is not everything. Perhaps there is also a right to have two parents and not
simply two genitors.' In evoking human rights in order to justify
bringing a child into the world by all possible means, the minister
was slipping from the right to life to the right to choose the means
with which to give life, which was indefensible. This interpretation
was based on an 'intensification of the notion of the individual,
seen as a monad tightly closed in on itself. However,' she argued,
'the social is never the aggregate of each individual's rights but an

arbitrary entity based on rules, in which filiation/descent is never reducible to the purely biological' (Héritier 1985c: 32).

However, the speaker was worried. French law had added biological truth to the three standard modes of access to filiation (natural, expressed wish and possession of status) and a judgment that had just ratified a repudiation of paternity threatened to set a precedent. She then lamented the fact that it had given 'an individual [the right], depending on his desires and convenience at any particular moment, to acknowledge and then to repudiate a filial relationship . . . Who can ever calculate the damage done to children', who 'are deprived of an essential part of what makes a person by a repudiation that deprives them of their identity?' By introducing the biological criterion into the process of establishing filiation, 'we have lost sight of an essential rule by which societies function, namely that there is no social institution that is founded exclusively on nature.' The article titled 'Jupiter's Thigh' begins with a restatement of the view that all human societies are based on the need to reproduce themselves, which is strictly a matter for mixed-sex couples, that cloning is utopian and that Lévi-Strauss had concluded that the collective system of child-rearing had been an historic failure (Lévi-Strauss 1956). Filiation is at one and the same time universal, social and not biological. Furthermore, ethnography teaches us that the introduction of a third person with in vitro fertilisation is absolutely nothing new: brothers share the same wife in Tibet, and wombs could be rented in Ancient Rome as they can be among the Baganda in Africa. The reference to biological truth in the recent French legislation marked a break with the past, and 'because of the new primacy of the notion of the individual, everyone now understands that they can cite as evidence the biological or the social as they see fit and in accordance with their interests at any one time' (Héritier [1985a]1996a: 275). Since surrogate mothers, sperm donors and posthumous insemination were not new phenomena, it was not helpful to legislate on filiation, although it would be desirable to do soon the possibility of repudiation. On donor anonymity, she said that 'investigation shows that it is perfectly possible, when filiation is defined in law, to live in harmony with oneself and with others while dissociating the functions of father-pater and father-genitor and those of mother-mater and mother-genetrix.' Nevertheless, couples today named a cousin or brother as a donor. The article in *L'Homme* concluded thus: 'it would not be unhelpful to question . . . the wisdom of a desire to keep things within the family'. Eleven years later, this article had become Chapter X of *Masculin/féminin I* (1996a), and the author added that the rule established by the Centre for the Study and Conservation of Human Eggs and Sperm, founded in 1973, was to deny this desire: besides avoiding conflicts within families, it might also be wondered whether such a desire reflected a predilection for incest of the second type.

Let us summarise Françoise Héritier's thinking at this period: a) Filiation is universal and it is always the fruit of a mixed-sex couple, b) it is always social, c) medically assisted procreation changes nothing, and there would be no need for legislation if the 1972 act had not added genetics to the three standard modes of access to filiation, since d) society must now protect the rights of beneficiaries; e) as for donor confidentiality, we can wait and see, f) but donors cannot be relatives. These themes would stay with her until the end of her life.

Since 1984, the Collège de France seminar had been given over to matrimonial alliance strategies, while the lectures had focused on bodily humours. Françoise Héritier had extended the investigation of kinship, blood and sperm to representations of conception and sterility and then to those of the bodily and humoral substrates (flesh, bone, fat, blood, sperm, saliva, lymph, milk) and the way in which human societies explain the circulation thereof. Her inquiries took in Africa and Polynesia and ventured as far as the Sumerian and ancient Egyptian and Greek civilisations before reaching China and America in the 1986–1987 lecture series, and South-East Asia, Australia and the Inuit world in subsequent years. The lectures gave rise to numerous papers and other writings that were as much drafts as finished articles. One of the first, 'Semen and Blood' (Héritier 1985d), was published in *La Nouvelle Revue de Psychanalyse*, founded by Jean-Bertrand Pontalis (1924–2013), which, despite being the organ of the

French psychoanalytical association, was aimed at a wide readership. J. Pouillon, a member of Lévi-Strauss's LAS, was on the editorial board, and he invited Françoise Héritier to write an article for the journal. For her, this was an opportunity to bring together the ethnographic data with which we are by now familiar. For the Samo, men and women possess 'a water of sex' originating in the marrow of all the bones in the joints and spine that is transmuted into blood and sperm. The sperm is transformed into blood in women's bodies. Conjugal relations provide women with an excess of blood that they lose during their periods. When relations lead to impregnation, the man is drained of his substance, and he complains of being stiff and aching the next day. The sperm, transformed into blood, forms a foetus that has to be supplied with blood by assiduous sexual relations for the first six months of the pregnancy. The mother uses the blood, which she is no longer losing, as the raw material for making the child's body but does not transmit anything specific from her, since the blood comes from male ancestors. Once the baby has been born, the mother transmutes the substance from her bones into milk – being cold; she is unable to produce sperm and can produce only milk. The process requires all her available heat, which explains why she does not menstruate during the lactation period.

Having reached this point, it was necessary to compare this explanation with those from other cultures, as was the case with the principles of Crow-Omaha terminology. Thus it was that Françoise Héritier investigated among the Sanskrit, Sumerian, Egyptian and Otomi concepts and found the same idea of semen stored in the bones. The ancient Chinese concept is said to be a variant of this, since bones that had been washed and reburied were said to increase fertility. These interpretations were 'held to be true, since they are sufficient to account effectively for the facts laid out on display'. In all cases, bones, which are hard and hollow, protect a whitish substance (the marrow) that is close in consistency to sperm and is perceived in various cultures to be of the same nature.

In 1984 and 1985, in this final period of the socialist government, Francis Bailly (1939–2009) of the Fédération Syndicale Unitaire organised 'popularisation lectures' on the general theme 'of the meaning and place of knowledge in society'. These lectures gave rise to three volumes to which Françoise Héritier contributed with a chapter entitled 'Les logiques du social: Systématiques de parenté et représentations symboliques' (Héritier 1987a). In his introduction, F. Bailly evoked a society that, seeking

> to become aware of itself, is satisfied with neither the established disorder (as expressed in the phrase: the sloppiness of liberalism) nor the conservatism that has withdrawn into a form of organisation that . . . fossilises the various forms of domination to the benefit of those who hold power. [And] Academics should become actors who are more aware of their objective role. (Bailly 1987)

His revolutionary programme encompassed Françoise Héritier's contribution, in which she had written that her aim was 'to make available to all . . . extraordinary knowledge . . . , to fight against conservatism' and not to allow 'those in power' (men) to sleep. Nevertheless, in contrast to the organiser's optimistic statements, there was no 'established disorder' for our author but rather an order – an unjust one certainly, but one that was the very foundation of the social world (Héritier 1987a).

CHAPTER 6

INSTITUTIONAL ACTIVITIES
MITTERRAND II

• • •

MITTERRAND – THE SECOND PRESIDENCY

The left governed for two years with a socialist programme
(1981–1983) and then for a further three (1983–1986) without
advancing that programme any further. In 1986, in addition to
the High Council of Francophonie and the Consultative Ethics
Committee, Françoise Héritier was appointed chair of the National Centre for Literature (Centre national des lettres) and
became a member of the High Council on Population and the
Family (1986–1992). The presentations at the Collège seminars
continued the theme of marriage alliances, while her lectures
there focused on food and seed. Her course at the EHESS was
entitled: 'Making Visible and Being Heard: The Symbolism of
Appearances', a discussion of the Other, who was as much the
figure of standard ethnography as one much closer at hand: the
immigrant. The French fertility rate had begun to decline a century before the other European countries, and it was Poles, Italians and Spaniards who had made good the consequent labour
shortages. At the dawn of the twentieth century, five hundred
thousand refugees arrived from Armenia (1915) and a hundred
thousand came from Russia. Then pogroms in Turkey brought a
wave of Greek refugees (1922), eight hundred thousand Italians
sought refuge from fascism in France, and in January 1939 the
border was opened up to five hundred thousand Spanish repub-

licans. Other refugees arriving after the Nazis' victory were to be handed over to them by the Vichy regime (1941).

After the war, the flows of migrants from Spain resumed, and the Portuguese started to arrive. Taking over from Italians in the construction and automotive industries, there were seven hundred thousand Portuguese in France by 1970. From 1954 onwards, France began to take in settlers returning home from North Africa; more than a million eventually returned to France, to whom must be added the official figure of more than fifty thousand *Harkis* – that is, Arab and Kabyle auxiliaries in the French army. Until the mid-1960s, charter flights continued to bring in manual workers, notably from Kabylia.

The economic and social landscape was transformed by the first oil shock and some significant technological advances. From 1973, immigration was assumed to have been suspended. However, the most recent waves of manual workers were living in all-male hostels, and they were poorly integrated. The Italians, Poles and Portuguese had come with their families and, under pressure from the international community and out of sheer humanity, Jacques Chirac (1932–2019), the prime minister appointed by V. Giscard d'Estaing, signed the family reunification decree on 29 April 1976. Raymond Barre (1924–2007), who succeeded Chirac as prime minister in 1976, suspended it at the end of 1977. Migrant support associations then took the case to the Council of State, which quashed his decision, since 'it follows from the Preamble to the Constitution that foreigners normally resident in France have, like French citizens, the right to lead a normal family life'. The only problem was that economic growth had declined from 9% in 1950 to around 2%. In 1967, G. Pompidou, the prime minister, declared on television: 'if the day comes when we have 500,000 unemployed people, there'll be a revolution.' In May 1968, there were 350,000, a million in 1977 and two million in 1984. At the same time, development in the former colonies was virtually at a standstill, and young people were looking to leave. For the next twenty years, the supposed economic recovery remained on hold, and integration was further complicated by the fact that the state school system had fallen apart, and traditional solidarity was sufficient for the immigrant communities. Redundancies in manufacturing industry increased, and 80% of those made redundant were from outside metropolitan France. Non-strikers of French origin and immigrant strikers clashed with each other during the strikes of 1982, 1983 and 1984, and the Front National obtained 9% of the votes cast during the 1983 municipal elections. In 1983, following incidents of police violence and a racist murder, the first 'March of the Beurs' (*beur* is a term used to refer to a person born in France of North African immigrant parents) crossed the country, covering a total of 1,500 km (1983). Intellectuals were mobilising, including Françoise Héritier, and it was during this period that the focus of her seminars at the Ecole des Hautes Etudes shifted from an investigation of symbolic spaces (1984–1985) to the theme of the Other and the foreigner (1985–1986), the Other of the others (1986–1987) and the symbolism of appearances (1987–1988 and 1988–1989). Given over to deliberations on 'anthropology in the city', those held between 1990 and 1994 combined deliberations on AIDS, the feminist problematic and the representation of those Others often called 'illegals'. These same questions were also addressed at some length at a joint seminar with M. Augé and Jean Bazin (1941–2001).

The socialists were still in power when, in March 1985, the association 'Espace 89' organised a major conference on 'French identity' that attracted two thousand participants. Françoise Héritier gave a paper entitled 'La leçon des primitifs' (Héritier 1985e). Since her session was entitled 'Identity Crises', she clarified the former term with the aid of C. Lévi-Strauss, who in 1975 had defined identity as 'a virtual home to which it is vitally important for us to refer ... without it ever actually existing.' On this occasion, F. Héritier outlined a schema that remained present in all her future talks: there are among human beings some implicit, primary concepts that never change and that underlie all intellectual output. The origin of these invariant concepts lies in the rootedness of objects and phenomena, in the irreducible characteristics of the body and the cosmos, and they function as pairs of opposites (identical/different, continuous/discontinuous, one/many) and correspond to abstract properties of the real world. They are few in number and simple. Thus, it takes a man and a woman to make a baby, and individual sexual unions result in generations that are linked together. That is the universal aspect. In the second part of her talk, she asked: since identity exists only through a person and not through a group, what is a person? Her answer to her own question was that in the West a person is the conjunction of a body and a soul, while for the Samo a person is the merging of nine constituent elements, including blood. Now in both Greek (Aristotle) and Hindu (the Upanishads) thought, blood is a transmutation of food, and sperm is its perfected form. Thus by consuming the same foods, the outsider who is integrated by name, and not through the transmission of blood, creates for himself an identity that is shared with a group. Conversely, one of the fundamental characteristics of otherness is that the Other does not eat like oneself. Having imparted this lesson, Héritier's talk moved on to the concrete aspect of the matter: 'The immediately useful value in terms of consanguinity and neighbourhood is that of three generations.' Once they have settled in Samo territory, Dogon, Pana, Marka and Mossi are all Samo. An outsider who arrives is given land. In the next generation, marriages are contracted. By the third generation, immigrants are no longer seeking their spouses in their community of origin. And one 'point' that she highlighted as 'important' was that: 'the host community first of all takes the immigrants' daughters as wives, but does not give its own daughters until the following generations' (Héritier 1985e: 62). Similarly, among the Polish migrants in Picardie studied by Jean-François Gossiaux (b.1943), the first generation was totally endogamous. In the second generation, endogamy persisted in the case of individuals born in Poland, but mixed marriages were preferred for those born in France. By the third generation, all marriages were mixed, and the children, now wholly French, left the villages.

A few months later, M. Piault, president of the French Association of Anthropologists (AFA), organised a conference entitled 'Towards Multicultural Societies', the promotional leaflet for which noted that 'xenophobia and racism are all too often the response to economic and social problems' (Piault 1987). This was the Association's second conference, and it was sponsored by UNESCO and many other important institutions. From the 9th to the 11th of January 1986, two months away from a general election, more than a hundred participants gathered to listen to the eight short speeches given by their representatives, including one from the Ministry of Culture, who declared, 'in the name of Jack Lang', that his budget for supporting research 'had risen threefold since 1981' and that the Ethnological Heritage Mission had benefited from it. There followed the two 'overtures' delivered by Françoise Héritier and E. Terray before the participants were divided into seven workshops and gathered together again three days later to listen to the closing speeches given by Augé, Piault and Vernant.

The four pages of the address given by Héritier on 9 January 1986 returned to the ideas outlined in March 1985, including Lévi-Strauss's definition of identity as a 'virtual home', but she went on: 'here we are brought back to politics … We have to make our voices heard as citizens.' She reminded her audience that, in November 1985, the President of the Republic had established a High Council for the Population and the Family, which he had charged with the tasks of telling the story of immigration and reflecting on the conditions under which the right to vote and French nationality were granted to foreigners. Declaring 'the second conference of the French Association of Anthropologists open', she concluded thus:

Jean Daniel wrote in an editorial in the *Nouvel Observateur*: the debate is no longer between those who wish to deport or punish immigrants but between those who wish them to be integrated and those who would respect their diversity. Nobody in this debate is suspected of xenophobia and hate. On the contrary: some call on immigrants to become part of the national community, others say they should live as guests, while yet others believe that that community should now be extended, as in the USA, to become a multi-ethnic, multicultural nation. . . . If this is now the real debate, we need to complement it with our experiences and analyses. (Héritier 1987b: 38)

On 16 March 1986, the parliamentary right won a convincing victory in the legislative elections. J. Chirac was appointed prime minister by F. Mitterrand, who remained president. For the next two years, France was governed by the so-called 'cohabitation' regime, with a left-wing president and a right-wing prime minister. Although they had won the election, the traditional right's share of the vote nevertheless fell by two percentage points as the Front National increased their share from 0.35% in the 1981 legislative elections to 9.65% in 1986. By virtue of a dose of proportional representation, the Front National held thirty-five seats in the National Assembly, the same number as the Communist Party. This prompted the socialist deputies and their counterparts among the traditional right to agree to abolish the proportional element of the electoral system by the next elections.

In power, the right privatised sixty-five industrial groups and attempted to reform the university system. However, the proposed reform failed, since it led to demonstrations during which a student was killed. The reform was buried, and the minister resigned. It was easier for the government to make it more difficult to obtain a residence permit, and the decision to deport an illegal immigrant was now made by the local prefect rather than a judge. On the left, the Socialist Party had helped to set up SOS-Racisme in 1984 as a satellite organisation with the aim of attracting young people to the party. In response to the measures introduced by the right-wing government, the association put on concerts and created its yellow hand logo with the slogan 'Hands off my mate', which was fashionable for a while.

In December 1988, Héritier concluded an enormous conference on the theme of 'Outsiders in the city' by reiterating her thoughts on the 'Same and the Other', and in May 1990 she again devoted a lecture given in Porto at the invitation of the president of Portugal (Mário Soares) to the subject of immigrants. She concluded:

Man does not exist alone, the question of mankind's destiny is that of the destiny of others. . . . Mankind's destiny . . . is the collective project of the political nation which, sadly, is experiencing great difficulty in opposing the centrifugal forces of the ethnic nation. Mankind's destiny is to learn to live with one another and to put in place the ethical and political means to do so. (Héritier 1990b)

Françoise Héritier was to devote many other lectures to this motto. And perhaps encouraged by her words, Mário Soares (1924–1917) was to speak with equal generosity at the Congress of Europe in The Hague on 9 May 1998:

Europe cannot behave like a fortress under siege. The Union must be open and capable of assuming its historic responsibilities towards the world. It must therefore be able to integrate the immigrants who appeal to it . . . , while at the same time respecting their cultures, languages and religions and assuring them of the rights and duties that the European Convention on Human Rights grants them.

After the 1986 elections, the Ministry of Research came under the control of the right-wing government, and the sociologist Jacques Lautman (b.1934) succeeded M. Godelier as director of the CNRS. Godelier had attempted, without success, to bring psychoanalysis within the orbit of the CNRS, which, as a sort of consolation, gave rise to a conference entitled 'Encounter with Psychoanalysis: The Functions of the Father' (May 1987). M. Augé wrote the preface to the conference proceedings, and Françoise Héritier was a member of the organising committee and responsible for the session entitled 'Kinship, Filiation and Transmission', where she added nothing to what had already been presented to readers (Héritier 1989a).

Her personal life was troubled. Separated from M. Augé, she sought refuge with her brother and then found an apartment in Montparnasse, and to go to the Collège she took,'like [she said] an old friend', the number 89 bus.

AIDS (1989)

In 1981, the US Centers for Disease Control and Prevention, headquartered in Atlanta, Georgia, announced the deaths of five immune-suppressed male homosexual patients. Other cases were reported in Europe; these too were homosexuals. The talk then was of a homosexual cancer (because of the purplish skin lesions), and amyl nitrite ('poppers') was suspected of being the cause until it was realised that heterosexual patients who had had blood transfusions were also affected and that the disease was transmitted through sexual fluids and blood and from mother to child during pregnancy, birth and breastfeeding.

In 1982, this disease was named AIDS (Acquired Immune Deficiency Syndrome). In 1983, when the Institut Pasteur published the first description of the virus HIV-1, the World Health Organisation (WHO) recorded ninety-two AIDS patients in France. In 1984, there were three hundred, included the famous philosopher Michel Foucault (1926–1984), who died on 25 June. In September of that year, D. Defert, his partner, founded the Aides association (Defert 2014). Although scientists developed a screening test in 1985, the public feared contagion. Having come to Paris to receive experimental treatment, the actor Rock Hudson (1925–1985) made his illness public in July 1985. Subsequently, he had to return to the USA in a private aeroplane because no airline would accept him as a passenger. The first drug treatment was discovered in 1986. Although patients no longer died in three months, the WHO announced that the epidemic had already caused 15,000 deaths. France was the second most severely affected country with, it was said, 'two hundred thousand people infected with the virus.' Declaring himself officially a candidate for the presidency of the Republic at the 1988 elections, Jean-Marie Le Pen (b.1928), interviewed on television on 6 May 1987, recommended that 'the old sanatoriums be reopened in order to turn them into "aidatoriums"'. The opinion poll that followed this interview indicated that 39% of French people were in favour of this isolation, and 35% were against. There were not ten alternative courses of action. There would either be confinement under conditions that would be appalling, or the government would have to gamble on people behaving responsibly. The stakes were very high, and the politicians made some courageous choices. Inviting the population not to engage in 'risky behaviour', Michelle Barzac (b.1943), J. Chirac's Minister for Health and the Family, had the 1920 law prohibiting the dissemination of information on birth control repealed, and she launched a campaign to encourage the use of condoms. On 26 June 1988, Françoise Héritier took part in the first interdisciplinary symposium on 'Blood' organised by the Collège de France's Fondation Hugot.

In 1988, J. Chirac, the prime minister, ran for president against F. Mitterrand and the Front National candidate, J.-M. Le Pen, who obtained 14.5% of the votes cast. Re-elected on 8 May, Mitterrand dissolved the conservative-controlled National Assembly (14 May). The next government was the so-called 'openness' government led by Michel Rocard (1930–2016), which acquired its name because there were no plans for nationalisation or any other change. It included a minister 'for the Family, Women's Rights, Solidarity and Repatriates'.

Six months passed before the presidential decree of 8 February 1989 established the French Agency for the Fight Against AIDS (l'Agence française de Lutte contre le Sida), the National Agency for Research on AIDS (and viral hepatitis) and the National Council for Acquired Immune Deficiency Syndrome, whose twenty-six members were charged with the task of 'submitting any useful propositions to the government'. F. Mitterrand himself telephoned Françoise Héritier to offer her the position of chair. She was a socialist, she knew Africa (the origin of the AIDS pandemic) and she worked on bodily humours and fluids. Moreover, she had already been involved in putting together an exhibition entitled 'Le sang des hommes', which opened on 29 March at the Musée des Sciences et des Techniques de la Villette. In the same month, Marc Fellous (b.1938), head of the Institut Pasteur's Human Immunogenetics Unit, invited her to present her research at the Méribel meetings in Savoie. And although Françoise Héritier was busy with a thousand and one things, and particularly museums (Héritier 1991b), during her time as chair of the National

Council from 1989 to 1994 some twenty advisory notices and reports were produced (Héritier 2013c). She was supported in this task by a secretariat, managed by Emmanuel Desveaux (b.1956) and then by Catherine Duby-Kouchner.

The committee engaged in preventive work but also undertook information campaigns (the HIV virus cannot be transmitted by shaking hands) and above all sought to combat the stigmatisation of AIDS patients, since even nurses and nursing did not dare go near them. Incidentally, the journalist Jean Lebrun (b.1950) noted that the huge increase in the number of cremations in France dates very precisely from patients' internalisation of their exclusion, which says it all (Lebrun 2018).

The banks wanted to make a screening test obligatory before agreeing to a loan. Urged on by its chair, the Council sprang into action, and Mitterrand opposed the banks. Insurance companies were also trying to identify individuals at risk. Eluding the attentions of the recently established Commission on information technology and civil liberties (CNIL), founded in 1978, they even created an interconnected file detailing behaviours. Once notified of its existence, for whistle-blowers already existed, the National Council located it, and the courts ordered that it be destroyed. Prisons were also described as places with a high risk of contamination, although considerable amounts of blood were donated by inmates. The 'contaminated blood scandal' was yet to erupt. In 1990, the Commission and its chair visited half a dozen prisons, recorded 2,235 cases of AIDS among 88,000 inmates (a rate of 5%) and observed considerable disparities in the possibility of following a treatment programme as well as a total lack of confidentiality. Françoise Héritier persuaded Mitterrand to move responsibility for prison health services from the Ministry of Justice to the Ministry of Health. There was still some preliminary work to be done on combating resistance, from neighbourhood associations, for example, or the ex-prostitutes' bus. Finally, there was Africa, and the chair of the National council organised the fight against the influence of crazy beliefs, such as 'having sex with virgins or pre-pubescent girls cures AIDS', which, in Héritier's view, could be explained by a social perception in which women, who give life, were seen as an 'interchangeable mass'. She remained a member of the Council after standing down as chair and denounced the selfishness of the West, which reserved the treatments for itself and left the task of prevention to Africa.

The academic year 1987–1988 was a very full one for Françoise Héritier, with lectures, three seminars each week, the publication of four articles, ten conferences and the responsibilities mentioned above. After that, however, her academic activities tailed off somewhat. The Collège de France's yearbook even indicates that her course did not take place in the academic year 1988–1989, and it was not until around April 1989 that Françoise Héritier resumed her myriad activities; undoubtedly her illness was the reason for her absence.

At that time, she was much translated into Italian, Spanish and Portuguese, but for English-speaking readers there was only her contribution to M. Izard and P. Smith's book, which was of interest only to the narrow circle of anthropologists. In 1989, Ramona Naddaff (b.1959), Nadia Tazi (b.1954) and Michel Feher (b.1956) edited the three volumes of *Fragments for a History of the Human Body*, an important publication that included two articles by Françoise Héritier (1989d, 1989e), who by this means crossed the barrier of the Atlantic.

In December 1989, the government set up a High Council on Integration directly attached to the offices of the prime minister. Its principal activity was to compile an annual report on 'the integration of foreign residents'. Françoise Héritier was appointed to serve on the High Council, and on the 31st of the same month F. Mitterrand made her Chevalier de l'Ordre de la Légion d'Honneur. Françoise Héritier accepted the honour without qualms. She often expressed her admiration for the president's intelligence (Wehn-Damisch 2008), and then there were her parents, and here we touch upon a personal element that was undoubtedly important: 'the lack of recognition from my parents saddened me a great deal .... I gave them all my books. They never opened them. My Légion d'honneur impressed them all the same' (Héritier 2012e).

CHAPTER 7

COMPLEXITIES OF ALLIANCE, INCEST OF THE SECOND TYPE AND SPIRITUAL AND MILK KINSHIPS

● ● ●

L'Exercice de la parenté had attracted the attention of senior scholars such as Philip Burnham (b.1942), Douglas White (b.1942) and Gérard de Delille (b.1944). It had also proved stimulating for young researchers, and at Héritier's seminars they presented research modelled on her theoretical framework. In 1990, the first volume of *Les complexités de l'alliance* brought together some of these papers. There were nine in all, preceded by an introduction by Héritier, who concluded that, some specific divergences notwithstanding, the results were consistent with a form of consanguineous endogamy resulting from an accumulation of marriage prohibitions. Thus while the Samo case was not the *hapax* that Robert Barnes had assumed it to be (Barnes 1982), it was, nevertheless, clear from the very first of these papers that the situation was more complex. Serge Bouez's subject was the Ho people of Bihar, who occupy a mediatory position between the prescriptive Dravidian systems and the complex systems of Northern India. The values of the caste system had been grafted on to an older system, so the author simply concluded that the choice of spouse fluctuated between the Hindu and tribal ideologies. Taking Senufo altars as her starting point, Nicole Sindzingre (b.1952) identified groups that practised semi-complex alliances, but she presented no genealogical statistics. Jean-Pierre Chauveau's (b.1944) Gagou society, with their Crow terminology, had a system for regulating alliances that was close to the model, but although the author emphasised the importance of 'adjustments', no detailed genealogical survey data were presented. The model was also left hanging in the air in M. Dupire's (1920–2015) contribution, which traced the evolution of the matrimonial practices of the Serer-Ndut people, who use the Crow terminology and among whom local reinforcement and diversification of alliances succeed one another. In contrast to Héritier, Michael Houseman (b.1951) minimised the opposition between unconscious practices and strategic choices and came down in favour of the second term in the case of the Beti people of Cameroon, who prohibit marriages between genealogically related individuals– that is, they typically marry away from the father's and the mother's lineages. There is no dispersion of alliances but regularities identified by statistical analysis of marriages between distant consanguines. However, the official kinship system is overloaded, and it is only through a relative lack of compliance with the prohibitions that loops are created. It is not until Danielle Jonckers' (b.1947) patrilineal and patrilocal Minyanka people of Mali that we come across a group whose system is clearly one in which alliances are renewed every three generations. Similarly, the set of 485 marriages among P. Burnham's Gbaya people of Cameroon is characterised by a regularity achieved through a high level of polygyny (the daughter of a second or third wife is given away in marriage). Again in Cameroon, E. Copet-Rougier's Mkako people, with their Omaha terminology, share the Samo prohibitions; since the descendants of those who have left the group continue to take spouses from it, they are an example of the model made concrete. The book ends with a chapter by R. Tom Zuidema (1927–2016), in which it is surmised that Inca terminology had certain Omaha characteristics, with matrimonial alliances beyond the 4th degree. The book's main contribution is that E. Copet-Rougier and P. Burnham show that distant consanguinity takes precedence over territory, which answers an objection raised as early as 1966, and to which the Samo case did not provide the conditions for a response: consanguineous loops are not created by a cumulative effect in a restricted space.

At the same time, Izard and Pierre Bonte (1942–2013) took over the management of a team compiling a *Dictionary of Anthropology and Ethnology* (Paris: PUF 1991). Bonte wrote the entry on 'kinship', E. Copet-Rougier those on 'alliance', 'clan' and 'residence' and Héritier those on 'family' and 'incest'. The entry on the 'family' takes up the thread of the first chapter of G. Murdock's *Social Structure*: the primary conjugal cell is always the basic unit, and in polygamous families several units share the same spouse. Héritier adds that this institution has a 'particular biological basis: the fact that oestrus occurs every month and that human females are constantly receptive' (Héritier 1991c: 273). This is one the few encyclopaedia articles dedicated to the family that does not ignore this fact. It should also be noted that Héritier had taken part the previous year in a round table discussion on 'Sexual differentiation in humans and animals'.[1] In her article, she tells us that a family needs 'a man's continuous presence' and then comes the argument advanced by Lévi-Strauss; namely, that the prohibition of incest establishes exchange and peace, and the division of labour establishes dependency between the two sexes. There is nothing new in this encyclopaedia entry on the family, but the entry on incest is more distinctive, since Héritier uses, perhaps for the first time in writing, the expression 'incest of the second type'. Here it was the entry in the *Encyclopedia of the Social Sciences* (1932) on incest by Reo Fortune (1903–1979) that inspired her. Although incest is generally perceived as an illicit relationship between two partners of opposite sexes, Françoise Héritier argues that the empirical reality shows that the concept should be extended to the establishment of a relationship not between two persons but with a partner of the same sex via an intermediary. In the Hittite world, in Leviticus and the Koran, and among Christians, contact with the 'identical' substances of two sisters is forbidden and it is a fact that exchange theory does not explain this prohibition. According to Héritier, the explanation is that human beings, having in the beginning taken as the

starting point for their thinking observation of the difference between the sexes, conceive the world as resulting from a balance
between the identical and the different. One of the consequences
of this is the prohibition on that which would bring together two
identical substances; thus this incest of the second type encompasses the first type.

In 1991, a second volume of *Les complexités de l'alliance* (Héritier 1991e) was introduced by Copet-Rougier, who noted that
marriage constructed inequalities by creating a distinction in the
heritage of opposite-sex full siblings. The book includes four articles on alliances in Europe, four on Arab marriage systems and
a mathematical transcription of the elementary structures. In
May–June 1989, P. Bonte had organised a conference on kinship
in the Mediterranean, at which Héritier spoke about the elective kinship (Héritier 1994a) to which the 1989–1990 seminars
were devoted, while in the following year the theme was about
brotherhood relationships. The main reference on the question
of so-called Arab marriage at the time was an article by Robert
Murphy (1924–1990) and Leonard Kasdan revealing segmenta-
tion (Murphy 1959). For his part, Lévi-Strauss had wondered in
1958 whether Arab marriage should be classified with the complex or semi-complex systems (Lévi-Strauss 1959), and Héritier
was to ask the same question, whereas Suzy Bernus (1928–1990)
advanced the hypothesis that the Tuareg system was based on
cognatic descent groups (Héritier 1992b). In fact, in so far as the
terminology denotes Ego must marry his father's brother daughter, Tuareg alliance can be classified as an elementary structure,
although at the same time it shatters the category because this
choice tends to lead to fissions rather than reciprocity. Here, in
this second volume, P. Bonte approaches Arab marriage by disregarding alliance in favour of brother-sister and brother-brother
relations and concludes that they are based on a proximity of
status and genealogy that is framed by an ideology of honour,
'which is lost by women and acquired by men'. The same applies
in South Kanem (Chad), where Edouard Conte observed that
the agnatic genealogy clashes with Koranic ideology, in which all
categories of cousins are marriageable and that distant and close

alternate. The alliance circles of an endogamous group of Isla-
mised Dogon in the Tabi Massif studied by Marie-Hélène Cazes
reveal a preference for the matrilateral cross cousin and for the
patrilateral parallel cousin. Erik Guignard, recognising the sibling group as a unit of exchange, noted that ternary closure cycles
were pre-eminent, but at the cost of abandoning the prescriptions of Arab marriage in favour of cognatic kinship. The second
part of the book, devoted to an investigation of kinship in European societies, opens with a study of Corsica. Gérard Lenclud
(b.1941) discovered consanguineous marriages there that are
governed by a desire to reproduce a line in which the women neither receive a dowry nor inherit land. Martine Segalen (b.1940)
reported on fifty domestic groups in the Bigouden area of Brit-
tany and noted that the practice of relinking alliances served to
thwart the high level of mobility among domestic groups in an
egalitarian inheritance system. F. Zonabend noted that the practice among the Haguais of Lower Normandy was for late marriages with alliances between cousins born of full siblings, the
aim of which was to compensate for inegalitarian inheritance
practices implemented during the parents' lifetime. P. Lamaison,
finally, questioned the relevance of the 'complex structure' category, since peasant societies had fractured during the transition
from egalitarian to inegalitarian societies and had done so again
during the transition to the urban world. Instead, he proposed a
typology of combinations of 'marriage and devolution' that more
accurately reflected the historical dynamic of reality. In fact, the
initial intention to establish a Lévi-Straussian theory of exchange
came to a standstill objectively when so-called Arab marriage
was interpreted as an ideology whose logic, completely unconnected with kinship, reinforced a patrilineal system of descent,
and the Corsican and Breton cases similarly identified descent
rather than alliance as the primary social atom.

In 1993, a third volume of the *Complexités de l'alliance*, introduced by Héritier, was devoted entirely to Africa (Héritier
1993a). Having given herself over since the outset to an inquiry
into kinship, the theme of the 1987 seminars was 'violence'. In
the following year, Françoise Héritier returned to kinship in the

form of papers on 'Filiation and adoption'. Neither her lectures nor her seminars took place in 1988–1989, and the theme in the following year was 'spiritual kinship' (Héritier 1995b). The 'kinship years' at the Collège can be considered to have come to an end with the 1991 seminar series on 'Relations de germanité et fraternités dérivées' (German relations and derived fraternities) (Héritier 1991f).

In March of that year 1991, Héritier outlined her construction in Italy to an audience composed of Latinists and Hellenists (Héritier 1993b). She followed that with a paper given in Lille in the more sociable setting of a conference organised by an association for research on the family. In May she was invited to give the closing address at the annual conference of the Canadian Anthropology Society, where her subject was the 'anthropology of the body'. On her return to France, she presented 'the foundations of male domination' in Marseille.

During this period, she was concerned with the development of the South, chaired the National AIDS council and the task force examining the fate of the museums managed by the Ministry of Education (Héritier 1991b), was a member of several other organisations and had also got involved in defending so-called illegal or undocumented immigrants. In 1992, a new theme emerged at the seminars Collège in the shape of 'the ages of life' (Héritier 1992c), and it continued the following year. It should be noted that although a broad interpretation of these 'ages' or 'stages' would include birth, childhood, the crisis of adolescence, old age and so on the papers presented were confined to the then fashionable theme of 'age groups'. For her part, Françoise Héritier, who had been dealing with conception and maternity since time immemorial, focused on adolescence (Héritier 1976c, 2001b, 2012a) but also spoke on women of mature age (Héritier 1990a). We should note papers and talks on death (Héritier 1992d, 1995a), the menopause (Héritier 1998a, 2007c), and, in a context in which participants were speaking of the sociology of youth, her opening address at the 'Generation' conference held by the Canadian Association of Sociologists and Anthropologists in 1999 emphasised the fact that society was moving from the co-

existence of three generations to that of four generations, before
going on to speak of 'immigrants', who, as we have seen, contract
so-called 'mixed' marriages (Héritier 2005e). But it is in *Retour aux
sources* (Héritier 2010a) that there will be the most commentaries
on the ages of life and which even include the naming of babies.

Although she was a member of the High Consultative Council
on Population and the Family, Françoise Héritier was not happy
with it. The idea of immigrants' right to vote was forgotten after
the 1986 elections, and the reports compiled by this High Council had titles such as 'the balance between family life and working
life' (1987) or 'the effects of biological progress on population
size' (1988). Furthermore, Léon Tabah (1923–2000) and Christine Maugüé (b.1963) compiled a report on filiation from which
Françoise Héritier was excluded (1991). On leaving the High
Council in 1991, she complained that: 'it took me a long time to
get the High Council to understand certain –elementary– things,
like the fact that the new modes of procreation would not have
any impact on the filiation system.' In five years, her main published contribution consists of the four pages of 'Introduction to
the debates' at the seminar on the Future of the Population.

The Collège seminar in 1993–1994, entitled 'On Incest', was
attended by practitioners. They included the neuropsychiatrist
Boris Cyrulnik (b.1937), the paediatrician and psychoanalyst
Aldo Naouri (b.1937) and the juvenile court judge Dominique
Vrignaud, and Héritier published a book with them (Héritier
1994b). The incest theory was aired again in Portuguese in an
interview with Miriam Pillar Grossi and then in Italian, and the
main event in March of that year was the publication of *Les deux
sœurs et leur mère: Anthropologie de l'inceste* (Héritier 1994c). The
introduction to the book restates the ontology previously set
out: observation of the anatomical differences between the sexes
is the basis for the primary categories of identical and different,
etc., and contact with identical bodily substances has negative
effects (disease, drought etc.). Like *l'Exercice de la parenté*, the
book is then divided into three parts.

In the first part, entitled 'History', Héritier analyses early laws
and religious proscriptions on incest in the Middle East and

Mediterranean area and centuries of legal debates on the question. The same conceptualisation is present among the Ashanti, Nuer, Merina, etc. peoples. Finally, while the Hittite explicitly specify prohibitions on sexual relations 'with two sisters and their mother', this is because they are formulated from the male point of view. Like *l'Exercice*, the second part is given over to an examination of Héritier's research among the Samo people, whose kinship system she dissects in order finally to show that a spouse can be taken from the lineage of one of the wives of a polygamous grandfather. In the third part, Héritier marshals her arguments and concludes the book with the case of Woody Allen (b.1935), who, scandalously, married the adopted daughter of his former partner.

In sum, the infraction in incest of the second type is to be situated not between the two partners in an individual act but rather within the conjunction of two acts with the same actor, and 'Levi-Strauss's theory needs to be completed to reveal incest and its prohibition as closely linked in each culture to a total set of representations which relate to the person, to social organization, to the world and to relationships between these three universes' (Héritier 1994c: 22).

In May–June 1989, Françoise Héritier had attended an important conference on 'Marriage within close degrees of consanguinity' organised by P. Bonte at the Laboratoire d'Anthropologie sociale. Her paper was entitled 'Identity of Substance and Milk Kinship in the Arab World' (Héritier 1994a). The ethnographic evidence presented at this conference described, in particular, cases in which the prohibitions on marriage or sexual relations were linked neither to consanguinity nor to affinity, and Héritier's paper reconsidered the fact that 'a mother's milk comes from the man's sperm', which renewed the presence of the identical.

However, *Les deux sœurs et leur mère* offered readers an opportunity to examine at their leisure realities hardly touched upon previously. What was to be said about Egypt, for example, where documents attested to brother-sister marriages? Françoise Héritier responded that there would sometimes be cultural preferences for a certain degree of proximity to the identical since, she concluded, the prohibition of the second type is not a universal fact, the only such fact being the salience of the primal opposition between the identical and the different derived from the apprehension of sexual duality. C. Lévi-Strauss, to whom the book is dedicated, thanked her straightaway on 29 March 1994 and then wrote to her on 5 April to say that he had read it 'in three days' and that he found the book 'rigorous, clear and visionary', while at the same remarking mischievously that 'not all societies have enforced the identical and the different with the same degree of zeal' (Lévi-Strauss 2018b: 221–27).

With a preface by Copet-Rougier, the volume on *La Parenté spirituelle* (1995), which ends the cycle dedicated to alliance, gathers together the papers presented in 1990 by J. Pitt-Rivers, I. Chiva, Paul-Henri Stahl (1925–2008), Agnès Fine (b.1944), S. d'Onofrio, Anita Guerreau-Jalabert (b.1940), and Danièle Bohler (b.1936). These papers examine the relationships between kinship structure and spiritual kinship (twinning, godparenting, 'brother-in-law' relationships/compérage). The prohibited relations between relatives are extended to include the identities of substance created by these forms of spiritual kinship such as milk kinship or the union of individuals brought together by the ties established with godparents in the Christian world. As they are condemned as incestuous, D'Onofrio suggested that they should be categorised as 'incest of the third type'.

NOTE

1. Albert Ducros and Michel Panoff's CNRS seminar for the year 1990: 'meeting between Social sciences and organic sciences'.

CHAPTER 8

MASCULINE/FEMININE

●　●　●

KERCHACHE'S DREAM

The first government of the Fifth Republic (1959) had established a Ministry of Cultural Affairs (André Malraux) that was separate from the Ministry of Education and had laid claim to the art museums while leaving those of science and natural history to the Ministry of Education – that is to say, four major establishments in Paris, including the Museum of Mankind, together with one hundred and seventy regional museums. Minister of education since 1988, Lionel Jospin (b.1937) appointed Françoise Héritier chair of an audit commission (of which M. Godelier was a member). In February 1991, she submitted her report to L. Jospin (Héritier 1991b), who was rather more concerned with the demonstrations against his proposed reforms than with the museums.

At loggerheads with the president Mitterrand, the prime minister M. Rocard was replaced by Édith Cresson (b.1934), who became the first woman to hold that position in France. The Maastricht Treaty (1991) concealed divisions within the country that became manifest in March 1992 with disastrous regional elections for the socialists. The victorious right saw its share of the vote fall by six points to the benefit of the Front National (13.72%) and the Greens (14.67%). E. Cresson was replaced by Pierre Bérégovoy (1925–1993) and L. Jospin by the popular Jack Lang (b.1939). As minister of culture, Lang had established the Celebration of music day, the Heritage Days, Celebration of movies days, etc. and managed to increase his budget to 1% of total government spending. He immediately withdrew the reforms proposed. If peace returned to the streets, in March 1993 the right won 85% of the seats in the National Assembly. This victory marked the start of another two years of 'cohabitation' between a right-wing prime minister – Édouard Balladur (b.1929) – and a left-wing president (Mitterrand). The Socialist Party's first 'primary', held in February 1995, saw L. Jospin anointed as the party's candidate in the forthcoming presidential elections. François Hollande (b.1954) was to recall Françoise Héritier's 'commitment' (2001d) to the cause of this socialist candidate, who on 7 May 1995 was beaten by J. Chirac, who succeeded F. Mitterrand.

Having seen the new president five years earlier flourishing a magnificent book on *L'Art africain* (L. Stéphan, J. Kerchache, J.-L. Paudrat – Paris: Mazenod, 1988), the gallery owner Jacques Kerchache (1943–2001) had become his advisor on matters of non-Western art. J. Chirac wanted to see such art displayed in the Louvre but clashed with the museum management. In October 1996, he announced that a museum of non-Western arts was to be established. And in the meantime, the Louvre inaugurated its Pavilion des Sessions with an exhibition of 'exotic' works, most of them loaned by the Musée de l'Homme (Dupaigne 2006).

BUFFERS TO THOUGHT, VALENCE, PSYCHOANALYSIS

It is only, she said, from 1996 onwards that Françoise Héritier 'used systematically' the expressions 'buffer to thought' and 'differential valence of the sexes' (Héritier 2013b: 36). Borrowed from the chemistry lexicon (the valence of an element is a measure of its combining power with other atoms to form chemical compounds or molecules), the expression 'differential valence' both conveys the predisposition of mental categories to make us feel positive or negative emotions and underlines the fact that those relating to the masculine are always valued more highly. She goes on: 'differential valence is not to be confused with male domination' (Héritier 2000a: 24). 'Domination' is the term used

by M. Godelier and P. Bourdieu and, according to her, it has the
drawback of causing a 'war' similar to that between the classes
while at the same time disregarding reproduction, when in fact
that is precisely why men take possession of women. Although
Françoise Héritier insisted that this 'differential valence' was 'an
artefact and not a fact of nature', she said that she was, nevertheless, 'pessimistic about its disappearance', since it was this valence
that linked the three basic pillars of the social world; namely, the
exchange of women (and prohibition of incest), the sexual division of labour and a recognised form of stable sexual union.

J. Pouillon retired in 1996 and J. Jamin, elected to succeed him
in the secretariat of *L'Homme*, set about the task of putting together the issue of the journal paying tribute to his predecessor.
He suggested to Françoise Héritier that she should 'interpret' anthropology's relationship to psychoanalysis. This was a task that,
in my view, she sidestepped with a literary response (Héritier
1997b). As a member of the editorial team of the *Nouvelle Revue
de Psychanalyse*, J. Pouillon had invited her to write a piece for
the journal. This was the article: 'Le sperme et le sang' (Semen
and blood) (Héritier 1985d, 1989d), which addressed themes
that are by now familiar to readers but which, at that time, were
new to psychoanalysts, who asked for more. In response, she
served them up other portions of Françoise Héritier – that is to
say: 'filiation, body fluids and incest of the second type'. In fact,
psychoanalysis – as such – appears on two occasions. One is in
the obituary of Christian Geffray (1954–2001), an intellectual
shooting star and the author of *Trésor: Anthropologie analytique
de la valeur* (le Seuil, 2001), of which she wrote: 'Until then, I had
not found the various attempts to bring together the two orders
of knowledge [psychoanalysis and anthropology] truly convincing.' C. Geffray 'succeeded in marrying structure and the unconscious' (Héritier 2001a: 8). The second appearance took place
when the Association Française des Anthropologues asked her to
speak at its annual conference on 22 May 1996. She chose to offer
an appraisal of precisely this theme in a paper entitled 'Anthropologie et psychanalyse: Quelques propos'. She began by declaring that she 'subscribed to Georges Devereux's point of view . . .

that postulates that all the illusions or fantasies that are observed clinically have their equivalence, somewhere, in types of cultural behaviour' (Héritier 1997a: 10). Having fleshed out this, she refers to 'The Acquisition and Control of Fire', an article by Freud that opens with a reference to the Mongolian prohibition on men urinating on ashes. Fire is said to be a symbol of the constantly recurring passion of love (sex), which would explain the renunciation. For Héritier, however, the significance of the text is that

> early humans, obliged to understand the external world by using their own bodily sensations, had not failed to notice ... the analogies: fire rises, burns and is extinguished by water.... It seems to me that here we have, contained within the human body and offered to the human mind as the first object for analysis, those fundamental self-evident notions that cannot be broken down into smaller units.

and which therefore become '*buffers to thought*'. She goes on: for Freud 'one of the purposes of mythical activity may be to represent, in disguised forms, mental processes that have a bodily manifestation. I advance the same idea' (Héritier 1997a: 14). A second point of convergence is that 'the materialist Freud relies in *The Future of an Illusion* on the consubstantiality of the brain and of nature in order to legitimise man's claim to knowledge of his environment'.

However, she went on to point out '[Freud's] blindness to the importance of the feminine: the (Freudian) fear that, in urinating, a man may extinguish his own desire arises from that blindness, since it in fact represents the prohibition on completely satisfying female desire, which would amount to the absorption and destruction of male vitality'. And then there are two further, even more fundamental objections. Since the prohibition of incest relates to the bringing into contact of two identical substances, 'what is important in the story of Oedipus is less the carnal encounter between a son and his mother than the son's encounter with the father in the body of the mother', and 'Freud bases the higher status of the masculine on the absence or presence of a penis and women's concomitant envy of the phallus.' However, 'the male desire to appropriate the physiological power to give life seems to me to explain male domination rather than women's envy of the phallus.'

MASCULINE/FEMININE: LA PENSÉE DE LA DIFFÉRENCE (1996)

The first Centre for Women's Studies was set up in 1972 at the University of Provence, and in October 1973, the Hellenist Pauline Schmitt-Pantel (b.1947) and the eighteenth-century specialist M. Perrot taught a joint course entitled 'Do Women Have a History?' In June 1975, the conference entitled 'Les Femmes et les sciences humaines' (Women and the Human Sciences) took place. Then C. Dauphin and V. Nahoum-Grappe went to Houston to attend the first International Congress of Women (1977), and the former wrote an entry on 'Women' for the celebrated *La Nouvelle Histoire* (Paris: Retz, 1978). Soon P. Schmitt-Pantel came back from the USA with the concept of *gender*, and a research group on the history and anthropology of women focused particularly on the matriarchy and, above all, read female American anthropologists.

M. Godelier, director of the CNRS human sciences department in 1982, was to say: 'When I was able, I helped' (Godelier 2007). And help he did. He commissioned Anne Martin-Fugier (b.1950) to produce a report on 'Women and feminist research', and then established a five-year thematic action plan (CNRS) with an academic committee made up exclusively of female researchers. In December 1982, the University du Mirail hosted a conference attended by nine hundred women. The 'Women's Culture and Power' group (1982) soon published a manifesto, signed by ten women, in the prestigious journal *les Annales* (1986), and it was twice translated into English (M. Perrot et al. 1986). Then followed the *Histoire des femmes en Occident* (History of Women in the West), edited by G. Duby in association with M. Perrot, P. Schmitt-Pantel, Christiane Klapisch-Zuber (b.1936), Arlette Farge (b.1941), Geneviève Fraisse (b.1948) and Françoise Thébaud (b.1952). Sixty-three female contributors (and twelve males) produced five volumes published in five languages between 1990 and 1997.

It is astonishing to realise how detached Françoise Héritier was from this scene. Although they referred frequently to Godelier's work, the protagonists largely ignored her, possibly justifiably so, since Françoise Héritier often pointed out that she did anthropology and not 'the anthropology of women', refuted the myth of a primal matriarchy and gave a paper entitled 'On the Improbable Power of Women' (Héritier 1993e). Even though it was the subject of her seminar from 1994 to 1997 (Héritier 1995c), she did not contribute to *De la violence et des femmes* (ed. C. Dauphin and A. Farge – Paris, 1997).

However, everything changed with *Masculin/Féminin I: La Pensée de la différence* (1996a), a collection of twelve articles published between 1979 and 1993, the content of which we are already familiar. As humans emerged from pure animality, their thinking was trained on the anatomical substrate, and the difference between the sexes structured the concepts of the identical and the different. The differential valence that justifies male dominance is a culturally universal fact common to both sexes' cognitive categories. A girl displaying masculine tendencies is a 'failed boy', while a man displaying feminine tendencies arouses contempt. The inequality gives fathers and brothers the right to control the women who are exchanged, which C. Lévi-Strauss 'took to be natural'. Among the possible logical combinations derived from kinship systems shaped by the biological facts, the one in which $P=FM\neq FP$ is absent. For Françoise Héritier, the Omaha system was simply 'the most accomplished' terminological combination of men's domination over women (Héritier 1996a: 66–67). The ultimate origin of the hierarchy was situated in 'female fertility', which led to an 'appropriation that for women ratifies the loss of their freedom', and the differential valence of the sexes was the essential framework providing an explanation for the social 'tripod' (prohibition of incest, sexual division of labour and stable union). Ultimately, Françoise Héritier advances the hypothesis that there exists a 'form of contract between men' to preserve the hierarchy while at the same time declaring that to change the relationship between the sexes would be to disrupt 'thousand-year-old intellectual structures'.

The book was immediately translated into Italian and Portuguese; its contents were discussed in magazines, or in the very traditional *Bulletin de la Société française de philosophie* (Héritier 1997c). When she finally went on the radio, Françoise Héritier swapped her status as professor for that of public intellectual (Héritier 1997c). This is perhaps a French characteristic, since it is difficult to imagine another country where a specialist in kinship would be invited to discuss questions such as the fate of illegal immigrants at peak listening hours. In fact, in March 1996, three hundred foreign nationals whose papers were not in order occupied a church and demanded that their situations be regularised. Their hunger strike lasted two months, and they were joined by campaigners (including E. Terray).

Foreseeing that the imminent parliamentary elections were likely to go badly, J. Chirac dissolved the National Assembly on 21 April 1997; the gamble did not pay off, as the so-called 'pluralist' left defeated the right. The government resigned, and a third period of cohabitation ensued, this one a mirror image of the previous ones, with a right-wing president and a left-wing prime minister (L. Jospin). And, following the signing of the European Treaty of Amsterdam in October 1997, which legislated on the promotion of equality between men and women, the prime minister commissioned a report on the feminisation of the vocabulary.

Héritier's 1987–1988 Collège de France lectures concluded: 'in the *conceptual chains* that link in a self-structured way representations of masculinity and femininity, matter, the animality, body fluids, food and, beyond, filiation, ancestrality, alliance and identity, two models are encountered that cannot be understood as both similar and contradictory unless the complete series of *transformational chains* is brought into play' (Héritier 1988). Since the lectures did not take place in the academic year 1988–1989, the yearbook for 1989–1990 set out about *transformational chains*: 'the basic self-evident notions that are not divisible and around which will accumulate . . . common syntactical processes and microscopic structures leading to a succession of states that organise them at a macroscopic level'. This theme was taken up again in 1990–1991 with the use of expressions such as 'associated signifying fields', 'associative chain' and 'self-structured concept chains' that were to be brought to the fore. The 1991–1992 lectures indicated that the undertaking consisted of following them up. In 1992, the article 'Du comparatisme' put forward, as an 'autonomous object of reflection', these 'associated concept chains', which, after the theoretical approaches explored by G. Murdock and C. Lévi-Strauss, were proposed as a 'third option remaining to be explored' (Héritier 1992a: 9). Finally, in 1998, in 'L'Anthropologie symbolique du corps: Pour un autre structuralisme' (The Symbolic Anthropology of the Body: Towards a Different Structuralism) (Héritier 1998b), Héritier spoke again of an inquiry into '*associated signifying chains*', based on the 'postulate' that it was 'the entire body of possible representations in the same field' that made sense. The hard core of basic self-evident notions placed limits on the possibilities that might emerge and of course also 'a few solutions are unthinkable because their realisation would be incompatible with others' (the example obviously being the non-existence of the seventh terminology ($FM=P \neq FP$) that would imply the predominance of the female over the male: 'assuming that it would be realised in a society with a coherent system of designation, residence, filiation and rules governing alliance, succession and inheritance') (Héritier [1998b], D'Onofrio and Terray 2018c: 26). We cannot develop here the work program proposed by Françoise Héritier on the signifying chain, but I would consider that her outline was the highest point of her theoretical reflection.

RETIREMENT (1999)

The second volume of papers given at the 'Seminar on violence' was published in August 1999 (Héritier 1999c), and Françoise

Héritier retired in December. She wrote about pain (Héritier 2000c, 2002a), and her health prevented her from reaching the maximum retirement age. Jean-Luc Jamard (b.1942), E. Terray and Margarita Xanthakou (b.1943) compiled *En substances: Textes pour Françoise Héritier* (Jamard et al. 2000) (forty-six contributions), and she was offered a large female nude by Michael Bastow (b.1943), an artist whose work she was to comment on (Héritier 2011d).

Three years earlier, C. Lévi-Strauss had published in *La Repubblica* 'The lesson to be learnt from the mad cows' (24 November 1996). In the UK, two hundred thousand cattle had been infected with a prion that caused a neurodegenerative disease. It originated in cattle feed made from bone meal, and the disease was transmitted to humans through the consumption of meat from infected animals. In his article, Lévi-Strauss dreams of a humanity giving up meat and of alternative lifestyles developing in vast abandoned spaces (C. Lévi-Strauss 2008[1996, 2001]: 48). He also repeats what he had been hammering away at since 1955: 'humanity now manifests itself in the form . . . of a proliferating and overexcited civilisation.' A famous passage from *Tristes tropiques* was also cited by F. Héritier (Héritier 2010e: 70), and it was to a 'chair in the anthropology of nature' that the assembly of professors of the Collège de France elected the Americanist Philippe Descola (b.1949) in 2000 at Héritier's retirement.

Les deux sœurs et leur mère was published in Italian in January and in English in November 1999 (Héritier 1999d). In retirement, Françoise Héritier was now a public intellectual committed to fighting the 'sexist domination', which led her to be featured often in the media. However, she was also directing the seminar of the 'Corps et affects' (Body and Emotions) team at the Laboratoire d'Anthropologie Sociale and co-directing a seminar at the EHESS on the theme of the transition from the Roman to the canonical kinship system.

On 13 April 2000, J. Chirac inaugurated the Pavilion des Sessions gallery with an exhibition of one hundred and ten masterpieces from Africa, Asia, Oceania and the Americas. Although the director of the Louvre, Pierre Rosenberg, insisted that the objects were awaiting the opening of the Quai Branly museum, the matter was settled because his term of office came to an end in 2001. There were loans from Mexico, and France acquired a large Guinean Banda and some Nok sculptures (which were to stir up large controversies). However, most of the exhibits came from the Musée de l'Homme and the Musée des Arts d'Afrique et d'Océanie, whose building had been closed in 1996.¹ The site for the new museum of non-Western art on the Quai Branly had been chosen in 1998, and work began in 2001. In 2002, the establishment was announced as a new museum of mankind devoted to prehistory and anthropology, conceived by a commission of which Françoise Héritier was a member.

The transfer of three hundred thousand items from the Museum of Natural History began in 2003, and the European ethnology collections were put into store, to be displayed eventually at the future Musée des Civilisations de l'Europe et de la Méditerranée, which opened in Marseille in 2013. The Quai Branly was to be inaugurated in June 2006. Situated parallel to the Seine, the museum faces the Trocadéro on the other bank of the river.

In accordance with the reforms of the French state, the institution outsources as many of its activities as possible and made *Gradhiva* its house journal. Under the presidency of Stéphane Martin, a graduate of the Ecole Nationale de l'Administration, a seconded ethnologist headed up a research and education department. This post was held successively by M. Godelier, E. Désveaux, Anne-Christine Taylor (b.1946) and Frédéric Keck (b.1974). In 2018, with a view to repatriating human remains, Philippe Charlier (b.1977), a well-known forensic scientist, was appointed to the position.

About mid-May 2000, Françoise Héritier was at the Federal University of Florianópolis, where she met Carmen Rial and M. Pillar Grossi, both of whom had completed their PhDs at the University of Paris V. A specialist in gender studies, the latter had disseminated Françoise Héritier's ideas in Brazil. Françoise Héritier gave two lectures in Florianópolis. On the 29th of that month, she gave a lecture at the University of Paraná, the next day at the State University of Rio de Janeiro and the National Museum. On the 1 June, she gave a lecture at the French Consulate in São Paulo and a second one on the same day at the Federal Universities of São Paulo. On her return to France, she attended a three-day international conference on stem cells. Finally, university holiday time came, and she availed herself of the opportunity to make progress with writing the second volume of *Masculin-féminin*. Thus she was continuing to operate on the basis of the academic year, and in September 1999, she was featured in the first of five radio programmes before newyear (2000). On 5 October, Françoise Héritier starred on the 'Horizon portrait' page of the daily newspaper *Le Monde*. Everything was there: the apartment overlooking Montparnasse, the coffee table on which *Une femme*, a novel by Annie Ernaux (b.1940), took pride of place (even though it had been published twelve years earlier, 1988), the painting given to her by her colleagues, the announcement of the publication of the book *En Substance*, the discrimination she had suffered in the early stages of her career when her application to join the Upper Volta mission was rejected and, finally, the Collège de France: 'I remember a working party . . . one of us suggested that everything had to be put down on paper. G. Duby, who was chairing the meeting, proposed that someone should take notes: "Could you do that?" I was a professor at the Collège de France, but I was also the only woman present!' *Le Monde* also shed light on the title of an interview given to the Catholic daily *La Croix* about civil solidarity pacts (PACS): 'No society accepts homosexual parents.' She clarified this statement: 'I was saying that it had not been practised until now . . . The anthropologist's role is to identify the issues!' The interview also touched on her work on violence and her friendship with M. Perrot (Héritier 2000d).

At the end of October, Françoise Héritier took part in the 'Gender and Women's Rights' session at the *On Global Ethos* conference at the United Nations University in Tokyo. On 13 November, she was lecturing in Lyon, and this even was followed on by the Annual Ethics Symposium. The recently founded 'Femmes et sciences' association managed to snare her and appoint her an honorary member before she met up with her friend S. D'Onofrio in Palermo for a conference on kinship. The calendar year ended with a lecture given at the Institut d'Etudes Politique in Paris.

The following year (2001), the retired professor published thirteen articles, four prefaces, a review, twenty talks and lectures, and she gave six interviews. G. Dieterlen had died in November 1999 at the age of ninety-seven, and Françoise Héritier contributed verbally to the round table tribute that took place in June but did not write anything. An interview with F. Hollande in October 2001 for the journal *Témoin* is worthy of mention (Héritier 2001d). Less concerned to question the secretary of the Socialist Party than to demand his approval for some leftist sentiments, Françoise Héritier laid charges against the 'technocratic vocabulary' that reduced development to 'the provision of goods and services to consumers' and against the building of roads for heavy goods vehicles, when what was required was piggyback transportation. Héritier's reference point was NGOs and civil society, the underlying theme being denunciation of a policy that was likened to 'company management'. And of course she was in favour of the Tobin tax proposed by the Association for the Taxation of Financial Transactions and Citizens' Action (founded in 1998). And then finally: 'one of the reasons why action in favour of equal rights for men and women must be maintained is that the brutal exclusion of women is the matrix for all the others' (Héritier [2001d]2009c: 255).

In January 2002, Françoise Héritier spoke of violence, and several lectures followed on this theme. In February, she hailed the new legislation on names (June 2001) in an article entitled: 'La transmission du nom revisitée': whereas previously the 'power of the father's name' had prevailed absolutely, 'filiation is hereinafter to be established simultaneously by both parents, who have the right to choose either the father's or the mother's name'. And she wagered: 'when the mother's name was added to the child's surname, it was that of the mother's father. Hereinafter it might be that of the mother's mother, which she will perhaps have received from her own mother: in this way, we shall see strictly uterine lines established' (Héritier 2002b: 176–77).

After five years of a third period of cohabitation with a right-wing president and socialist prime minister, the parties decided that it should not begin all over again, and a referendum in the year 2000 cut the president's term of office from seven to five years. The first round of the presidential election was held on 21 April 2002. The extreme left obtained 5.5% of the vote's case, the Communist Party 3.6%, the leftist republican Jean-Pierre Chevènement 5.33% and the Greens 5.25 %. In short, with this 20% and the 40% who abstained, only 16.18% of the votes were cast for L. Jospin, who ended the first round in third place. Everyone professed astonishment, but all they had to do was count. Thus although J.-M. Le Pen (16.86 %), the Front National candidate, was hard on the heels of J. Chirac (19.88%), a march with more than a million demonstrators restored normality, and Chirac was re-elected on 1 May with 82.21% of the votes.

The legislative elections of June 2002 were also won by the right-wing parties, and with less than 5% of the votes, the Greens and the Communist Party had 3 and 21 deputies, while the Front National had none, despite an 11.5% share of the vote. Objectively, a section of the French population was no longer represented in the National Assembly. Right-winger Jean-Pierre Raffarin (b.1948) succeeded L. Jospin as prime minister, and the European Union devoted its Seville summit to 'migratory flows' just as one hundred and thirty undocumented migrants occupied the Basilica of Saint-Denis on 17 August.

Many commentators criticised *Masculin/féminin: La Pensée de la différence* (1996) for leaving little room for hope. Given that the prohibition of incest, the sexual division of labour and a stable form of union were all linked by the differential valence, the unequal status of women was not dependent on the socio-economic situation. 'To think is to classify', wrote C. Lévi-Strauss in *The Savage Mind* (1962), and since the binary order that is inimical to cognitive categories is intra-language, women themselves are actors in the structure of domination. Consequently, in returning to the subject behind the structure in *Dissoudre la hiérarchie*, the second volume of *Masculin/Féminin* (2002c), Françoise Héritier toughened both her tone and the content: there is a 'global, ideological, political, religious, institutional and familial, public and private' consensus on 'maintaining a part of humanity in a state of inferiority . . . from the most industrialised to the most archaic places in the world'. The articles gathered together in this book include those in which the author examines origin myths in order to point out that many of them show men's obsession with wanting to reproduce themselves exactly, but women, who they have to employ as their intermediaries, have 'the outrageous privilege' of preventing them from doing so by also producing girls. As we saw, all the myths relate how men imposed the law and the dissymmetry because women do everything the wrong way round (Héritier 2001g). The book insisted that if the demeaning dissymmetry arose spontaneously from the 'perception [of anatomical difference] mediated by the senses' (Héritier 2002c: 127–31), its roots and cause were to be found in the periodic exclusion of women due to their reproductive activity. The process of procreation gives rise to an inequality, which, according to Françoise Héritier, collective modes of organisation are able to counteract, thereby engendering hope. 'The hierarchical model is not eternal,' and rather than notions of 'parity' (which place women in the role of victims), Françoise Héritier puts her faith in the 'lever' of the legalisation of women's right to own and control their bodies by managing their fertility, which is the cause of their appropriation by men and the differential valence (Héritier 2002c: 11). Thus she tells us: 'The present text sets out to explore not what underlies domination but what can free us from it.' Control of reproduction is what transforms relations between the sexes. Since history is changing society's relationship to its own reproduction, equality is becoming thinkable and therefore possible. Obviously, a large part of the world has not – yet – experienced this extension of women's rights, and, most importantly, Françoise Héritier repeats: 'Contraception was legalised only because the leaders and rulers were ignorant of what was happening' (Héritier 2002c: 187, 278). After all, 'authorisation was granted unwittingly . . . those drafting the legislation did not realise that it struck at the very heart of the differential valence of the sexes on which male power is based.' Calling for a 'partnership' between men and women, she incidentally raises the problem – without resolving it – of the transition to a different hierarchy, since, as she points out, unbalanced relationships are a characteristic of all dual structures in nature.

These are the basic points of the book, but *Dissoudre la hiérarchie* examines a variety of different issues. There are, for example, deliberations on cloning: since the domination exerted over women is – currently – a non-modifiable invariant, widespread adoption of the practice would increase female servitude and, by dissociating reproduction from exchange, would undermine the very existence of the social world (Héritier 2002c: 138). The official prohibition of human cloning 'is [she concludes] an act that radically renews humanity, similar to that by which early societies prohibited incest' (Héritier 2003a).

The book came out the 1ˢᵗ September 2002 at a time when, from June of that year onwards, her illness undoubtedly prevented her from appearing in person to talk about it. It was not until January 2003 that a very intensive promotional campaign got under way, with five meetings, six interviews and around twenty lectures. Françoise Héritier also agreed to take part in a large debate (2003b). And, in addition, there were three typical talks on kinship, one of them on the occasion of the first seminar by her successor at the Collège de France, Philippe Descola (17 December 2003), and active participation in the 'Corps et Affects' (Body and Emotions) conference organised by her friend M. Xanthakou in October 2003 (2004a). Immediately afterwards, she went to Saint Joseph University in Beirut for the conference 'Intercultural Dialogue and Conflict Resolution'. Her paper, in my view a pivotal one, was entitled: 'The Universality of Human Rights and Cultural Particularity' and was given for the first time in 2003 (23–26 October 2003) (Héritier 2004f), repeated at an Amnesty International study day in April 2005 and for the Angers Philosophy Society in March 2009 and then a final version was published in a book that she edited with Jean-Loup Amselle (b.1942) (Héritier et al. 2010f). In December 2003, she was in Rabat to close a conference on 'Women and Science: Knowledge and Development' with a paper she had first given in Rouen. Her final talks of the year comprised three television appearances, in which she talked about the National Ethics Committee, discussed the end of life and was interviewed by the theatre critic of the *Figaro*, Frédéric Ferney (b.1951).

There were also honours. She was asked the Association pour la recherche en Anthropologie to give the 11th Robert Hertz lecture (18 June) and by the Société des Africanistes to give the Marcel Mauss lecture (Héritier 2003c). She received the prize awarded by the Nouveaux Droits de l'Homme (December 2002) and was also the first recipient of the Irène Joliot-Curie Prize, which sought to promote 'the place of women in research in France' (June 2003).[2]

After sixty-nine years, the Société des Africanistes was in a parlous state. Changes had to be made, and the committee decided to establish an annual lecture. This was the Marcel Mauss Lecture. G. Balandier gave the first one in 1999, Elikia M'Bokolo (b.1944) gave the second in 2000 and on 15 October 2003 Françoise Hériter gave the third one, entitled 'A Symbolic Anthropology of the Body' (Héritier 2003c). Between 1985 and 1993, three articles and eight talks had borne exactly the same title, which in 2007 was once again to be the title of a DVD. It might well be wondered in what respects this series (A Symbolic Anthropology of the Body) differs from 'Corps et affects' (Body and Emotions), the name of the team at the Laboratoire d'Anthropologie Sociale that Françoise Héritier directed. The seminar papers' themes were also congruent with the title, since the subject for debate one year was 'sexualities'; in another it was 'rapes and enforced pregnancies in times of war' and in a third it was 'the prostituted body' and so on. In short, the title 'Body and Emotions' encompasses a multitude of subjects relating to the treatment of the body. In contrast, 'A Symbolic Anthropology of the Body' sets out to specify an ontology with which we are already familiar: the different bodies of men and women, bodies as the material that formed the basis for thought, and the fluids and foods organised accordingly and in various modes.

Following its defeat in 2002, the left won the presidency of the regional council in 24 of the 26 French regions in the elections of March 2004. The right reorganised, but in a referendum held on 29 May 2005, 54.68% of voters rejected the proposed Constitution of the European Union, and J. Chirac chose as his new prime minister Dominique de Villepin (b.1953), formerly the foreign minister and then the interior minister, who had been popular since his 2003 speech against the Iraq war. Nicolas Sarkozy (b.1955) took over from him as interior minister, a post he had already held, and found himself faced with a situation that thrust him into the limelight. After two youths had been electrocuted while they hid in an electricity substation after fleeing from police during a disturbance, France erupted into twelve days of riots from 1 November 2005, during which more than a thousand vehicles were torched. Faced with persistent youth unemployment, and ten years after the introduction of the labour market integration contract, which the government had withdrawn, D. de Villepin introduced the First employment contract, which was aimed at the under-26s and passed by the French parliament on 31 March 2006. More than a million university and high school students took to the streets in protest (and formed themselves into a single age group on this occasion). President Chirac suspended an act that had already passed into law, and it was eventually abolished.

Recognition of diversity and equality between the sexes was an easier battle to fight than that against unemployment, since it was a subject on which there was widespread agreement. Article 23 of the Charter of Fundamental Rights of the European Union states that: 'Equality between men and women must be ensured in all areas.' Accordingly, a Ministry for Equal Opportunities was created in 2004. Gripped by this legalistic frame of mind, Françoise Héritier produced one of her most strongly expressed pieces: 'Women's rights in the debate between the universality of human rights and cultural particularity', which we have already mentioned. As we saw, the first version, written in 2003 for a lecture in Beirut (Héritier 2004f), was used on a number of other occasions until 2009 (Héritier et al. 2010f).

The article takes as its starting point the declarations on equality between the sexes (Jakarta 1994, Beijing 1995, Dakar 2000) and draws on World Bank data showing that access to education for women improves economic productivity; nothing new or original there. From then, Héritier attacks the position that holds that 'the status reserved for women falls within the province of cultural fact and tradition and must therefore be respected, as religions are' because, it is argued, such interference is a product 'of the boastfulness of powerful Western states that wish to impose their cultural model on others', which leads to acceptance of the view that 'countries have the competence to formulate . . . their own policies on the advancement of women in the light of their cultures, values and traditions'. Noting that cultural relativism was invented by anthropologists in order to establish respect for differences, Françoise Héritier goes on to observe that 'it is always in connection with the extension of human rights to women that this argument is advanced', while exactly the same archaic dominant model is encountered everywhere! The text explains the primal realisation of the physiological difference, the identical and the different, the binary nature of the cognitive categories that still connote female inferiority, etc. and that a universal order was finally established that functions by depriving women of their freedom and access to knowledge and positions of authority. This is why the argument that customs should be respected is absolutely a snare and a delusion: there is no such thing as cultural relativism because we are dealing here with 'a culture shared by all of humanity', and 'it has to be changed because women are human beings in exactly the same way as men' (Héritier 2010f: 34).

In May 2006, Reine Prat submitted a report to the Minister of Culture that concluded with a proposal for 'non-sexist writing', which heralded the start of campaigns for so-called 'inclusive' writing. Françoise Héritier viewed the proposal with disfavour (Héritier 2017h). In 2001, she remarked: 'For six years, I was *le représentant français* on the academic council of the United Nations University'(and not *la représentante*) (Héritier [2001d]2009c: 236), and in 2013 she referred to: 'My journey as a *chercheur* (researcher)' (and not the feminine *chercheuse*). Nevertheless, she was not hostile to all linguistic innovation, because she sponsored a petition to submit a complaint to the Economic and Social Council concerning the absence in French of a word to denote a parent mourning the loss of a child: 'a parent of a dead child is still that child's father or mother but why is there no equivalent of widower or widow?'. As for the rest, the Prat report contains statistics 'enriched by reading reference works', and the section entitled: 'Throughout Our Readings' places *Masculin/ Féminin II* between three books by Judith Butler (b.1956) and one by C. Taraud.

In mid-January 2004, Françoise Héritier travelled across Morocco on a trip that took her from Mohammed V University in Rabat in December to the International Book Fair in Tangier (Morocco). This was the second event of this kind after Brazil in 2000; the next one was to be in Germany in January 2005. In October 2006, she travel again to receive an honorary PhD degree from the University of Ottawa, and M.-B. Tahon organised a conference around her work (Héritier 2010g) before she went to meet Pierre-André Tremblay (b.1954) at Laval University. She returned to Buenos Aires in May 2007, on the occasion of the publication of the Spanish translation of *Masculin/féminin II* and gave the closing lecture at the International Book Fair. And then except for a trip to Brussels, she stopped travelling. For the next ten years, lectures and papers were no longer given anywhere other than France. Once again, her illness was the cause. This is why, she said, somewhat forgetfully, to Laure Adler in May 2017: 'I haven't travelled so much' (Héritier 2017e).

PHD SUPERVISOR

When Françoise Héritier was elected to the Collège de France in 1982, the time had passed when G. Balandier and then G. Dieterlen and D. Paulme supervised all PhDs on Africa, G. Condominas supervised the South Asian PhDs, L. Dumont supervised those on India and C. Lévi-Strauss supervised a few on the Americas. Thus the specialists on the Americas now included J. Malaurie, J. Soustelle and R. Jaulin, while the Africanists included C. Tardits, E. de Dampierre, L.-V. Thomas and Claude Rivière (b.1932). These names paved the way for others, and between 1980 and 1990 young Africanists could choose one of the old guard or one of the younger additions to the list of possible supervisors, who included M. Izard, M. Augé, E. Terray, Pierre-Philippe Rey (b.1941) and then Jean Copans (b.1942), J.-L. Amselle, among others. Besides P.-P. Rey (who had supervised 102 PhDs), two champion supervisors stand out: M. Godelier, who supervised twenty-five PhDs between 2008 and 2017 alone, and M. Augé. If the catalogue of PhD theses is to be believed,[3] Françoise Héritier, who 'never took advantage of her fame' (Pascale Bonnemère and explained Pascal Dibie in Faure 2017), played a more modest role, supervising only a dozen or so PhDs throughout her entire career.[4] This is almost the same number as Bronislaw Malinowski (with thirteen) and, like him, she helped her students by contributing prefaces.

Her first doctoral student was an American militant feminist, Sherrill Mulhern, who never submitted, and the last one investigated the correlations-based approach that Françoise Héritier had long used with her '*files*'. Between the two, there was, notably, Priscille Touraille (b.1970) 'Dimorphismes sexuels de taille corporelle: des adaptations meurtrières?' (Sexual Dimorphism in Body Size: Fatal Adaptations? The Models of Evolutionary Biology and the Silences of Human Behavioural Ecology) (Touraille 2008). In it, Touraille advances an argument that Françoise Héritier was to take up publicly:

> Women's food has always been subject to prohibitions. This applies particularly to those periods when they might well need to have a surplus of proteins, when they are pregnant or breastfeeding . . . . Consequently, they draw enormously on their bodies' reserves . . . . This 'selection pressure', which has probably lasted since the emergence of the Neanderthals, has given rise to a number of physical changes . . . . Some researchers believe that the physical differences between men and women in terms of stature, weight and strength, might not be an original biological characteristic

but 'a constructed difference' due to selection pressure exerted by men. (2007d)

If this is the case, it would obviously be a major discovery. However, it has also on occasions been refuted. Thus, for example, another feminist, Peggy Sastre (b.1981), wrote that the hypothesis of 'a constructed difference' caused by 'an imposed selection pressure' 'totally contradicts a hundred and fifty years of research ... the same sexual dimorphism is observed among virtually all primates'.[5] Nevertheless, Françoise Héritier returned to the subject in 2009: 'Priscille Touraille's work shows that the morphological difference in weight and height between men and women is a question not of nature but of access to food. . . . It will take generations for women to reach their real height' (Héritier 2009e). The same argument, bolstered by some observations by the neurobiologist Catherine Vidal (b.1951), was advanced again in 2013.

NOTES

1. In anticipation of a National museum of the History of Immigration, which was inaugurated in 2007.
2. F. Héritier, acceptance speech, Irène Joliot-Curie Prize. Can be viewed at: https://videotheque.cnrs.fr/doc=1109.
3. (http://www.sudoc.abes.fr/DB=2.1/SET=9/TTL=41/NXT?FRST =51).
4. PhDs submitted under the supervision of Françoise Héritier : Marc-Eric Gruenais, 'Autorité et territoire: histoire d'un apanage Mossi (Haute-Volta)', 1984. Annick Wouters, 'Etude de la parenté chez les Ntsong du Kwilu, en liaison avec le substrat symbolique (Zaïre)', 1988. Laurent Barry, 'La parenté recomposée: figures Peul de l'alliance sur les hauts plateaux de l'Adamaoua (nord Cameroun)', 1996. Lucien Scubla, 'Histoire de la formule canonique du mythe et de ses modélisations', 1996. Manuela Tartari, 'Les représentations du corps dans la pratique funéraire de crémation, de l'antiquité au monde moderne', 1997. Angela Procoli, 'Le récit mythique d'une réparation identitaire: le cas d'une formation au management des ressources humaines au Conservatoire national des arts et métiers', 1998. Lidia Calderoli, '"Déposer la masse"

pour demander la paix: représentations et pratiques de la forge chez les forgerons moose de Wubr-tēnga (Burkina Faso)', 1999. Noélie Vialles, 'La logique du sang', 1999. Gilles Tétart, 'Mythologie de l'abeille et du miel en Europe: anthropologie comparée', 2001. Maria Beatrice Di Brizio (supervised jointly by F. Héritier and Wiktor Stoczkowski), 'Contextualisation des usages théoriques et heuristiques de la notion de couvade', 2015.

5. Let us say to P. Sastre: but why would other primates not share the same characteristic with the same cause? P. Sastre, 'Entretien avec Peggy Sastre'. *Le Figaro*, 25 November 2017. Retrieved 8 February 2019 from http://kiosque.lefigaro.fr/le-figaro/2017-11-25.

CHAPTER 9

SOCIALIST ACTIVIST

● ● ●

NICOLAS SARKOZY BECOMES PRESIDENT

After two successive terms of office, Chirac was no longer a candidate for the presidency; on January 2007, the UMP anointed N. Sarkozy its candidate for the 2007 presidential elections, while as far back as November 2006, 65% of Socialist Party activists had voted for Ségolène Royal (b.1953). Royal was the first female candidate selected by a 'party of government', and Françoise Héritier criticised the press: 'calling Ségolène Royal by her first name, implies that she is of inferior status', and 'I'm not sure that the main point of interest with regard to male politicians is their good looks and clothes' (Héritier 2007e).

On 12 February 2007, *Libération* ran the following headline: 'Defeat Sarkozy, now. The left must think about the second round and not target the wrong enemy.' This was an appeal by eight intellectuals – including three anthropologists: Terray, Abélès and Héritier – which they made because the Greens and the extreme left were inveighing against Royal in the hope of lowering her score (the number of votes obtained determines the level of the subsidies the State grants to the parties).

The more Ségolène Royal's credibility is undermined before the first round, the less likely voters will be to respond to a desperate appeal to vote for her in the second. These people are behaving irresponsibly. If Ségolène Royal wins, we'll still be fighting the same battles. It'll be nothing to compare with the yoke of oppression that will descend if the current Minister of the Interior is elected.

In order to remove 'any risk of seeing a repeat of 21 April 2002, some of us will vote for Ségolène Royal in the first round, others will not . . . . However, if we are to win in the second round, our attacks will have to be directed against the main adversary' (Héritier 2007f).

On 10 April 2007, *Le Monde* offered Michèle Le Doeuff (b.1948), C. Vidal and Héritier a platform: 'Women are physically too weak', in which Héritier presented again the arguments of P. Touraille (2008). To follow, two hundred intellectuals proclaimed 'Take responsibility' as they called on the French people in the *Libération* of 18 April 'to get behind Ségolène Royal in the first round'. There were thirty-one anthropologists among their number, including Héritier. *Le Monde* and the *Nouvel Observateur* published the same appeal. Three days later (22 April), Sarkozy and Royal obtained 31.18% and 25.87% respectively of the votes cast, and J.-M. Le Pen 10.44%. It was obvious that many voters feared being governed by the extreme right, as it was that S. Royal was not to be president. Sarkozy was elected on 6 May and François Fillon (b.1954) put together a government that included a 'Ministry of Immigration, Integration, National Identity and Solidarity Development', which was declared 'contrary to the republican tradition' by a group opposed to it, which Françoise Héritier joined.

OLD AGE

When Françoise Héritier returned from Buenos Aires book fair, Teri Wehn-Damisch (b.1936) shot the film entitled *Françoise Héritier, la pensée de la différence* (2008d). Three sequences were with Michèle Perrot, M. Augé or her doctor, Jean-Charles Piette, and six with Héritier alone in a bus, on the Paris-Atlantique TGV, at the country house in Bretagne, in the Bibliothèque Nationale de France and at the Collège. The film was shown at the Bibliothèque Nationale on 16 January 2009, at the EHESS on 4 February 2009, and twice on television. One learns that Françoise Héritier took 'her number 89 bus' to go to the Collège and then that her rejection for the Upper Volta mission was 'her first humiliation as a woman'. The Morbihan house provided her with an opportunity to comment on the chromo of the ages of life. We see her viewing her inaugural lecture, and the film-maker shows her handing photos to Augé. Héritier, who was now walking on crutches, evokes old age, and her last words – 'we are living in incredible times' – do not make up for the feeling of nostalgia and sadness hanging over a film that deals less with advances in understanding than with the tragedy of the human condition. The courage of the heroine who allowed her damaged body to be filmed is to be applauded. It brings to mind both Wim Wenders' film of Nicolas Ray's final days (1980) and the Dylan Thomas of 'Do not go gentle into that good night' (1951), since her public appearances proliferated from then onwards; before the end of the year, ten interviews had been published in the press and she had been heard on the radio on six occasions. A second film came out in 2009, this one commissioned by the CNRS (Sion 2009).

In March 2009, S. D'Onofrio edited *Françoise Héritier, Une pensée en mouvement*, a collection of interviews (Héritier 2009c). The first part of the book is devoted to her career and is followed by 'The differential valence of the sexes', 'Types of incest and substances', 'Anthropology in the city', 'The future of the sciences', and postface by D'Onofrio. In one of the chapters, 'Research in peril', she declared that 'the utilitarian vision and short-term productivity targets are draining away resources, whereas an apparently insignificant discovery may become absolutely crucial to a society's industrial future.' And yet the funding of CNRS teams has remained unchanged or been reduced, and in an epilogue she declared (in the manner of Bourdieu): our sciences 'are dangerous' because they 'shine a light on elements that the authorities do not necessarily wish to see brought into a public space' (Héritier [2004e] 2009e: 324). Throughout its entire length, *Une pensée en mouvement* describes 'the selective blindness of societies' that can ultimately be attributed to the 'dominant archaic model' and to the constitution from birth onwards of a girl or a boy and the processes leading to the internalisation by girls of the differential valence of the sexes: 'that hormones work to make boys noisier and more combative than girls is a proven fact. However, it is the value attributed to things that makes all the difference' ([2004b] 2009c: 372).

In April 2009, Héritier, writing in *Le Monde*, put both the secretary of state for the family (Nadine Morano, b.1963) and the children's advocate (Dominique Versini, b.1954) in their place. After the signing of the Convention on the Rights of the Child in 1989, the journalist Claire Brisset (b.1945) had first been appointed to this post in 2000, and Héritier had become a member of the advisory board set up to combat incest and child abuse and advise the government on questions such as school age. The children's advocate had managed to get the minimum age for marriage for girls set out in the French Civil Code raised from sixteen to eighteen in April 2006. When these members' terms of office came to an end, president Chirac had appointed D. Versini to the post of children's advocate. In *Le Monde* of 21 March 2009, she wrote: 'Furthermore, we are moving towards a sort of social filiation that will replace biological filiation.' And so Françoise Héritier repeated for her benefit the lessons she had given to the former minister of justice: 'in all societies, filiation is a social act.' Contrary

to the statements made by the children's advocate, it is our societies that introduced the biological dimension with the amendment to the Civil Code, since, in response to a supposed 'social demand', the legislature added a further criterion to those that had prevailed previously, namely legitimate or natural birth (in or out of wedlock), expressed wish (adoptive filiation and acknowledgement of paternity) and possession of status (reputation of being the child of) [by adding that of biological truth].

In doing so, 'and this is the crucial point; it allowed this fourth criterion to be used to repudiate the other three'. In most cases

[it is] used not for constructive but for destructive purposes, amidst conflicts of interest linked largely to matters
of finance and inheritance or as a manifestation of a reversal
of feelings previously experienced. A denial of paternity is
a major wrong committed against a child and a reference
to this repudiation will be entered on all civil status documents. . . . The primacy of the biological dimension is a
snare and a delusion and the social nature of filiation should
be protected. (Héritier 2009e)

On the question of surrogacy, she argued once again in favour
of the social over the biological dimension because, 'If there has
to be legislation . . . filiation should revert to the parent(s) who
have expressed a wish to acknowledge the child as their own and
not to the donor of eggs or the lender of a uterus.' She remained
intransigent on the question of donor identity, the subject of her
second lesson:

Contrary to what Nadine Morano, secretary of state for the
family, is proposing, surrogacy must not take place within
a family, with a mother bearing the child of her daughter
and son-in-law, for example. We should remember that in
civil law marriage between affines in the direct line is prohibited: a woman may not marry her daughter's husband.
Would she then have the legal possibility of bearing his
child? . . . what is emerging is the threat against which the
human species has always guarded itself, namely a society
without recourse to otherness in order to create the social
bond. (2009e)

This was the point of view she set out in 2010 to the National Assembly's bioethics committee (2010l).

On 12 October 2009, three hundred undocumented immigrant workers occupied a temporary employment agency. There
were soon three thousand demanding regularisation of their situation, and Héritier became involved in the campaign:

We stand with the six thousand undocumented workers who have been on strike for more than three months . . . . They live and work in France in arduous jobs in construction, public works, catering, cleaning, and so on. . . . Many of them pay income tax and social security contributions but do not have access to the benefits to which they are entitled, including healthcare and housing. The others are not declared . . . . They have had the courage to leave their underground existence. We join them in demanding recognition of their rights.

The letter had thirty-eight co-signatories, including four anthropologists: Balandier, Fassin, Terray and Héritier (2010k).

Thus although Françoise Héritier was a campaigner, M. Perrot clarified: 'she was a feminist, but she didn't really shout from the rooftops.' Héritier explained: 'I was part of the women's liberation movement in the beginning, but I very quickly stopped because authority relationships were becoming established.'She noted that 'a world governed by women would not be better' but insisted that 'we have to work to make people understand the benefits to be gained from equality' (Héritier 2015b). These are the words of a non-violent activist. In 1998, 1999 and 2000, she had taken part in the forum of the Universal Academy of Cultures, of which M. Perrot was a founder and which was chaired by Nobel Peace Prize winner Elie Wiesel (b.1928). Having joined the sponsorship committee of the 'French Coordination for the Decade for a Culture of Peace and Non-Violence' in November 2000, she supported the establishment in 2001 of the association 'Non-Violence XXI'. A few months before her death, she defined her concept of political action:

I would never get involved in violent activities that might lead to the death of a human being . . . . I use words in an attempt to make people understand . . . . And even though they're only small changes, added together, they will enable us to see big changes. I've experienced enough now to see the difference from when I was twenty. (2017g)

And, on the subject of women: 'It's the outdated ideas and attitude that we have to change. . . . That will take time. . . . That gap can only be filled through education', and 'it's from this particular relationship between the sexes that the very idea of inequality amidst difference, which is the source of all the humiliation and all the oppression, was originally developed' (2010g).

Françoise Héritier was to be a co-signatory of three appeals drawing attention to events abroad. The first was an 'SOS human rights in Ivory Coast' in *Le Monde*, 4 November 1999, with Augé, Jean-Pierre Dozon (b.1948), M'Bokolo and Terray, which demanded the release of two politicians in Ivory Coast, whose president was overthrown the following month. International pressure forced the country to hold elections, which were won in October 2000 by the historian Laurent Gbagbo (b.1945), for whom Augé had acted as a go-between with the leaders of the French Socialist Party. When Gbagbo refused to accept his electoral defeat in November 2010, *Le Monde* of 29 December published a magnificent 'open letter to President Laurent Gbagbo' in which Augé 'implored' his friend Gbagbo to listen to him. However, it was to be the victor's soldiers, supported by French tanks, that dislodged the president. The second signature was the appeal by fifty-two personalities styling themselves 'the godmothers', who, in August 2013, called for an international criminal tribunal for the Democratic Republic of the Congo, where women were routinely raped. A delegation was received at the UNO, and in 2016 Héritier was still calling for such a tribunal to be established (Héritier 2016a). Finally, 'Fight anti-Semitism and condemn Israeli policy' (*Libération* 11 May 2015) was signed by sixty-five intellectuals, including two ethnologists: Favret-Saada and Héritier.

Thus although Héritier did not get involved to any great extent in international conflicts and remained silent on Burkina Faso, she devoted the last three years of her seminar to deliberations on violence. The fruit of those years was two volumes entitled *On Violence*, a collection of some twenty-three papers that examined cases of violence and the rejection thereof and reflected on pain and investigated the genealogy of ethics (Héritier 1996b, 1999c). Héritier wrote two forewords, a preface (vol.1) and a conclusion (vol.2), a total of 90 pages. The contents of other papers are sum-marised, including the account of the Xhosa people's attempt to return to 'the previous world', and there is ontology: 'living beings have essential needs', one of which is 'to be able to relax in peace' and thus to 'trust' the people around them. 'For prim-itive groups, humanity stops at the boundaries of the family, the band or the ethnic group', and the problem is that 'the trend towards globalisation has not been accompanied by its correla-tive, namely a complete extension of the scope and definition of human groups.' Above all, she warned against 'attempts to ascer-tain whether man is naturally, that is to say biologically, violent and intolerant'. The question 'naturalises' violence, she argues, whereas it is in fact polysemous (and can even be good), and the distinctive feature of mankind is to be simultaneously violent and non-violent. If evil exists, it lies in the desire for ethnic cleansing or the crazy and impossible desire to be sufficiently self-contained to be one's own identity and origin. Finally, if the generally ac-cepted violence against women is inherent in all cultures, violence in general is symbolically gendered, the victim being feminised. In place of relativism, she advocates a code of ethics based on the universalism of human rights and a presumptive subject who, un-derstanding himself as constantly evolving, accepts an otherness that is never thought of as absolute (1999e). This credo is repeated many times: 'cultures are built on syncretisms arising out of their confrontation with other cultures' (Héritier [2005a] 2009c: 304).

MONSTROUSNESS

Although struggling physically, Héritier maintained a busy sched-ule in 2010, with twenty talks, two co-editions, two edited vol-umes of popularising articles and a third, more specialist book, seven articles, two prefaces and fifteen participations or inter-views in the media, to which must be added, among other things, a hearing before a National Assembly commission (Héritier 2010l).

In January, she began reading the books shortlisted for the Closerie des Lilas literary prize, awarded in April each year for a novel written in French by a woman. The panel of judges comprised five founders and a number of public personalities. Between 2010 and 2014, and between the ages of seventy-six and eighty, Françoise Héritier sat on the panel alongside the actress Arielle Dombasle (b.1953), Nathalie Rykiel (b.1955 and daughter of Sonia Rykiel/Zonabend of the Sorbonne group), Cécilia Attias (b.1957, former wife of President Sarkozy) and the young secretary of state Rama Yade (b.1976). The 25th of February saw the publication of *La Différence des sexes explique-t-elle leur inégalité?* which summarised her work for young readers. The book explains the 'buffers to thought', that women produce identical and different bodies and that mental constructs dating back some 500,000 years ('papa put his little seed in momma's tummy') are still in place and can be changed only by collective action (2010m). On 9 March, T. Wehn-Damisch again showed her film at the seminar of the psychiatrist Daniel Frydman (b.1945), while on the same day the film's heroine was invited on to France Culture's 'Jardins secrets' programme. The broadcast was introduced thus: 'Brigitte Lefèvre pushes the door to the secret gardens of personalities from the worlds of the arts and journalism and so on.' Thus we have to believe that Héritier was now part of that world. It was undoubtedly with pleasure that she agreed to answer the questions put to her by Laure Mistral, who, with the support of Amnesty International, wrote *La Fabrique des filles*, in which she decoded sexist stereotypes for the general public (Héritier 2010n).

On 5 May 2010, at a 'Cafés curieux' event put on by the company Electricity Network Distribution (ERDF), the audience of women listened to Françoise Héritier as she 'urged them to commit themselves' in a lecture on women and work, which was repeated twice that year. A member of the advisory board of the National Council on Disability since 2005, Françoise Héritier returned to ERDF on 10 June, since the consortium organised a study day following the signing of the United Nations Convention on the Rights of Persons with Disabilities. The speakers commented on people's life stories, and it fell to her to talk about that of a woman who became an amputee at the age of fourteen. This was a far cry from the anthropology of Lévi-Strauss, whose only biographical writings concerned a Hopi chief. However, in taking disability here and now as a subject, anthropology was deepening its knowledge and understanding, since Héritier's approach was to move outwards from the particular to the general. Her talk pointed out, firstly, that the gaze of others, whether compassionate or ill-intentioned, is always stigmatising and is answered by a 'tenacious and implacable will to reject being identified by one's handicap'. That will find expression in an amputee playing 'Orpheus magnificently' or young people dancing 'in a discotheque in wheelchairs'. She then observed that the life stories highlighted the fact that, when it came to looking after a disabled child, it was always the mothers who gave up their careers. She noted, further, that 10% of the population had a disability of some sort and then outlined the stages of integration. Since 1987, companies had been obliged to recruit 6% of their workforce from registered disabled. The act of 4 February 2002 invoked national solidarity and had since been supplemented by the act of 11 February 2005 and the UN Convention of 2010. She then turned to the ways in which disability was treated, whether with compassion, as shown by fossils of edentulous individuals who survived because their food was chewed for them, or in law: 'each human being enjoys the same rights as his or her fellow creatures', ending with the question: how far should solidarity go? This was an opportunity to tackle the extension of prenatal diagnostic testing to Down's Syndrome: 'the question is whether the problems associated with handicap should be dealt with by eliminating the risk or whether, in the name of national solidarity and dignity, it might be preferable to fund research and establish ways of meeting the needs of those with handicaps in an acceptable fashion.' Her desire for 'a genuine public debate' on the definition of what constitutes 'the good life' was an optimistic one, and she supported the 'Palliative Care and Support in Pregnancy' association, but it was the case that 90% of future parents 'choose to terminate a pregnancy when informed of an adverse prenatal diagnosis'. After humanistic thoughts, finally, the anthropological deliberation: what are the representations that compel us to think of a disability as discriminative? The response was that such representations were based on a '[conceptual] requirement to conform to the physical and psychological model of the species'. This explained why in many societies a sovereign had to represent 'the perfect man in both body and mind ... in whom the species recognises itself' and why in some societies 'his body, under scrupulous examination, must have no malformations or blemishes' (Héritier 2010d). In contrast, myths, stories and representations reveal the universal presence of a dissymmetric body, with a single leg and one eye, or divided lengthways. In her article on the subject, entitled 'Moitiés d'hommes, pieds déchaussés et sauteurs à cloche-pied', she concluded that the one-sidedness (of the lame person or the unshod foot) 'is nothing other' than a 'figurative representation of the fundamental asymmetry, namely the difference between the sexes' (Héritier 1992e). Decoding one-sidedness, C. Lévi-Strauss arranged on a vertical axis, 'in the manner of a musical score', the man with swollen feet (Œdipus), the lame man (his grandfather, Labdacos) and the man who was shaky in his gestures because of being left-sided (his father Laius) and arranged their characteristics in 'bundles' of identical structures on a horizontal axis. He presented this chart as an example of a structural analysis, interpretation of which was its own justification (Lévi-Strauss 1958a). Françoise Héritier's decoding, in contrast, engages again with meaning; on this occasion, she arranged 'mankind's most profoundly physical characteristic, namely the difference between the sexes' on the side of the monstrous as, incidentally, does Plato in the *Symposium*, where it is a divine punishment. And it is because they are the converse of the perfect body that hermaphrodites, albinos, amenorrhoeic women, hunchbacks and lepers harbour an evil power that is 'supposed to dry up the rains and impede fertility', and they are not buried (Héritier 2010a). Surprised not to encounter any individuals disabled from birth in Samo territory, Françoise Héritier observed that they disappeared. The functionalist explanation 'justifying' these infanticides on the grounds of exigency in a world of scarcity did not account for these cases, and her symbolic theory of a requirement to conform to the model is undeniably more satisfying. The requirement to conform is also cultural, and monstrousness is a punishment for infringements like adultery with a brother's wife, or a grandmother who procreates when her grandchildren are beginning to do so (Héritier 1981a: 354). With references ranging from an Akkadian treaty to Ambroise Paré via Mexico and West Africa, the article entitled 'La mauvaise odeur l'a saisi' had established as early as 1987 the universal correspondence between sperm, milk and an unweaned infant's health. Everywhere 'sperm dries up milk and spoils its taste' (Héritier 1987c), and the article showed that this in no way constituted a moral sanction or punishment but was the active principle of a natural causality. This was why there was no arrangement that could conceivably be made in respect of non-conformists 'monsters'. The extension of prenatal diagnostic tests to Down's Syndrome was driven by the search for 'the perfect baby' and the same requirement to conform.

Between the two talks at ERDF (5 May and 10 June), Héritier was invited on 10 May 2010 to give the Ethnology Society's Eugène Fleischmann Lecture, which was to be published in 2013 as *Le rapport frère-sœur, pierre de touche de la parenté* (*The Brother-Sister Relationship, Touchstone of Kinship*) (Héritier 2013b). This theme was the object of the 1996 seminar, although no publications resulted from it. However, the lecture further developed an article (Héritier 2000a). Right at the outset, Héritier declares: 'There is no doubt that the hard core of the logical organisation of the standard terminological types ... is the full sibling relationship, because it is the primordial locus for experience of the identical and the different within an equivalence, namely that of the shared status of child of the same parents.' The brother/sister relationship may be neutral or 'positioned hierarchically from the brother to the sister or from the sister to the brother'. The Hawaiian, Eskimo, Iroquois and Sudanese systems do not use a dominance principle but – essential fact – it 'comes into play behind the scenes', and the terminological discursiveness of the matrilineal Crow regimes does not reach its limits, since the real birthright of male siblings is, in practice, recognised in order to reintroduce inequality with sisters (Héritier 2013b: 25). The lecture alluded to the audience's everyday lives: whereas other systems privilege the status of being a brother's older or younger sibling, 'there is no neutral term in French to denote a member of the sibling group'. 'Sameness' is the principal characteristic of the brother/sister relationship who share the identity of consanguinity and an identical relationship with their parents, but in no society does this 'sameness' transcend the difference between the sexes.

Kroeber established that the terminological treatment of siblings depends on taking into consideration alter's sex and the relative age and sex (depending on whether alter's sex is identical or different to that of Ego). In 1958, and drawing on studies of 800 societies, Murdock ended up with seven models: 69 societies in which sameness and generation are the sole organisational criteria (one term signifying siblings for both sexes); 86 societies in which two terms denote oldest and youngest sibling without any distinction of sex; 74 societies that distinguish the sex of the oldest siblings and has three terms: oldest brother, oldest sister and youngest sibling; 177 societies that have four terms: oldest brother, youngest brother, oldest sister and youngest sister; 156 societies based only on the distinction of sex (two terms); 201 societies that have four forms, taking into account the sex of the locator: brother for a woman, brother for a man, sister for a woman, sister for a man; and 37 societies that implement the three criteria. Since the classification does not identify the internal strength of the combinations, Héritier wanted to go further. Although 'one should encounter a relatively equitable distribution between societies', the corpora set forth the marriage prohibitions from a man's point of view, since 'it is men who exchange women'. If this is 'hardly surprising', it is because it is regarded as 'not questionable' (Héritier 2013b: 31). Lévi-Strauss's atom of kinship (a brother, a sister, a husband), in which the woman subsumes the positions of daughter, sister and wife, supplants the symmetrical structure of a brother, a sister, a husband (and the daughter born of their union), whereas the Samo genealogical survey, 'immersing it in reality', shows the frequency of cases in which a woman who rejects the levirate or is leaving a husband 'drags along in her wake several daughters or sisters'. This dynamic exposes the feeling of a shared 'destiny that [these women] do not experience with their brothers'. However, when examining the positive or negative relations between men, Lévi-Strauss ignores these ties. Héritier augments the material elements – there are parents and children, older and younger siblings and two sexes – by adding the species' neoteny: parents protect and have authority over their children and, by virtue of being born earlier, the older children have the same duties and pre-eminence vis-à-vis the younger children. While there are no cases of a sister/brother relationship being correlated with a mother/son relationship, there are many cases in which an older brother's relationship with his sister is likened to a filiation. The fact that making sex a criterion in determining the nature of the relationship positions women as the youngest children brings us back to the buffers to thought, to the gendered difference observed at the dawn of humanity, etc. The invention of filiation systems is proof of the universal knowledge that a sexual relationship is necessary for a pregnancy, as is the belief that men put children into women's bodies. Not only do women not produce sperm because they lose blood, but in hunter-gatherer societies they had the right to kill (by trapping or strangling) but not, in accordance with the principle of avoiding combinations of the identical, to shed blood. The valence that determines the value attributed to tasks depending on the sex to which they are allocated goes back to this gathering/hunting opposition, which was forbidden to women but which, although risky and uncertain, was valued (women gatherers provided 80% of the groups' food). The structural systems of kinship were established in parallel with this asymmetrical relationship, and the differential valence of the sexes is a universal principle that makes women dependent on the birthright model. In theory, the hierarchy in the Crow type runs from sister to brother, but in 'actual situations that have been described in some detail' this is not how it functions, since 'the actual order of birth takes over'. As she was discovering the Samo terminology, Héritier immediately asked herself what the 'driving force' of this structure was and put forward the idea 'that this gendered male dominance is indeed its ultimate goal' (of the terminology). The audience did not escape a reminder that, of all the possible ways of creating equivalence or distinction between parallel and cross relatives, the only one that is never used is that in which cross relatives are classified as direct relatives while at the same time distinguishing them from parallel relatives. However, Héritier pointed to another blind spot shared by Kroeber, Lowie, Lévi-Strauss and Murdock; none of them had seen that 'amitalocality' (residing with a father's sister) does not exist, but it would be the logical counterpart to the common practice of avunculocality. The reason is that, accompanied by a logical series of interlocking relationships, amitalocality would have led to the pre-eminence of the feminine.

With the exception of Marxism, it is seldom that a sequence of intellectual discoveries and a programme of social transformation coincide to this extent, but while Marx and Engels had no reason to complain on their own behalf, it is touching to see Héritier question herself: 'I'm also suffering', before concluding: 'we are entitled to believe that that which has been created by the human mind could have been different and could be destroyed . . . . Nothing that falls within the scope of intellectual consciousness is immutable' (Héritier 2013b: 55). This optimistic conclusion is further developed: 'access for women to contraception and hence to control of their own fertility is the force driving gradual progress towards equality of status' (Héritier 2000a: 36). And in another lecture: 'As Westerners, we are no longer deprived of the right to control our own bodies . . . . The following two stages remain: access to power and an end to sexism . . . . A number of major obstacles remain, both in people's minds and in the domestic sphere' (2004g). And so it was that the daily *Ouest-France* ran the following headline above the interview she gave: 'Next step, share the housework' (2010o).

SURROGATE PREGNANCY

Surrogacy was already permitted in a dozen countries (UK, 1985, Israel, 1996, etc.), and others were putting in place regulatory bodies or recognising it implicitly (Belgium, Netherlands, etc.). In France, the highest court in the French judiciary (*Cour de Cassation*), basing its opinion on the principle of 'the unavailability of the human body', put it in the same category as illegal adoption, and 'incitement to abandon a child' was an offence under the French Penal Code. Reproductive tourism was on the rise, to which the government responded by refusing to recognise as parents anyone returning to the country with a child born to a surrogate mother. Lawyers argued that surrogacy was akin to the use of assisted reproductive technology (ART), while the debate was further intensified by the prospect of recognition for same-sex marriage and the possibility of gay parenting. In June 2008, the Sénat, the upper house of the French parliament, proposed that surrogacy should be legalised provided it was done for purely altruistic reasons. Two justice ministers – a former one (Robert Badinter) and a future one (Christiane Taubira) –were both in favour. In 2009, opinion among politicians was roughly divided along party lines, with the left-wing opposition broadly in favour of surrogacy and the right-wing majority broadly against. Except for her reservations about 'surrogacy within the family', Héritier's view in April 2009 was that of her political camp. In May 2009, the Council of State delivered an opinion in which it recommended that the prohibition on 'surrogate mothers' should remain while at the same time proposing a flexibility for children born abroad. Eight months later, the publication on 25 February 2010 of the little book *la Différence des sexes* was accompanied by a lot of media hype, including an interview with *l'Express*, which the magazine entitled: 'The right to a child does not exist.' These were Héritier's own words:

> Show me a case of totally disinterested surrogacy! ... The question posed by sterility is as old as the world. All societies have offered responses to it. In Oceania, for example, it is not uncommon for a child, or even two, to be given to other families .... I'm not against surrogacy on ethical grounds, but let us not mistake financial motivations for female or humanist solidarity!

And she went on to declare that 'The right to do something is too often confused with an entitlement to something. I understand very well that our society does not tolerate frustration, but this right to a child simply does not exist.' On the other hand: once '"the mental barrier" has been lifted . . . , I don't see what might prevent a homosexual couple from having the same rights and the same capacity to raise a child.' And then she declared once again:

Assuming that it is necessary to legislate on this practice . . . we should begin by recalling that filiation should be attributed to those who have 'expressed a wish' to be a child's parents and not to the donor of eggs or the woman loaning her womb . . . . However, it should not be possible for these elective parents to refute filiation because the child does not meet their expectations. (Héritier 2010c)

Finally we were witnessing the reversal of what had hitherto been a norm: 'Mater certa semper est, pater incertus semper.' Thanks to assisted reproductive techniques, a father is always certain, whereas surrogacy creates dissociation: 'one woman donates the egg, another carries the foetus and gives birth and another raises the child.' This constitutes, she insisted in *Le Point*: 'a radical change in the history of humanity that is taking place under our very eyes' (2010p).

The legalisation of surrogacy being under consideration, on 30 June 2010 the National Assembly's bioethics committee called M. Godelier, A. Cadoret and Héritier to a hearing (Héritier 2010l). With assisted reproductive technology, parents may be the child's genetic fathers and mothers, be the genetic parents in part only (implantation of sperm or egg) or have no genetic link to the child at all. Françoise Héritier noted that two of these practices had always existed, the gift of a child being a frequent palliative for sterility. Invoking 'the transition to the emotionally conceivable', she thought that the transition had been effected in the case of homosexual marriage but not in that of surrogacy for heterosexual couples and that 'it is possible that legalisation would cause the mental barriers to be taken by force', since 'consensus does not mean unanimity or even majority'. This was the position of most of the members of her party, and like them she feared there could be 'abuses' and argued 'in favour of a regulatory body'. Nothing surprising there, but she concluded with the observation she had made five months earlier, namely that the new technologies made paternity certain and maternity uncertain because it could now be divided three ways; this was a matter 'to be reflected on'. She did that a year later but without any theoretical advances (Héritier 2011f).

RETURN TO THE SOURCES (2010)

The major event of the year 2010 was the publication on 14 October of *Retour aux sources*, which is her *Ambiguous Africa* (G. Balandier 1956/published in English as *Ambiguous Africa – Cultures in Collision* in 1976) or *Tristes tropiques* (C. Lévi-Strauss 1955). As in these cases, the book 'combines a return to ethnology and to the field with some personal stock-taking and soul-searching' (Héritier 2010a: 13). Like the books published in the *Terres humaines* series, *Retour aux sources* offers some glimpse of a life story. Thus, indeed a work of biography, it is primarily an ethnic survey of the Samo people. Readers learn once again, of course, that girls 'must learn from a very young age that frustration and waiting will be their lot in life', or that all cases of infertility in couples are ascribed to the woman, etc. In 2010, the naïve innocence of the 'ethno-pretext' was a thing of the past, and the text indicates that there is inequality among the Samo, that the actors are in competition with each other and that the norms and law are harsh and even unjust. Pages are devoted to botany, agriculture, cuisine, the status of the blacksmiths, land rights . . . In this sense, *Retour* rediscovers the spirit of Daryll Forde's 'African Monographs' but is extended to include an historical dimension that had been neglected in the past, since the conversion to Islam is a fundamental element, perceived by those concerned as the advent of modernism and individualism. And it is pointed out that the women tend to be more traditionalists than the men (2010a: 29, 52).

Héritier returned to Lévi-Strauss's conception in order to define her discipline: ethnography denoted the work of describing a given society or a specific fact, ethnology was an exhaustive task of analysis applied to a population, and social anthropology, through the use of the comparative approach, aimed at generalisation. This 'ambitious task can be completed successfully only by isolating spheres: myths, for example, as Lévi-Strauss did for a set of American myths'. The distant gaze adopted by Héritier does not renounce the gains made possible for the discipline by the comparative approach, and if the discipline can be regarded as a science, it has achieved that status by dismissing 'total man' as an object. And to the objection that: 'Our disciplines are condemned to subjectivity and to their results being invalid', she replied: 'It would be better to turn the question round: are there any truly objective disciplines? With the exception of mathematics, the answer is no.' At a time when ethnology's status as a science was being challenged from 1980 onwards, this was praise for a discipline defended in the same way as in Lévi-Strauss's *View from Afar* (Lévi-Strauss 1983). Ethnographers capture in writing the cultures of others because 'no actor' is capable of expressing in an all-encompassing discourse all the partial discourses that constitute his society's ideology or: 'everybody knows how to use a system of thought that nobody is able to convey in its entirety. And it is the task of the ethnologist to tie things together.'

The book closes with a restatement of the firm belief that reason is universal and that both the explicit and tacit rules of Samo social life are no exception to this; the Samo social fabric is an expression of the 'sympathy' or harmony that, for the Samo people, exists between cosmology, the social world and the biological world. Individual representations of it are not mindful of this system, which governs the acts of everyday life as much as it fulfils a need, shared by all of humanity, to give meaning to inexplicable facts that have been and remain 'buffers to thought'. Thus it is that heredity theories reveal a correspondence between these representations and a spouse selection system. Moreover, *Return to Laughter* (1954) by Elenore Smith Bowen, the pen name of Laura Bohannan (1922–2002), who Françoise Héritier admired so much, had certainly inspired her although, unlike *Retour, Return to Laughter* does not map out a thought system. While the monographic clarity with which the ethnologist's view from afar is celebrated – 'brought to light the general philosophy of a coordinated entity' (2010a: 183) – does this reconfiguration not owe something to the work of M. Griaule? But this is a Griaule without Ogotemmeli, since we are dealing here with a diffuse, uniformly shared body of knowledge without a repository: in short, a shared belief manifested in practices that only the ethnologist's view from afar is capable of revealing. However, the question then arises of knowing whether all the Samo believed in all the items of information presented in this narrative.

The Ministry of Immigration, Integration and National Identity was disbanded in November 2010, with the immigration remit handed to a Ministry of the Interior, Overseas, Regional and Local Authorities and Immigration. To link security with the French overseas territories and immigration was not a very clever move but proved to be even less so when the title of the new ministry initiated a 'great debate on national identity', which was abandoned after protests in which Françoise Héritier played a part. On 8 May 2011, she was on France 3 TV to discuss 'Europe and the challenge of the Lampedusa immigrants'. 'What should be done, Françoise Héritier?' She replied:

> France alone cannot take in all the world's destitute, as M. Rocard said. He is often quoted, but the second part of his statement is usually forgotten: 'but we should take in our share'. What strikes me is that Colonel Gaddafi is forcing the immigrants he doesn't want back into Tunisia . . . which is creating enormous difficulties for that country, which takes in twenty times more refugees than Europe.

The failure of the 'great debate' led to the appointment of Claude Guéant (b. 1945) as Minister of the Interior. On 4 February, he declared: 'We must protect our civilisation . . . . Unlike the socialists, I don't think that all civilisations are equal.' When heckled, he explained: 'Not all cultures are equal when it comes to our republican principles .... Does the Socialist Party believe that a civilisation that subjugates women, that denies individual freedoms ... They must answer!' Héritier did so in *Le Monde*:

1. The statement originates in a 'reflex shared by all of humanity: every society raises its children to trust those close to them and to distrust others'

2. 'These primal emotions can be controlled only through analytical reasoning.

3. Globalisation has initiated a hitherto unheard intermixing of cultures ... anthropology must be added to the curriculum of our schools as a matter of urgency' because

4. M. Guéant regards 'cultures as autonomous, mutually irreducible blocs'. However, from its origins, humanity had been able to make peace only by bringing hostile groups closer together through the establishment of the prohibition on incest.

CHAPTER 10

FEMINISM AND FANTASY

● ● ●

FEMINISM

Writing *Retour aux sources* did not curb Françoise Héritier's commitment to the feminist cause. There were interviews in the press and on radio and television that were as much attempts to popularise academic discourse as forceful summaries of her views. Drawing on several disciplines and ten authors, *La construction de la différence* sets out to review Simone de Beauvoir's assertion that 'One is not born, but rather becomes, a woman.' 'Sex' being defined here as: 'a group of individuals able to reproduce only with members of the other group' because 'the laws of genetics and physiology create males and females in our species', the authors concluded that sex is not the same thing as gender. Gender is produced by the environment and the scrutiny of parents and the wider society during the process of 'constructing the difference'. The contribution of the neurobiologist C. Vidal was to be repeated immediately with Françoise Héritier on the occasion of an audiovisual recording entitled: 'Men and Women, Not the Same Brain?' (Héritier 2010q). In conversation, they corrected two popular ideas. Paul Broca (1824–1880), discoverer of the area of the brain that bears his name, inferred from the smaller size of the female brain compared to that of men that women were 'intellectually inferior' and more recently, female neurologists had claimed that since the left hemisphere is involved in analytical reasoning and the right in representations and emotions, the differences between men and women resulted from the predominance of one of the hemispheres. Héritier and Vidal showed that these ideas were wrong, since the two hemispheres are in constant communication with each other and that the decisive factor is the type of connections established between the neurons. Children come into the world with an undeveloped brain and neural pathways, and their neural circuits are constructed as they develop by incorporating the influences of their environment. It was these discoveries that informed all the contributions to the book. True, tests show that women score higher on language exercises while men have a better spatial sense. However, this difference is created by the practice of initiating boys into playing team sports in the open air, which helps them learn to find their bearing in space, while girls are not encouraged to engage in such activities but tend to stay at home, a situation more conducive to fostering oral communication, etc. A subject's gender is said to be fixed by the age of about two and a half, except for cases in which the parents have transmitted an ambiguous identity. The end of childhood leads to the emergence of the three components that constitute an individual's identity; namely, gender, sexual orientation and representations of the appropriate social behaviour. The construction of identity continues through interactions, leading the subject to adopt strategies that enable him or her to be regarded as a man or a woman (Héritier 2011h).

January 2011 saw the publication of *Ces yeux qui te regardent, et la nuit, et le jour: Regards sur la violence faite aux femmes* (2011g). After thirty years of feminism, the book's tone was not one of theoretical deliberation but rather of confrontation. Murder of girls at birth, live burials, 'honour killings', mutilations and so on: Héritier was no longer addressing women's status as the dominated sex but arguing against customs that she denounced as criminal. She observed that human beings were 'the only species in which males kill females'. This was to be a new leitmotiv. It should be noted that the book's publication was also the occasion for a reprint of the *Declaration of the Rights of Woman and the Female Citizen* (1791) by the anti-slavery campaigner, revolutionary and feminist Olympe de Gouges (1748–1793).

On 13 May 2011, Françoise Héritier was awarded the Grand Cross of the National Order of Merit by President Sarkozy. Only 137 French men and women have been received into that level of the order since it was established (1963).

'The Sofitel affair' broke the next day. The first round of the presidential elections was to take place on 2 April 2012. Dominique Strauss-Kahn (b.1949), who according to the opinion polls was would get 60% of the votes in a contest with the incumbent Sarkozy, was arrested by the police in New York. Formerly minister for economics in the Jospin government, he had been head of the IMF since 2007. On 14 May, he was indicted for the rape of a chambermaid in his hotel. Françoise Héritier was to comment on the affair on three occasions: 'The word rape reawakens the war of the sexes. Are all men sexual predators? Certainly not. . . . but vigilance is still required' (Héritier 2011h). Then she used the same phrase in a very popular magazine and in the daily newspaper *Le Figaro*: 'With the DSK affair, we have seen the archaic model resurface.' She went on to say that: 'This archaic model' is based on denying women ownership and control of their own bodies and access to knowledge and power and that what links all this together is contempt. And then: 'What we've hardly worked on at all politically – and it's fundamental – is this fourth pillar: the devaluation of women' (Héritier 2011i). Was she saying that the commentators had denigrated the complainant? She does not clarify that point. The charges against Strauss-Kahn were dropped in August 2011. However, it had not been possible for him to stand as a candidate in his party's primary, and the First Secretary of the Socialist Party, Martine Aubry (b.1950), announced her candidature in June. Although her illness forced her to spend lengthy periods of time in hospital, Françoise Héritier agreed to take charge, jointly with Caroline De Haas (b.1980), of the Aubry team's 'Women' theme.

In November, it was in fact F. Hollande who won the Socialist Party's primaries with 56% of the votes. Françoise Héritier then joined the group supporting him. In 2001, incidentally, when he had been general secretary of the Socialist Party, he had seemed to have understood the statement that 'the oppression of women is the matrix for all other forms of oppression' ([2001d]2009c: 255). On 6 May 2012, Hollande was elected president of the Republic. Appointed prime minister, Jean-Marc Ayrault (b.1950) formed the first French government with equal numbers of men and women (18 ministers), which has henceforth been the order of the day in all spheres. A chevalier of the Order of the Legion of Honour, then officer and then commander, Héritier was promoted on 20 April 2014 to the rank of grand officer, and the President decorated as many women as men. She was eighty-one, and there were only three hundred people still living who had been so honoured. Even Lévi-Strauss had never been promoted beyond commander.

MARRIAGE FOR ALL

Françoise Héritier was now a popular figure, and she made an increasing number of appearances on radio, TV and in the press. She talked about herself, spoke of the future, about 'hair' and cinema, although she stopped filling in the 'activities' section for honorary professors in the Collège de France's yearbook. And yet her activities were scarcely negligible: a new film was shot in January 2013 (Héritier 2013f), and the following month she was invited to attend a hearing of the Senate. The introduction in 1999 of the so-called civil solidarity pact (*Pacte civil de solidarité*), which is available to same-sex couples, seemed to resolve the problem of giving homosexual couples a legal status. Identical to marriage in most respects, it did not grant couples the right to adopt a child. The question was a divisive one. The right was opposed, and the Socialist Party refused 'to legislate in haste'.

According to Héritier, the general public 'began to move in favour of homosexual parenthood' in about 2004–2005 (Héritier 2010c). Her own position had itself evolved. In 1985 in the article entitled 'Les mille et une formes de la famille', a section on 'Mariage légal entre femmes' indicated that 'among the Yoruba of Nigeria, a sterile rich woman may marry other women', and she noted further that: 'it is out of the question to see these unions, the aim of which is to constitute a normal family, as a particular form of female homosexuality' (Héritier 1997e). A clumsy expression, since it contrasts homosexuality consequentially with 'the normal family'. Five years later, the entry on 'La Famille' (1991c) made the same argument. She knew, as an anthropologist, that nothing like homosexual parenthood had been seen in the history of humanity and said so again. However, people interpreted this as indicative of a reactionary position, and Héritier took up the cudgels and declared in 2001:

> Originally, marriage was the concrete expression ... It would be wiser and less unjust to give all couples the same rights when it comes to parenthood. We should not be afraid of social innovation. (Héritier 2009c: 170)[1]

Then in 2005, along with Marie-Elisabeth Handman (b.1942), her colleague at the Laboratoire d'Anthropologie Sociale, she gave an interview on the 'Homosexual marriage and parenthood' website created by students at the Institut des Sciences Politiques (Héritier 2005f). Handman had asserted in front of students that homosexual couples existed among the Azandé. Héritier picked up on this assertion. Her response to it was blunt: 'This way of presenting things is quite unacceptable. What has to be acknowledged is that there is no known society that recognises the existence of homosexual unions of the same value as heterosexual unions.' She went on to outline the classic ethnography of homosexuality. In New Guinea, pre-pubescent males have to receive a donation of sperm obtained by sodomy or fellatio from older males; however, it would be inconceivable to continue these activities once the supply of sperm has been built up. Among the Nuer, sterile women 'buy' themselves a wife who produces children for them through the intermediary of a slave. Finally, the rae-rae in Tahiti and the Amerindian berdaches 'get married' to young men, who, once they reach adult age, leave them for a wife. In all these cases, and in others, the homosexual behaviour is confined to episodes in the life course; there is no example of a society in which lasting homosexual relationships have ever been made official. For small groups, the sex ratio is the problem, and any shortage of girls has to be made good by taking them from elsewhere; in the words of Edward Tylor (1832–1917), humanity has had to choose between 'marrying out and being killed out'. This gave rise in turn to the incest taboo and the exchange of women. The crux of the matter is that the progeny of heterosexual marriages forge ties between two lines, whereas homosexual marriage does not transform 'enemies into consanguines'. With the civil solidarity pact (PACS), homosexual unions became 'conceivable' and marriage was to follow. Besides, 'for anthropologists, social innovations are always welcome. Otherwise, there would not be any different societies. . . . This is why we look on them positively' (Héritier 2005f).

However, following marriages 'between persons of the same sex' contracted abroad, the *Cour de cassation* delivered a judgment stipulating that 'marriage is the union of one man with one woman' (March 2007). In response, and after having declared five months earlier that 'a family is a father and a mother', S. Royal, now the socialist candidate, included 'homosexual marriage' in her manifesto for the 2007 presidential elections, which she lost.

In 2009, *Une pensée en mouvement* accused psychoanalysis 'of essentialising the categories of masculine and feminine', whereas this opposition 'grafted on to the apparent sex is defined by the culture' (Héritier 2009c: 169). On 23 November 2012, she declared once again: 'Homosexual marriage has never existed before but it's in the nature of humankind to innovate.' At the same time, opinion among politicians was moving in favour of homosexual marriage although many remained sceptical about adoption, which made the problem a constitutional one, since one was not possible without the other. F. Hollande, anointed the Socialist Party's candidate for the 2012 presidential elections, promised to legislate in favour of gay marriage if he was elected,which, in May, he was. The Catholic bishops, the Chief Rabbi, the Muslim Grand Council and the National Council of French Evangelicals informed him of their opposition, and the Pope encouraged Christians 'to take up the challenge'. Taking no notice, the secular Council of State delivered a favourable judgment on the draft bill tabled by the Minister of Justice. On 17 November, La Manif pour tous, the main umbrella organisation for the movement against homosexual marriage and adoption, brought two hundred thousand people on to the streets in protest; this was followed by a demonstration organised by the LGBT associations supported by the left. The question of medically assisted procreation (MAP), reserved for heterosexual couples experiencing difficulties in conceiving (1994), was ignored in the draft bill. However, opening up marriage to lesbian couples might have made this condition irrelevant, and what would be the situation with surrogacy for gay couples? François Hollande affirmed: 'Yes to MAP, no to surrogacy.' And indeed the draft bill was not amended to make provision for this practice, which most feminist movements denounce as commodification of the womb.

Since November 2012, the National Assembly's Law Commission had been hearing witnesses. After legal experts and the Academy of Medicine on 13 November, the witnesses invited for the afternoon session were the philosophers Thibaud Collin (b.1968) and Elisabeth Badinter (b.1944) and the anthropologists M. Godelier, Anne Cadoret (b.1945) and Héritier. Only the first of these, Collin, argued against surrogacy, and Badinter finished her statement by saying, 'I am in favour of surrogacy, unlike my friend Héritier.' The editors of the *Cahiers de l'Herne Françoise Héritier* (D'Onofrio 2018c) included the transcription of the parliamentary commission. It begins by contradicting those who 'refer on occasions to an anthropological truth in order ill-advisedly to reject marriage for homosexual couples', since 'as ill-luck would have it, anthropology is not taught in our schools'. If it were in the curriculum: 'our compatriots would learn that filiation systems are varied and that they should not be confused with the begetting of a child'. Having informed the hearing that our social systems are derived from mental creations dating back some two to one hundred thousand years and that 'continue to inform our existence', she outlined the notion of 'buffers to thought', neoteny, the occurrence of the mental opposition (identical and the different), that in order to have children men have to have recourse to women's bodies reduced to mere vehicles, that Lévi-Strauss had established that the social bond was based on exogamy as the positive aspect of the prohibition of incest, that heterosexual marriage is the institution developed to organise that exchange, that the differential valence makes minors of women and, finally, that she had deduced from Lévi-Strauss's theory thathomosexuality has never been accepted because it does not establish lasting ties between clans. However, humankind 'no longer needs to base peace on the exchange of women', and homosexual marriage has therefore become something that can be formulated because it is now a matter of individual choice, and 'there is no reason to reject changes in the social order simply because our ancestors did not live in that way' (D'Onofrio 2018c: 77). Thus although Héritier explained that she was in favour of same-sex marriage and the possibility of adoption, she repeated her opposition to surrogacy, which, in her view, was a means of exploiting poverty, even though it was not the woman who made the decision but the husband, in India, for example, and that in 5% of cases the children were rejected by the prospective parents.

On 13 January 2013, between three hundred and fifty thousand and a million people marched in protest against the draft bill, and the Academy of Moral and Political Sciences 'noted' that it was 'firmly opposed to the draft bill'. On 29 January, the Minister of Justice opened the debates. After the Assembly hearing, the Senate's Law Commission invited Héritier to a hearing on 5 February 2013. Once again, she explained her position. She was then asked whether it was possible to 'brush aside these famous buffers to thought?' She replied that some would lose their power over millennia (Héritier 2013a; D'Onofrio 2018c: 75–81).

After 109 hours of debates, the National Assembly completed its scrutiny of the draft bill on 9th February 2013 at 5:40 in the morning. On 12 February, the deputies passed this 'reform of civilisation' by 329 votes to 229. France became the fourteenth country to permit gay marriage on 18 May, when the *Journal official* printed the text of a law that opened up 'marriage and adoption to all couples, whether they be of different sexes or the same sex'. The first gay marriage took place in Montpellier on 29 May 2013.

PROSTITUTION

In the meantime, Héritier became involved in another far-reaching battle. As the Goncourt *Journal* (1851–1896) and that of M. Leiris (1922–1989) indicate, men's use of prostitutes was long considered normal, even among 'progressives'. However, the brothels had become notorious for their collaboration during the German Occupation, and Marthe Richard (1889–1982) succeeded in getting them closed down when France was liberated (with the notable exception of those in the colonies). Prostitutes were forced out on to the streets. Then during the 1960s, Eros Centres were offered in Germany, the Netherlands and Spain. French prostitutes demanded recognition of 'their rights', and a world congress adopted a 'Charter' (1985). At the same time, the AIDS pandemic meant that 'sexual matters' became of crucial significance, and for Michèle Barzach (b.1943), Minister of Health, reopening the *maisons closes* was 'the best means of sanitary control', when opinion polls regularly indicated that 63% of French people were in favour. The battle was not won for those who declared themselves 'abolitionists'. In 1999, Sweden introduced legislation that made it illegal to buy sexual services. Norway and Iceland followed, and the idea was adopted by the Socialist Party. 'The PS wants to criminalise punters' was the headline in *Libération* on 6 July 2006. Interviewed, Françoise Héritier replied systematically: 'education means teaching children that men's sex drive is not irrepressible and to accept that there is such a thing as female desire.' From infancy onwards, some bodies were accustomed to being satisfied while others were not, and she went on: prostitution

> exists only as a response to a demand that stems from the unquestionably irrepressible nature of male desire. It is always argued that it is a necessary evil. Why? My response

to that is that it is simply because there is a tacit agreement ... [that] everybody should acquiesce in the belief that the male sex drive has not to be contained ..., the only restriction being that of the social convention that stipulates that one does not make use of the bodies of women who are under the control of another man: brother, father or husband – except in times of war, when an attack on a woman's body is also an attack on the honour .... It is regarded as normal for men to unburden themselves on welcoming bodies because their desire is irrepressible. This unquestioned premise is false. That is what has to be called into question. (Héritier 2007g)

Prostitutes established a Sex Workers' Union and demanded professional status. Confronting them were organisations offering assistance for women seeking to escape sex work. On 13 April 2012, a fact-finding mission submitted a report to the National Assembly in which it was proposed that it should be made illegal to buy sex. It was supported by fifty-four voluntary associations gathered together under the umbrella title of Abolition 2012.

When asked: 'Has prostitution always existed?', Héritier replied:

The example of all hunter-gatherer groups ... shows that prostitution – with payment and women designated as prostitutes – did not exist there. As soon as you had the state, trade, the beginnings of urban life, I think everything was in place for prostitution to develop. ... In prostitution, the sex act would not take place if there was no payment. ... I think that the payment represents the debasement of a very old practice. When a girl was abducted and raped, a payment was due to the men of her family. This was the dol. The harm was suffered not by the girl but by her family .... I think that sometimes ... the payment was made to the girl. And it was a way of saying to her: 'You can no longer complain.' Later on, the habit became established: a girl was raped, she was paid, and prostitution began. (Héritier 2011b: 66).

Even tempered by 'I think that', repeated several times, there are a lot of assertions here. It is a 'story', and there are others (for example, why would men not have forced certain women (slaves) to prostitute themselves to other men?). Héritier then turned her attention to male desire:

> The societies in which prostitution is a common practice are those – like ours – that never call into question the lawfulness ofthe male sex drive . . . People gladly assert that the female libido is easier to control. Nobody has ever proved it. On the other hand, girls have always been taught to channel their desires; whereas in the case of boys, they are praised and valued. As for the men who would be isolated or disgraced by nature, they would need sisters of charity of a rather special kind to relieve their distress. What of isolated or disgraced women? To say that women have the right to sell themselves is to conceal the fact that men have the right to buy them. (Héritier 2011b: 68)

Appointed Minister for Women's Rights in May 2012, Najat Vallaud-Belkacem (b.1977) (whose personal website displayed extracts from Héritier's writings) declared as early as June that she was in favour of making it illegal to pay for sex. A number of intellectuals banded together to write in *Le Nouvel Observateur* that this was 'an ideological prejudice that rests on the debatable premise that sex with a price attached to it is an attack on women's dignity and that prostitutes are all victims and their clients', etc. Sex workers fought to have their rights recognised, and the bill to repeal the criminal offence of soliciting was passed at its first reading in the Senate on 28 March 2013.

The following month, the Abolition 2012 group organised 'an event' at the 'Machine du Moulin Rouge'. Héritier took part by a video link and repeated word for word the statement reported above, finishing with 'and it's really not a "job like any other" to consent to being raped several times a day by men who pay to do it . . . . It takes violence, pressure from a pimp and often the use of various drugs'. 'Abolition 2012' argued that demand had to be weakened in order to bring pressure to bear on supply and that it therefore had to be made illegal to buy sex, and in November 2013, a Parliament Report recommended precisely that. On 4 December 2013, the deputies passed a bill that, among other things, criminalised prostitutes' clients. Invited by the media to comment on the main social events of 2013, Françoise Héritier repeated herself (2013g). After seven months' delay, the Senate reviewed the draft law, withdrew the clauses on criminalisation and sent it back to the National Assembly. Finally, after it had been sent back and forth several times between the Senate and the National Assembly, the bill was voted into law on 6 April 2016, when the Assembly was able to dispense with its approval. The President of the Republic promulgated it on 13 April 2016. We can still read in the magazines and daily newspapers of the time that, when it came to the vote, deputies were chanting: 'To say that women have the right to sell themselves is to hide the fact that men have the right to buy them.'

Having been vocal on the questions of prostitution and surrogacy, Héritier did not express her views on the new Musée de l'Homme, which was to be inaugurated on 15 October 2015. It was the feminist struggle that preoccupied her, with at least one instance of involvement a month, either in the media or in conferences. In 2016, the spokesperson for the Zéromacho group, Patric Jean (b.1968), produced a four-hour documentary with her on her work and career (Héritier 2016b).

On 10 May 2017, Emmanuel Macron, aged thirty-nine, became the youngest French president in history. His party won the legislative elections held the following month. Héritier confined her comments to his promise to establish a ministry for women. She was not 'completely in favour of it', since 'it is impossible to imagine a ministry for men . . . and it turns women into victims and the protection it affords is perhaps not the last bastion of male domination, but one of the last' (Héritier 2017e). The argument is consistent with the theory, but still . . .

In October 2017, the 'Weinstein affair' broke. Harvey Weinstein (b.1952), an American film producer, supporter of the Democratic Party and sponsor of programmes fighting for racial equality, was accused of sexual harassment by two *New York Times* journalists. Five days later, the *New Yorker* published allegations by a further thirteen women. By 30 October, ninety-three women claimed to be his victims. His board of directors dismissed him, Macron withdrew his Légion d'honneur, universities annulled his degrees. An American actress urged women to recount their experiences of harassment on the Twitter hashtag #metoo, which received thousands of responses. After the publication of *Au gré des jours* (Héritier 2017b), Héritier appeared frequently in the media, including television, and she was questioned: 'the Weinstein affair? I think it's important for [women's voices] to be heard in the public sphere . . . . Things can be done to improve pay and social behaviour. But changing ideas and attitudes is a collective task that can succeed only through action.' She was 'pleased that it's the other side that's feeling shame'. So she was still championing feminism, but without rancour and with love and tenderness:

> it would be a pity to renounce love, all the pleasures that seduction brings, sexual attraction, assignations and life together. It is perfectly possible to construct a world in which relations between the sexes are based on mutual consideration, constant seduction and love without it at the same time involving the domination of one sex by the other. A woman will always be able to rest her head on a man's shoulder and a man to call her 'my precious' without that implying that one is at the service of the other. (Héritier 2017f, 2017g, 2017i)

On 8 November 2017, the exclusively female panel of judges for the Prix Femina awarded its prizes. Jean-Luc Coatalem (b.1959) was awarded the essay prize, but *Au gré des jours* was in contention. Then, for the first time, it was decided to add a 'special prize' for an entire body of work. It was awarded to Françoise Héritier.

It was time. Having been treated for almost forty years with cortisone and a counteracting cocktail of insulin and getting about only in a wheelchair (Héritier 2010d: 103), she now left home as little as possible except when she felt a need to make her convictions known. And since happiness is 'to love others and for them to return that love' (Héritier 2017e), there were visits from friends. On 13 November, M. Perrot paid her a visit. A little later, Françoise Héritier was admitted to La Pitié-Salpêtrière hospital in Paris, she died in the night of 14 to 15 November, a few hours before her eighty-fourth birthday. The Twitter accounts crackled, and the newspapers, magazines and radio and television programmes all carried tributes to her. On 22 November, the City of Paris announced that its 'Council has unanimously expressed its wish that a public institution in the capital should bear her name'. In September 2018, the Montreuil council officially opened the Françoise Héritier Primary School. On Monday 3 September, junior high school students in L'Isle-Jourdain (Gers) returned to a 'Françoise Héritier Junior High School', and on 26 September The Political Sciences Institute of the University of Toulouse inaugurated a lecture theatre named after her. The anthropologist who believed so passionately in education would have appreciated this. Since a diagnosis in 1983 that had given her only five years to live, she had produced ten books, fought for a better society and experienced many moments of happiness; a splendid lesson in the art of living.

THE TRILOGY OF 'FANTASIES'

Françoise Héritier loved life so much that it would be unfeeling to end with her death. So instead, let us conclude on a joyful note with the 'fantasies'. As a member of the panel of judges for the Closerie des Lilas prize, she selected the books on the basis of their 'persistence over time', and it is this same persistence that is the subject of *The Sweetness of Life* (Héritier 2012a). *Au gré des jours* (Héritier 2017b) arrived in the bookshops just a few days before her death. Between these two came the more scholarly *Le Goût des mots* (Héritier 2013d). She had always been prey to literary temptations. Contrary to her demonstrative style, it is through literary magic alone that her tribute to J. Pouillon (Héritier 1997b) conveys to readers the complete transformation of representations. Recounting her astonishment at surprising Lévi-Strauss, Pouillon and Pontalis in commonplace situations – on the platform of a Metro station or at Roland-Garros stadium – the restructuring of her representations is traced like a reversal of the process of turning totemic figures into superegos, as in chapter three of Marcel Proust's *Time Regained* (1927). Ten years later, in 2008, in a tribute to M. Augé, she once again had recourse to a literary style as she conjures up 'an introspection that shadows the fluid movement of thoughts – however fleeting they may be –', and she continues: 'this way . . . that we have of using a language and metaphors . . . of being "frozen with fear", of "one's mind being elsewhere". . . . These ready-made expressions conceal something profound, something connected with the body' (Héritier 2008c).

Thus *The Sweetness of Life* is constructed around a series of meditations accompanying a collection of sensations and excerpts from memories that combine images of childhood and adulthood. The first part, 'bits and pieces' or 'odds and ends', is a hymn in the style of Georges Perec's (1936–1982) *I Remember* (1978;English 2014). The second part is a piece of advice: 'We spend most of our time avoiding these most simple of pleasures.'. . . 'It is up to everyone, drawing on just a few words, to find the richness of the universe they harbour within themselves.' Her 'self-help' side made contact with the public, and there is no need to be disparaging: *On Friendship* (Cicero, 44) and the Buddhist dharma belong to the same literary genre. Having sold two hundred thousand copies in France, *The Sweetness of Life* was the second most read book in 2012. On 31 May 2012, its author was honoured to be the laureate of the Prix Simone-Veil and also of the Fondation Martine-Aublet, linked to the Musée du Quai Branly.

In October 2013, *Le Goût des mots* (Héritier 2013d) invited readers to pick up the thread, and after the fashion of Jean-Paul Sartre in *Les Mots* (1963) reverts to a child looking for the relationships of words to sounds. Héritier had already described this 'inquisitiveness' in 2009: 'I wondered, for example, why the word "spoon" as I heard it and as it was written corresponded to that particular object' (Héritier 2009b). As an adult, she clung to this 'partiality' when faced with:

> illiterate speakers of a language whose original feature is that it has tones. . . . The term 'tyiri', which I write without tone, can have five different meanings (chief, kidney . . .). I usually got it wrong . . . , the people I was speaking to could not for the life of them see how I could confuse two words which, to their ears, were so radically different. It was because I was seeing the word written down. They were guided only by their ears and not their eyes. Thus it seemed to me that a learnt characteristic (the transmission of sounds through writing) plays a significant role in our way of isolating and hearing the words in a language . . . . What we are dealing with here is actually a loss . . . . This gives rise to two questions. What do we retain of the faculty to create meaning from sounds that children have before they learn to write, as humankind had long ago? And how does the formatting function in the body? (Héritier 2013d: 11)

With the assistance of Rimbaud, Baudelaire and Bonnefoy, Françoise Héritier establishes that 'meanings and concepts, schemas and commonplaces are four methods, linked together in pairs, for understanding and manipulating reality' (Héritier 2013d: 49). Thus the first part, entitled 'L'entrée du jeu' (start of the game), is concerned with words: 'Avalanche sweeps along and tumbles downwards'. And why is 'Agamemnon a fat man full of soup?' Answer: 'he owes this definition, which is scarcely respectful of his royal dignity, to the heavy, brutal character of "Aga-" tempered by the pot-bellied obesity of "-memnon", which calls to mind almost literally a breast'. Experiencing sounds through the senses is ontologically meaningful. A second register lists the expressions and common places of the French language: 'rire à gorge déployée [to roar with laughter], avoir les nerfs en pelote [to be edgy or tensed up], bayer aux corneilles [to stand gaping], suer comme un bœuf [to sweat like a pig], mettre les pendules à l'heure [to set the record straight]' as well as some 'emotional shortcuts ... that are essential for communication' (2013d: 75). Françoise Héritier interprets these 'emotional shortcuts' in this way: 'when we say of a person that he is a "lèche bottes" [boot licker], behind the words, lies careful observation of the bowed posture of a supplicant.' A 'third register' demonstrates, by means of a narrative, how these expressions (impossible to translate) might be used sequentially:

> a–S'il n'est pas content, qu'il aille se faire voir ailleurs! [If he's not happy, he can go to hell!] b–Tu lui cherches toujours des poux. Ce n'est pas un mauvais cheval! [You're always picking a quarrel with him. He's not a bad sort!] a–Peut-être, mais je ne peux pas l'encadrer. [Maybe, but I can't stand him] b–Tu ne peux pas mettre un peu d'eau dans ton vin? [Can you not just climb down?].

Héritier concludes thus:

> I have tried to show how a human mind works when confronted with squaring the circle, since it has to play with words in order to use them in the most advantageous way ... while at the same time conserving the elemental spark of an understanding of the real world derived solely from pure sounds. The theoretical quadrants of the schema I have presented express this duality, which is both antagonist and necessarily complementary. (2013d: 104)

Detached from scholarly discourse, *Au gré des jours* (2017b) is simply a fugue-like series of emotions, scraps of memories and comments on recollection. It might be: 'listening idly to the radio in a car at night' or 'settling down with sheer delight to watch "King Solomon's Mines"' and so on. These 'madeleines' are innumerable, and readers stumble across recollections of their own, since three generations in the Western world have taken pleasure in watching a film while lounging on a sofa, and who does not recall listening with great pleasure to the radio during a long night car journey? The second part, entitled 'Façonnages' ('Defining moments'), recalls the stages of the author's life. We accompany Héritier as she joins the group of philosophers at the Sorbonne, deals with illness, finds sources of spiritual nourishment and, throughout, fights to improve women's lot. As she opens up, the academic and feminist will surprise most of her readers: *Yamilé sous les cèdres* (1923) by Henri Bordeaux (1870–1963) is cited on three occasions, and many prejudices will have to have been set aside before admitting to a love of the historical novels of Mary Renault (1905–1983).

While the trilogy touches on the essence of human beings whose lives are woven from sensations, emotions and thoughts, this listing of the 'strata of a profound self' brings us back to a 'renewed structuralism'. In 2004, Héritier declared:

> It is the body and its senses and the way they are manipulated at a very early age that establish the neural circuits and thereby create in individuals a form of primal automaticity (which can be subsequently refuted) that conditions both emotional and social responses. Thus emotions have a place in the symbolic construction of the real world. And through a feedback effect, other channelled emotions emerge from the structures thus constructed. (Héritier 2004c: 410)

Thus one of the tasks of ethnology is to 'reveal the mental structure of a given society's associations and organisations', since from this starting point it would be possible to connect social facts as different as the choice of spouse, the transmission of bodily humours and the disposal of bodies in accordance with the categories of heat and cold.

In his inaugural lecture at the Collège de France, C. Lévi-Strauss had claimed Jean-Jacques Rousseau as the precursor of his discipline. While he alluded to the herbalist and philosopher, it was Rousseau the introspective that he chose. Now the introspective listing to which Héritier abandons herself gives rise to a form of objectivity: here are the strata that established my neural circuits and embedded me in a culture to which I give expression while at the same time perpetuating it. This is the 'unexplored avenue' – the surrealists and their free association notwithstanding – of the conceptual networks that emerge 'as soon as one cares to open one's eyes and be mindful of their emergence. Thus if for me "chrysanthemum" conjures up hara-kiri, it is because of a culturally accepted association of that flower with Japan and then, through the intermediary of a book entitled *The Chrysanthemum and the Sword*, with the ultimate idea of hara-kiri' (2013d: 29).

In an earlier chapter, we saw how the advent of computer processing rescued Françoise Héritier from her embroilment in genealogical data. Can we not imagine that the 'chains of associated meanings' will one day be similarly open to decoding, thereby injecting clarity into the vagueness of particular cultural configurations, in the hope of producing a globally applicable proposition, albeit one that is constantly shifting and is consequently asymptotic? And is this not, confusingly, what is at stake, anthropologically speaking, in the Fantasies!

NOTE

1. This would be an interview with Emmanuel Giannesini dated 2001 in Héritier 2009 (D'Ofronio editor), but no other reference is given.

SELECTED WORKS BY FRANÇOISE HÉRITIER

•   •   •

Izard, Françoise, and Michel Izard. 1958a. *Aspects humains de l'aména-gement hydro-agricole de la vallée du Sourou*. Ouagadougou: Service de l'hydraulique – Institut des sciences humaines appliquées de l'université de Bordeaux.

———. 1958b. *Bouna: Monographie d'un village pana de la vallée du Sourou (Haute-Volta)*. Ouagadougou and Bordeaux.

———. 1959. *Les Mossi du Yatenga: Étude de la vie économique et so-ciale*. Bordeaux: Institut des sciences humaines appliquées de l'uni-versité de Bordeaux.

Izard, Françoise. 1965. 'Communication sur la culture samo.' In *Col-loque sur les cultures voltaïques* [Sonchamp, December 6–8]. [See Héritier 1967a.]

Izard, Françoise, and René Bureau. 1966a. 'Le Centre d'Analyse et de Recherche Documentaires pour l'Afrique Noire (Cardan).' *Cahiers d'Etudes Africaines* 6(1): 130–39.

Izard, Françoise. 1966b. 'Unités de comparaison et échantillonnage des cultures.' Colloquium on the means of research in comparative cultural anthropology, 19–22 September 1966. Paris: TS in the Mai-son des Sciences de l'Homme Library. [See Héritier 1992a.]

———. 1967a. 'Communication sur la culture samo' [Héritier 1965]. *Recherches voltaïques*, ed. Guy Le Moal 8: 127–40. Paris-Ouagadou-gou: CNRS-CVRS. Reprinted 2018 in *Françoise Héritier: Cahier de l'Herne n°124*, ed. Salvatore D'Onofrio and Emmanuel Terray, 13–22. Lausanne-Paris: L'Herne. [Hereinafter: ed. D'Onofrio. 2018c.]

Izard, Françoise, Michèle Huart, and Philippe Bonnefond. 1967b. *Bi-bliographie générale de la Haute-Volta, 1956–1965*. Paris: CNRS; Ouagadougou: CVRS.

Izard, Françoise, and Michel Izard. 1968a. 'L'enquête ethno-démographique.' In *Ethnologie générale*, ed. Jean Poirier, 257–87. Paris: Gallimard.

Izard, Françoise. 1968b. 'Remarques sur l'énoncé des interdits matrimoniaux.' *L'Homme* 8(3): 5–21.

———. 1968c. 'Note sur la situation de la documentation en Haute-Volta.' *Notes et documents voltaïques* 1(2): 9–14.

Izard, Françoise, and M. Izard. 1968d. 'L'habitat traditionnel voltaïque.' Ouagadougou: Ministère du plan et des travaux publics, 11–14.

Izard-Héritier, Françoise. 1973a. 'La paix et la pluie: Rapports d'autorité et rapport au sacré chez les Samo.' *L'Homme* 13(3): 121–38.

———. 1973b. 'Univers féminin et destin individuel chez les Samo.' In *La notion de personne en Afrique noire*, ed. Germaine Dieterlen, 108–19. Paris: CNRS.

Héritier, Françoise. 1974. 'Systèmes omaha de parenté et d'alliance: Étude en ordinateur du fonctionnement matrimonial réel d'une société africaine.' In *Genalogical Mathematic*, ed. P.A. Ballonoff, 197–213. Paris-La Haye: Mouton.

———. 1975a. 'L'ordinateur et l'étude du fonctionnement matrimonial d'un système omaha.' In *Les Domaines de la parenté*, ed. Marc Augé, 95–117. Paris: Maspero.

———. 1975b. 'Des cauris et des hommes: Production d'esclaves et accumulation de cauris chez les Samo.' In *L'Esclavage en Afrique précoloniale*, ed. Claude Meillassoux, 477–507. Paris: Maspero.

———. 1976a. 'L'enquête généalogique et le traitement des données.' In *Outils d'enquête et d'analyse anthropologique*, ed. Robert Cresswell and Maurice Godelier, 223–65. Paris: Maspero.

———. 1976b. 'Contribution à la théorie de l'alliance: Comment fonctionnent les systèmes d'alliance omaha?' *Informatique et sciences humaines*, June 29:10–46.

———. 1976c. 'Adolescence et sexualité.' *Le Groupe familial: Adolescence et monde contemporain*, October, 76: 3–12.

———. 1977. 'L'identité samo.' In *L'Identité*, ed. Jean-Marie Benoist and Claude Lévi-Strauss, 51–80. Paris: Grasset.

———. 1978. 'Comment la mort vint aux hommes: Récit étiologique samo.' In *Systèmes de signes: Hommage à Germaine Dieterlen*, 259–69. Paris: Hermann.

———. 1979a. 'Symbolique de l'inceste et de sa prohibition.' In *La Fonction symbolique*, ed. Michel Izard and Pierre Smith, 209–43. Paris: Gallimard. [Translation: 1982. 'The Symbolism of Incest and its Prohibition.' In *Between Belief and Transgression: Structuralist Essays in Religion, History, and Myth*, ed. M. Izard and P. Smith, 152–79. Chicago: University of Chicago Press.]

———. 1979b. 'Fécondité et stérilité: La traduction de ces notions dans le champ idéologique au stade préscientifique.' In *Le Fait féminin*, ed. Eveline Sullerot, 388–96. Paris: Fayard.

———. 1979c. 'Maschile/Femminile.' In *Enciclopedia Einaudi* 8: 797–812. Turin: Einaudi. [Translated as 'Le sang du guerrier et le sang des femmes: Contrôle et appropriation de la fécondité', *Les Cahiers du GRIF* 29: 7–21.]

———. 1981a. 'Le charivari, la mort et la pluie' (lecture given in April 1977). In *Le charivari*, ed. J.-C. Schmitt and Jacques Le Goff, 353–60. Paris: Mouton.

———. 1981b. *L'Exercice de la parenté*. Paris: Seuil-Gallimard.

———. 1981c. 'Le célibat, épouvantail des sociétés primitives' [title given by editor]. *Autrement* 32: 116–23. Modified text in *Masculin/féminin: La Pensée de la différence* as chapter XX and under the title: 'Figure du Célibat: Choix, sacrifice, perversité', 237–51. Paris: Odile Jacob. [Hereinafter: 1996a.]

Héritier, Françoise, and Marc Augé. 1982. 'La génétique sauvage.' *Le Genre humain* 3–4: 127–36.

———. 1984a. 'Stérilité, aridité, sécheresse: Quelques invariants de la pensée symbolique.' In *Le Sens du mal*, ed. M. Augé and Claudine Herzlich, 123–54. Paris: Éditions des Archives contemporaines.

Héritier-Augé, Françoise. 1984b. Leçon inaugurale, chaire d'étude comparée des sociétés africaines (delivered on 25 February 1983). Paris: Collège de France.

———. 1985a. 'La cuisse de Jupiter: Réflexions sur les nouveaux modes de procréation.' *L'Homme* 25(2): 5–22. [Slightly modified text in 1996a: 253–77.]

———. 1985b. 'Don et utilisation de sperme et d'ovocytes. Mères de substitution: Un point de vue fondé sur l'anthropologie sociale.' In *Génétique, procréation et droit*, ed. Nyssen et al., 237–53. Arles: Actes Sud.

———. 1985c. 'L'individu, le biologique et le social.' *Le Débat* 36: 27–32.

———. 1985d. 'Le sperme et le sang: De quelques théories anciennes sur leur genèse et leurs rapports.' *La Nouvelle revue de psychanalyse* 32: 111–22. [1996a: 133–51.] [Translation: 1989. 'Semen and Blood: Some Ancient Theories Concerning their Genesis and Relationship.'

In *Zone 5: Fragments for a History of the Human Body*, ed. Michel Feher, 159–75. New York: Zone Books.]

———. 1985e. 'La leçon des primitifs' [title given by editor]. In *L'Identité française: Colloquium on French Identity*, ed. Club socialiste Espace 89, 56–65. Paris: Éditions Tierce.

———. 1985f. 'Etudes comparée des sociétés africaines.' *Annuaire du Collège de France: Résumé des cours et travaux (1984–1985), 85e année*, 531–50. Paris: Collège de France.

———. 1986. 'Foreword.' In *La Civilisation inca au Cuzco*, Tom R. Zuidema, 7–9. Paris: PUF.

———. 1987a. 'Les logiques du social: Systématiques de parenté et représentations symboliques.' In *Sens et place des connaissances dans la société*, ed. Action Local Bellevue, 123–69. Paris: CNRS.

———. 1987b. 'Ouverture: Mes chers Amis.' In *Vers des sociétés pluriculturelles: Études comparatives et situation en France*, ed. M. Piault, 35–37. Paris: Orstom.

———. 1987c. 'La mauvaise odeur l'a saisi.' *Le Genre humain*, spring, 7–17. [1996a: 153–64.]

———. 1988. 'Nourriture, semence, filiation 2.' *Annuaire du Collège de France: Résumé des cours et travaux (1988–1989), 89e année*, 445–67. Paris: Collège de France.

———. 1989a. 'Parenté, filiation, transmission: présentation.' In *Le Père. Métaphore paternelle et fonctions du père: l'interdit, la filiation, la transmission*, ed. A. Muxel and J.-M. Rennes, 107–15. Paris: Denoël.

———. 1989b. 'Parenté et filiation: Aspects anthropologiques.' *L'Information psychiatrique* 5: 455–68.

———. 1989c. 'D'Aristote aux Inuit: La détermination du sexe et le sens de l'ambiguïté.' Institut Pasteur: 20ème rencontre de Miribel, March 1989. [1996a: 191–205.]

———. 1989d. 'Semen and Blood: Some Ancient Theories Concerning their Genesis and Relationship.' In *Zone 5: Fragments for a History of the Human Body, Part 2.*, ed. Michel Feher, Ramona Naddaff and Nadia Tazi, 159–75. Brooklyn, New York: Zone Books.

———. 1989e. 'Older-Women, Stout-Hearted Women, Women of Substance.' In *Zone 5: Fragments for a History of the Human Body, Part 3.*, ed. M. Feher, R. Naddaff and N. Tazi, 281–99. Brooklyn, New York: Zone Books.

———. 1989f. 'Etude comparée des sociétés africaines.' *Annuaire du Collège de France: Résumé des cours et travaux (1988–1989), 89e année*, 419–21. Paris: College de France.

————. 1990a. 'O destino do homem.' *Hoje e amanha*, October, 130. [French version ed. D'Onofrio, 2018c: 13–22.]

Héritier-Augé, Françoise, and Elisabeth Copet-Rougier, eds. 1990b. *Les Complexités de l'alliance, Vol. I: Les Systèmes semi-complexes*. Montreux: Gordon and Breach.

Héritier-Augé, Françoise. 1990c. 'La femme d'âge mûr dans les sociétés traditionnelles.' In *Journées de techniques avancées en gynécologie, obstétrique et périnatalogie: Fort-de-France, 11–16 janvier 1990*, 157–62. Paris: Arnette.

————. 1991a. 'La valence différentielle des sexes au fondement de la société? Interview by Nicole Echard et Catherine Quiminal.' *Journal des anthropologues* 45: 67–78. Reprinted in *F. Héritier: Une pensée en movement*, from interviews by Salvatore D'Onofrio, 85–98. Paris: Odile Jacob. [Hereinafter: 2009c.]

————. ed. 1991b. *Les Musées de l'éducation nationale, Mission d'étude et de réflexion, rapport au ministre d'État*. (March 1990. Version corrected February 1991.) Compiled with M. Godelier et al. Paris: La Documentation française.

————. 1991c. 'Famille.' In *Dictionnaire de l'ethnologie et de l'anthropologie*, ed. P. Bonte and M. Izard, 273–75. Paris: PUF.

————. 1991d. 'Inceste.' In *Dictionnaire de l'ethnologie et de l'anthropologie*, ed. P. Bonte and M. Izard, 347–49. Paris: PUF.

Héritier-Augé, Françoise, and Elisabeth Copet-Rougier, eds. 1991e. *Les complexités de l'alliance, vol. II: Les Systèmes complexes d'alliance matrimoniale*. Paris: Archives contemporaines.

Héritier-Augé, Françoise. 1991f. 'Etude comparée des sociétés africaines.' *Annuaire du Collège de France, Résumé des cours et travaux (1990–1991), 91e année*, 559–87. Paris: Collège de France.

————. 1992a. 'Unités de comparaison et échantillonnage des cultures.' *Gradhiva* 1: 3–22. [Text slightly modified of F. Izard, 'Unités de comparaison et échantillonnage des cultures.' Colloquium on the means of research in comparative cultural anthropology, 19–22 September 1966. Paris: TS in the Maison des Sciences de l'Homme Library, 34 pages.]

————. 1992b. 'Témoignages: Au laboratoire d'anthropologie sociale.' *Journal des africanistes* 62(2): 243–46.

————. 1992c. 'Etude comparée des sociétés africaines.' *Annuaire du Collège de France, Résumé des cours et travaux (1991–1992), 92e année*, 568–73. Paris: Collège de France.

————. 1992d. 'De la mort et de la naissance des rituels.' *Psychanalystes* 41: 35–45.

————. 1992e. 'Le Corps en morceaux, Moitiés d'hommes, pieds déchaussés et sauteurs à cloche-pied.' *Terrains* 18: 5–14. [1996a: 165–198.]

————. 1992f. 'Où et quand commence une culture?' *CinémAction* 64: 11–23.

Héritier-Augé, Françoise, and Élisabeth Copet-Rougier, eds. 1993a. *Les Complexités de l'alliance, vol. III, Économie, politique et fondements symboliques, Afrique*. Paris and Brussels: Archives contemporaines – Gordon and Breach.

Héritier-Augé, Françoise. 1993b. 'La costruzione dell essere asessuato, la costruzione sociale del genere e le ambiguità dell' identità sessuale.' In *Maschile/femminile: Genere e ruolinella cultura antica*, ed. Maurizio Bettini, 113–39. Roma: Laterza.

————. 1993c. 'Les cultures ne sont pas des mondes absolus. Interview with L. Greilsamer and M. Kajman.' In *Dossiers et documents du Monde*, ed. Grands Entretiens du Monde, 100–1. Paris: Le Monde.

————. 1993d. 'Au-delà de l'inceste. Interview by Véronique Nahoum-Grappe et Marc Lafargue.' *Chimères* 18: 87–106.

————. 1993e. 'Du pouvoir improbable des femmes.' In *Femmes et histoire*, ed. Georges Duby and Michelle Perrot, 113–25. Paris: Plon.

————. 1993f. 'Audition de Madame Françoise Héritier-Augé, Président du Conseil national du sida, accompagnée de Monsieur Alain Sobel, Vice-président du Conseil national du sida. Extrait du procès-verbal de la séance du 10 décembre 1992.' In *Rapport de la commission d'enquête sur l'état des connaissances scientifiques et les actions menées à l'égard de la transmission du sida au cours des dix dernières années en France et à l'étranger, n°3252*. Report submitted to the President of the National Assembly on February 4, 1993, deposit published in the Official Journal 5 February 1993, pp. 240–71. Paris: Assemblée nationale. [See 2013c.]

————. 1994a. 'Choisir ses parents dans la société arabe: la situation à l'avènement de l'islam: Identité de substance et parenté de lait dans le monde arabe.' In *Épouser au plus proche: Inceste, prohibitions et stratégies matrimoniales autour de la Méditerranée*, ed. Pierre Bonte, 149–64. Paris: EHESS.

Héritier, Françoise, Boris Cyrulnik, and Aldo Naouri, eds. 1994b. *De l'inceste*. Paris: Odile Jacob.

————. 1994c. *Les Deux sœurs et leur mère: anthropologie de l'inceste*. Paris: Odile Jacob.

————. 1995a. 'L'amour, la mort: Le sens de la virgule.' In *L'Amour, la mort*, ed. André Durandeau, 93–112. Paris: Harmattan.

Héritier, Françoise, and Elisabeth Copet-Rougier, eds. 1995b. *La Parenté spirituelle*. Paris: Archives contemporaines.

———. 1995c. 'Etude comparé des sociétés africaines.' *Annuaire du Collège de France, Résumé des cours et travaux (1994–1995), 95ᵉ année*, 587–602. Paris: Collège de France.

———. 1995d. 'Sterility, Aridity, Drought.' In *The Meaning of Illness, History and Sociology*, ed. Marc Augé and Claudine Herzlich, 97–112. Luxembourg: Harwood.

———. 1996a. *Masculin/Féminin I: La Pensée de la différence*. Paris: Odile Jacob.

———. ed. 1996b. *De la violence I*. Paris: Odile Jacob.

———. 1996c. 'Réflexions pour nourrir la réflexion.' In *De la violence I.*, ed. Héritier, 11–54. Paris: Odile Jacob.

———. 1997a. 'Anthropologie et psychanalyse: Quelques propos tenus lors de l'assemblée générale de l'AFA du 22 mai 1996.' *Journal des anthropologues* 71: 9–16.

———. 1997b. 'Eclat et facettes.' *L'Homme* 37: 17–20.

———. 1997c. 'Masculin/féminin: La pensée de la différence.' *Bulletin de la Société française de philosophie*, April–June, 2: 35–63.

———. 1997e. 'Les mille et une formes de la famille.' In *Nouveau manuel: Sciences économiques et sociales*, ed. P. Combemale and J.-P. Piriou, 51–53. Paris: La Découverte.

———. 1997f. 'For intérieur: With Olivier Germain-Thomas', Radio Broadcast France Culture, 27 April 1997. Retrieved from https://www.franceculture.fr/emissions/les-nuits-de-france-culture/la-nuit-revee-de-michelle-perrot-39-interieur-francoise-heritier-1ere-diffusion-27041997.

———. 1998a. 'Anthropologie de la ménopause.' In *Stéroïdes, ménopause et approche socio-culturelle*, ed. Claude Sureau, F. Héritier-Augé et al., 11–21. Paris: Elsevier.

———. 1998b. *L'Anthropologie symbolique du corps: Pour un autre structuralisme*. Buenos Aires: Anales de la Academia Nacional de Ciencias de Buenos Aires. [Reprinted in ed. D'Onofrio, 2018c: 23–32.]

———. 1999a. 'La citadelle imprenable.' *Critique* 620–21: 61–83.

———. 1999b. 'L'inceste dans les textes de la Grèce classique et post-classique.' *Métis* IX–X (1994–1995): 99–115.

———. ed. 1999c. *De la violence II*. Paris: Odile Jacob.

———. 1999d. *Two Sisters and their Mother*. Translated by Jeanine Herman. Brooklyn, New York: Zone Books.

———. 1999e. 'Les matrices de l'intolérance et de la violence.' In *De la violence II.*, ed. F. Héritier, 321–43. Paris: Odile Jacob.

Héritier, Françoise et al. 1999f. 'Controverse with C. Dauphin, A. Farge, L. Capdevila, J.-C. Martin, and R.-M. Lagarde on Femmes et violence.' *Le Mouvement social: bulletin trimestriel de l'Institut français d'histoire sociale* 189: 83–111.

Héritier, Françoise. 1999g. 'Denise Paulme-Schaeffner (1909–1998) ou l'histoire d'une volonté.' *Cahiers d'études africaines* 39(1): 5–12.

———. 2000a. 'Articulations et subsistances.' *L'Homme* 40(1–2): 21–38.

———. 2000b. 'A propos de la théorie de l'échange.' *L'Homme* 40 (1–2): 117–22.

———. 2000c. 'Réflexions sur la douleur.' In *L'Ethique de la souffrance*, ed. David Khayat, 104–17. Paris: Le bord de l'eau.

———. 2000d. 'Interview with Jean Birnbaum, l'anthropologie faite femme.' *Le Monde*, 5 October. Retrieved 10 December 2018 from https://www.lemonde.fr/archives/article/2000/10/05/francoise-heritier-l-anthropologie-faite-femme_3714381_1819218.html.

———. 2001a. 'Figure du père: Françoise Héritier, Entretien avec Nathalie de Baudry d'Asson.' *Revue des deux mondes* 5: 16–19.

———. 2001b. 'L'idée de crise adolescente est-elle universelle?' *Neuropsychiatrie de l'enfance et de l'adolescence* 49: 502–11 (Plenary lecture for the French Society for Child and Adolescent Psychiatry Conference, Reims University Hospital, 12–13 May 2000).

———. 2001c. 'Inceste et substance, Œdipe, Allen, les autres et nous.' In *Incestes*, ed. Jacques André, 91–133. Paris: PUF.

———. 2001d. 'L'humain Politique (interview with François Hollande).' *Témoin* 25: 13–46. [2009c: 235–57.]

———. 2001e. 'Christian Geffray (1955–2001).' *L'Homme* 20(4): 7–10.

———. 2001f. 'Modes, Civilisations, Cultures. Interview by Nathalie de Baudry Asson.' *Revue des deux mondes* 7: 27–30.

———. 2001g. 'Mythe: explication et justification du monde.' In *Origine de l'homme, Réalité, mythe, mode*, ed. Yves Coppens, 75–87. Paris: Artcom.

———. 2001h. 'Foreword' to *Mariages, ménages au XVIIIe siècle, Alliances et parentés à Haveluy*, Guy Tassin, i–x. Paris: Harmattan.

———. 2002a. 'Introduction, and Participation à la discussion.' In *Actes du colloque Les Cicatrices. Des plaies pensées?*, ed. Ibéa Atondi and Eloi Ficquet, 7–8 and 5–93. Paris: Ecole des Hautes Etudes en Sciences Sociales.

———. 2002b. 'La transmission du nom revisitée.' *Travail, Genre et Sociétés* 7: 175–79.

———. 2002c. *Masculin-Féminin II: Dissoudre la hiérarchie*. Paris: Odile Jacob.

————. 2003a. 'Foreword' to *Les fabrications possibles et pensables d'un produit humain: Procréation, filiation, institution*, ed. Université catholique de Louvain, 1–34. Louvain: UCL.

————. 2003b. 'Françoise Héritier répond: Controverse autour du livre de Françoise Héritier, *Masculin/féminin II. Dissoudre la hiérarchie*, by Agnès Fine, Pascale Molinier, Sabine Prokhoris, Alice Pechriggl, Marie-Blanche Tahon.' *Travail, Genre et Société* 10: 173–217.

————. 2003c. 'Une anthropologie symbolique du corps.' *Journal des Africanistes* 73(2): 9–24.

Héritier, Françoise, and Margarita Xanthako, eds. 2004a. *Corps et affects*. Paris: Odile Jacob.

Héritier, Françoise. 2004b. 'Regard et anthropologie: Entretien avec Claudine Haroche.' *Communication* 75: 51–111. [2009c: 349–73.]

————. 2004c. 'Un avenir pour le structuralisme'. In *Lévi-Strauss: Cahier de l'Herne 82*, ed. Michel Izard, 409–16. Lausanne-Paris: l'Herne.

————. 2004d. 'Claude Lévi-Strauss: Tristes tropiques.' In *Claude Lévi-Strauss: Tristes tropiques*, 109–10. Paris: Ministère de la Culture, célébrations nationales.

————. 2004e. 'Entretien avec Marc Kirsch.' *La lettre du Collège de France, 11 June*, 31–37. Paris: Collège de France. [2009c: 315–30.]

————. 2004f. 'Les droits des femmes dans la controverses entre universalité des Droits de l'homme et particularité des cultures.' In *Dialogue des cultures et résolution des conflits, les horizons de la paix*, ed. Selim Abou and Joseph Maïla, 101–14. Beyrouth: Presses de l'Université Saint-Joseph.

————. 2004g. 'Questions de parenté: Un parcours.' Lyon, Ecole Normale Supérieure (25 March 2004). Retrieved 2 September 2019 from http://ses.ens-lyon.fr/articles/francoise-heritier-et-questions-de-parente-25385.

————. 2005a. 'Entretien avec Philippe Lazar.' *Diasporiques* 36: 6–13. [2009c: 300–14.]

————. 2005b. 'Un parcours remémoré.' In *Histoires de vie et choix théoriques en sciences sociales: Parcours de femmes*, ed. C. Zaidman and F. Aubert, 117–58. Paris: l'Harmattan.

————. 2005c. 'Entretien: Parcours de recherche. Interview by Muriel Rouyer.' In *Raisons politiques*, November, 113–48.

————. ed. 2005d. *Hommes, femmes: La construction de la différence*. Paris: le Pommier.

————. 2005e. 'Âges de la vie, générations, seuils ct passages: ici et ailleurs.' In *Générations*, Marie-Blanche Tahon and André Tremblay, 157–79. Québec: Nota Bene.

————.2005f. 'Homosexual Marriage and Parenthood. Interview with Students from the Institut des Sciences Politiques.' Retrieved 29 April 2021 from http://sciencespo2005.free.fr/qui_sommes_nous.php.

————. 2006. 'A voix nue: Conversation with Caroline Broué.' [Broadcast on France-Culture, 19 to 23 June 2006 then broadcast again from 20 to 24 November 2017 and recorded on tapes by myself.] https://www.franceculture.fr/emissions/a-voix-nue/etienne-daho-15-premiers-jours-du-reste-de-ta-vie.

————. 2007a. 'Foreword' to *Cendrillon en Afrique: Ordre et désordre dans les sociétés d'Afrique noire*, Denise Paulme, 9–19. Paris: Galade.

————. 2007b. 'Foreword' to *Qui épouser et comment? Alliance récurrentes à Haveluy de 1701 à 1870*, Guy Tassin, I–XII. Paris: l'Harmattan.

————. 2007c. 'Foreword' to *Sexe, croyances et ménopause*, Daniel Delanoë, 2–7. Paris: Hachette.

————. 2007d. 'Les femmes ont déjà le pouvoir.' *Libération*, 10 April 2007. Retrieved 8 February 2019 from https://www.liberation.fr/cahier-special/2007/04/10/les-femmes-ont-deja-le-pouvoir_89987.

————. 2007e. 'Est-on prêt à donner le pouvoir aux femmes?' *Le Monde*, 2 February 2007. Retrieved 10 December 2018 from https://www.lemonde.fr/societe/article/2007/02/02/est-on-pret-a-donner-le-pouvoir-aux-femmes_862824_3224.

Héritier, Françoise et al. 2007f. 'Tribune: Vaincre Sarkozy, maintenant: L'ensemble de la gauche doit penser au second tour et ne pas se tromper d'ennemi.' *Libération*, 12 February 2007. Retrieved 8 February 2019 from https://www.liberation.fr/france/2007/02/12/vaincre-sarkozy-maintenant_84613.

Héritier, Françoise. 2007g. 'La domination masculine est encore partout: Entretien avec E. Lanez.' *Le Point*, 29 November. Retrieved 21 April 2021 from http://1libertaire.free.fr/FHeritier05.html.

————. 2008a. 'Entretien.' *La lettre du Collège de France*, 20 November, 9–15. Paris: Collège de France.

————. 2008b. 'Il était beau, grand, brun, les cheveux coiffés en arrière, un peu ondulés, avec un beau regard.' In *Le premier homme de ma vie: Onze femmes racontent leur père*, ed. Olivia Benhamou, 175–92. Paris: Laffont.

————. 2008c. 'Saisir l'insaisissable et le transmettre.' *L'Homme* 48(1–3): 45–54.

————. 2008d. *Françoise Héritier, la pensée de la différence*. Documentary film with Françoise Héritier by Teri Wehn-Damisch, France 5/Cinétévé/CNRS Images.

———. 2008e. 'Lévi-Strauss, l'anthropologie structuraliste.' In *Lévi-Strauss: L'Homme derrière l'oeuvre*, ed. Emilie Joulia, 57–75. Paris: Lattès.

———. 2008f. 'Pourquoi je suis structuraliste. Interview by Nicolas Journet.' *Science humaines* 8: 82–85.

———. 2008g. 'Interview à l'occasion du centenaire de Claude Lévi-Strauss (no date).' Paris: Canal Académie. Retrieved 8 June 2018 from https://www.canalacademies.com/emissions/en-habit-vert/levi-strauss-par-francoise-heritier-son-successeur-au-college-de-france.

———. 2008h. 'Françoise Héritier.' In *Comment je suis devenue ethnologue*, ed. Anne Dhoquois, 149–66. Paris: Le Cavalier bleu.

———. 2009a. Lecture: 'Un parcours de vie et de recherches.' 14 November 2009. Institut Emilie du Chatelet, as part of the series 'Forty Years of Research on Women, Sex and Gender'. Paris: National Museum of Natural History. Retrieved 2 December 2018 from http://www.institutemilieduchatelet.org/visualisation-la-video?id_video=63.

———. 2009b. 'Françoise Héritier et Chantal Thomas, deux passionnées de l'intelligence.' *Télérama*, 31 July. Retrieved 8 May 2018 from https://www.telerama.fr/idees/francoise-heritier-et-chantal-thomas-deux-passionnees-de-l-intelligence,45643.php.

———. 2009c. *F. Héritier: Une pensée en mouvement* [from interviews edited by Salvatore D'Onofrio]. Paris: Odile Jacob.

———. 2009d. 'Cl. Lévi-Strauss, un passeur exceptionnel: Remarks collected by Jean Birnbaum.' *Le Monde*, 4 November 2009. [Reprinted in ed. D'Onofrio 2018c: 204–5.]

———. 2009e. 'La filiation, état social.' *Le Monde*, 19–20 April, p.14. [D'Onofrio 2018c: 202–3.]

———. 2010a. *Retour aux sources*. Paris: Galilée.

———. 2010b. 'De la tendresse humaine.' *L'Homme* 50(1): 17–22.

———. 2010c. 'Le droit à l'enfant n'existe pas, interview by Claire Chartier and Vincent Olivier.' In *L'Express*, 25 February. Retrieved 8 May 2018 from https://www.lexpress.fr/actualite/societe/francoise-heritier-le-droit-a-l-enfant-n-existe-pas_850975.html.

———. 2010d. 'Pourquoi le handicap est-il discriminant.' In *L'éternel singulier: Questions autour du handicap*, ed. F. Héritier et al., 100–20. Bordeaux: Le Bord de l'eau.

———. 2010e. 'C. Lévi-Strauss: L'anthropologue et l'ethnologue français du xxe siècle.' *Mondes et Cultures: Compte-rendu annuel des tra-*

vaux de l'Académie des sciences d'Outre-mer, part LXX, vol. 1. Les Séances, 5 February 2010. 70–74. Paris: Académie des sciences d'Outre-mer.

————. 2010f. 'Les droits des femmes dans la controverse entre universalité des Droits de l'Homme et particularité des Cultures.' In *Diversité culturelle et universalité des Droits de l'Homme*, ed. Jean-Loup Amselle and F. Héritier, 19–40. Nantes: Céline Defaut.

————. 2010g. 'Un parcours de vie et de recherche.' In *Une anthropologue dans la cité*, ed. Marie-Blanche Tahon, 171–205. Outremont, Québec: Athena.

————. 2010h. 'Un homme que j'ai beaucoup aimé.' In *Le Monde spéciale édition: Claude Lévi-Strauss, Une vie, une œuvre*, ed. Le Monde, 84–89. Paris: Le Monde.

————. 2010i. 'Hommage à Claude Lévi-Strauss 1908–2009.' *Rayonnement du CNRS*, February, 53: 65–66.

————. 2010j. 'L'œuvre de Lévi-Strauss, une philosophie globale du sens à donner au monde.' *Totem: Journal du Musée d'Ethnographie de Genève* 56: 20–21.

————. 2010k.'Tribune: Ferme ta bouche, t'es sans-papiers.' *Libération*, 26 January. Retrieved 8 February 2019 from https://www.liberation .fr/societe/2010/01/26/ferme-ta-bouche-t-es-sans-papiers_606293.

————. 2010l. 'Sur la question des procréations médicalement assistées et de la gestation pour autrui.' Comité bioéthique de l'Assemblée nationale, 30 juin [Hearing of the National Assembly's Bioethics Committee, 30 June. Paris: National Assembly]. Paris: Assemblée nationale.

————. 2010m. *La différence des sexes explique-t-elle leur inégalité?* Paris: Bayard.

————. 2010n. 'Entretien avec Françoise Héritier, anthropologue.' In *La Fabrique des filles*, ed. Laure Mistral, 213–31. Paris: Syros, Amnesty International.

————. 2010o. 'Prochaine étape, partager le travail ménager.' *Ouest-France*, 4 June. Retrieved 8 May 2018 from https://www.ouest-fra nce.fr/europe/france/ouest-france-fete-son-20-000e-numero-612583.

————. 2010p. 'Un changement radical dans l'histoire de l'humanité se produit sous nos yeux: Conversation with Violaine Montclos.'*Le Point*, 18 March. Retrieved on 29 April 2021 from the site of http:// claradoc.gpa.free.fr.

————. 2010q. 'Homme et femme, pas le même cerveau? Conversation between C. Vidal and Fr. Héritier.' Director: Sylvie Allonneau.

Paris: Palais de la découverte et la Cité des sciences et de l'industrie, 28 mn 25. [Broadcast 8 December 2010 universcience then on radio France Culture 21 June 2017 – wrongly put as 2015 on France Culture site.] Retrieved 30 April 2019 from https://www.franceculture.fr/conferences/palais-de-la-decouverte-et-cite-des-sciences-et-de-lindustrie/homme-et-femme-pas-le-meme.

———. 2011a. 'Michel Cartry: Memoriam.' *Journal des* Africanistes 81(1): 151–54.

———. 2011b. 'À l'aube de l'humanité.' In *La plus belle histoire des femmes*, ed. F. Héritier, Michelle Perrot, Sylvia Agacinski and Nicole Bacharan, 19–76. Paris: Le Seuil.

———. 2011c. 'Y a-t-il des constantes de l'imaginaire autour de la vie et de la mort?' In *Nouvelles formes de vie et de mortune* médecine entre rêve et réalité, ed. Danièle Brun, 89–97. Paris: Études freudiennes.

———. 2011d. *La Femme en Majesté: Oeuvres de Michael Bastow*. Exhibition at the Forêt Verte Gallery, 8 March. Paris: Philias.

———. 2011e. 'Présentation: Trois leçons japonaises de Claude Lévi-Strauss' [Lévi-Strauss book from 2010.]. *Europe: Revue littéraire*, Janvier–Février 2013. 1005–1006: 65–70. [Signed from 2011.]

———. 2011f. 'De la paternité certaine à la maternité variable.' In *Humain: Une enquête philosophique sur ces révolutions qui changent nos vies*, ed. M. Atlan and R.-P. Droit, 267–74. Paris: Flammarion.

———. 2011g. 'La seule espèce où les mâles tuent les femelles.' In *Ces yeux qui te regardent et la nuit et le jour: Regards sur la violence faite aux femmes*, ed. F. Héritier and Nadia Kaci. [2011g: 21–38].

———. 2011h. 'Interview on Radio suisse Romande. La Première', 29 May 2011. Radio broadcast. Retrieved June 2018 from https://www.rts.ch/play/radio/comme-il-vous-plaira/audio/franoise-heritier-anthropologue?id=3628300&expandDescription=true.

———. 2011i. 'Rencontre avec Patrice De Méritens.' *Le Figaro*, 4 July 2011. Retrieved 9 June 2019 from https://www.lefigaro.fr/lefigaro magazine/2011/07/02/01006-20110702ARTFIG00566-l-affaire-dsk-a-montre-que-les-femmes-ont-encore-un-statut-inferieur.php.

———. 2012a. *Le Sel de la vie*. Paris: Odile Jacob.

———. 2012b. 'M. Guéant est relativiste. Interview by Nicolas Truong.' *Le Monde*, 12–13 February, 206–10. [Reprinted in D'Onofrio ed., 206–10, 2018c.]

———. 2012c. 'L'égalité des sexes, le premier des combats.' In *Manifeste pour l'*égalité, ed. Lilian Thuram, 70–77. Paris: Éditions Autrement.

———. 2012d. 'La notion de bien commun forge une collectivité.' *Grand Paris*, 3 July, 10–11.

———. 2012e. 'Pour être content de soi, il faut oser y aller. Interview with Hélène Fresnel.' *Psychologie Magazine*, June, 319: 133–36.

———. 2013a. 'Autour du mariage des couples de personnes du même sexe.' Paris: Sénat, audition par la Commission des Lois, 5 February 2013. Retrieved in 2019 from https://www.youtube.com/watch?v=WiagxyPjdkQ.

———. 2013b. *Le rapport frère-sœur, pierre de touche de la parenté, Conférence Eugène Fleischmann n°6* [10 May 2010]. Nanterre: Société d'ethnologie.

———. 2013c. *Sida, un défi anthropologique.* [Texts edited by S. D'Onofrio.] Paris: Les Belles lettres.

———. 2013d. *Le Goût des mots.* Paris: Odile Jacob.

———. 2013e. 'Grand et petite: Une question d'ethnologie' (16 January 2013). Director: V. Kleiner. Point du Jour, CNRS Images. Retrieved March 2019 from https://www.dailymotion.com/video/x69h4d4.

———. 2013f. 'L'ethnologie en héritage séries: Françoise Héritier.' Directors: Gille Le Mao and Alain Morel. Paris: Ministère de la Culture (DVD).

———. 2015a. 'Précédé d'un entretien avec Françoise Héritier.' In *Rouge Sang: Crimes et sentiments en Grèce et à Rome*, ed. Lydie Bodiou and Véronique Mehl, vii–xxiv. Paris: Les Belles lettres.

———. 2015b. 'Entretien avec Françoise Héritier, avec Tomoko Hihana, Vitalia Kholkina et Laura Rocco.' In Revue du Mauss, Le Journal du Mauss, 28 January 2015. Retrieved 10 May 2019 from www.journaldumauss.net/?Entretien-avec-Francoise-Heritier.

———. 2016a. 'Pour la création d'un TPI en RDC.' 2 minutes. www.50-50magazine.fr. Retrieved 10 May 2018 from https://www.youtube.com/watch?v=hFvqIdG3wAg.

———. 2016b. *Conversations avec Françoise Héritier.* Director Patric Jean. Paris: Black Moon Production. [DVD box set.]

———. 2017a. 'Un choc esthétique pour prendre conscience de l'horreur de la guerre. Interview à propos du livre, Déflagrations.' *L'Humanité*, 10 November. Retrieved 22 July 1918 from https://www.youtube.com/watch?v=bzibcJ6_Vm4.

———. 2017b. *Au gré des jours.* Paris: Odile Jacob.

———. 2017c. 'Foreword: Emmanuel Terray l'insurgé.' In *Mes anges gardiens*, Emmanuel Terray, 5–16. Paris: Seuil.

———. 2017d. 'L'action vers l'égalité des hommes et des femmes.' In *Pour changer de civilisation*, ed. Martine Aubry with 50 fifty researchers and citizens, 213–30. Paris: Odile Jacob.

————. 2017e. Radio interview, 'Françoise Héritier, l'activiste', by Laure Adler, France-Inter, 'L'heure bleue', 30 May. 42'16. Retrieved 5 December 2018 from https://www.franceinter.fr/emissions/l-he ure-bleue/l-heure-bleue-30-mai-2017.

————. 2017f. 'Entretien du 12 novembre 2017 avec Pierre Vavasseur.' *Le Parisien*, 15 November 2017. Retrieved 9 February 2019 from https://www.leparisien.fr/culture-loisirs/livres/a-84-ans-l-anthro pologue-francoise-heritier-souffle-la-vie-12-11-2017-7387383.php.

————. 2017g. 'Matière à penser. Les Discussions du soir: l'universel féminin. Entretien avec Frédéric Worms.' France-Culture, 13 February 2017. Retrieved 10 February 2019 from https://www.france culture.fr/emissions/les-discussions-du-soir-avec-frederic-worms/ francoise-heritier-luniversel-feminin.

————. 2017h. 'Boomerang: Hériter de Françoise Héritier. Conversation with A. Trapenard.' France-Inter, 23 October 2017. Retrieved 10 June 2018 from https://www.franceinter.fr/emissions/boomerang/ boomerang-23-octobre-2017.

————. 2017i. 'Il faut anéantir l'idée d'un désir masculin irrépressible, interview A. Cojean.' *Le Monde*, 5 November 2017. Retrieved 30 April 2021 from https://www.lemonde.fr/societe/article/2017/11 /05/francoise-heritier-j-ai-toujours-dit-a-mes-etudiantes-osez-fonc ez_5210397_3224.html.

REFERENCES

● ● ●

Adler, Alfred. 2010. 'Michel Cartry (1931–2008).' *L'Homme* 195–196: 483–96.

———. 2014. 'Souvenirs et réflexions: Petits fragments. Michel Izard, l'État en Afrique noire et Hegel.' *Journal des africanistes* 84(2): 230–41.

Allard, Michel et al. 1963. *Analyse conceptuelle du Coran sur cartes perforées.* 2 Vols. Paris-La Haye: Mouton.

Bailly, Francis. 1987. 'Foreword' in ed. F. Bailly, 1987. *Sens et place des connaissances dans la société*, 8–19. Paris: Éditions du CNRS.

Barnard, Alain, 1982. 'Review of *L'exercice de la parenté* by Françoise Héritier.' *Man* 17(4): 792.

Barnes, Robert H. 1976. 'Dispersed Alliance and the Prohibition of Marriage, Reconsideration of McKinley's Explanation of Crow-Omaha Terminologies.' *Man* 11(3): 384–99.

———. 1982. 'Kinship Exercises.' *Culture* 2(2): 113–18.

———. 1992. 'Review of *Les complexités de l'alliance: Les systèmes semi-complexes*', ed. F. Heritier-Augéand Elisabeth Copet-Rougier, *Man* 27(1): 212. [Héritier 1990b.]

Beattie, John. 1960. *Bunyoro: An African Kingdom*. New York: Holt, Rinehart and Winston.

Cai, Hua. 1997. *Une société sans père ni mari: Les Na de Chine*. Paris: PUF.

Cartry, Michel. 1968. 'La calebasse de l'excision en pays gourmantché.' *Journal de la Société des Africanistes* 38(2): 189–226.

Clastre, Pierre. 1962. 'Échange et pouvoir: philosophie de la chefferie indienne.' *L'Homme* 2(1): 51–65.

Collard, Chantal. 2000. 'Femmes échangées, femmes échangistes: À propos de la théorie de l'alliance de Claude Lévi-Strauss.' *L'Homme* 40: 101–16.

Condominas, Georges, and Simone Dreyfus-Gamelon, eds. 1979. *L'Anthropologie en France: situation actuelle et avenir*. Paris: CNRS.

Daniel, Defert. 2014. 'Hors-champs: Interview with Laure Adler.' Radio Broadcast, France Culture, 20 October. Retrieved 22 December 2020 from https://www.franceculture.fr/emissions/hors-champs/daniel-defert.

Delaisi De Parseval, Geneviève. 2017. 'Au gré des jours. Tome ultime.' *Libération*, 15 November. Retrieved 8 February 2019 from https://next.liberation.fr/livres/2017/11/15/au-gre-des-jours-tome-ultime_1610347/.

D'Onofrio, Salvatore. 2009. 'La structure dans les choses.' In *Une pensée en movement: Françoise Héritier*, ed. S. D'Onofrio, 401–17. Paris: Odile Jacob. [see Héritier 2009c.]

———. 2018a. 'Françoise Héritier ou l'éthique par la méthode.' *L'Homme* 58: 7–14.

———. 2018b. 'Un hommage à Françoise Héritier.' Fondation Maison des Sciences de l'homme/Palimpsest. Retrieved 26 January 2019 from http://www. ameriquelatine.msh-paris.fr/spip.php?article 916.

D'Onofrio, Salvatore, and Emmanuel Terray, eds. 2018c. *Françoise Héritier: Cahier de l'Herne n°124*. Lausanne-Paris: L'Herne.

Dosse, François. 1991. *Histoire du structuralisme*. Paris: La Découverte.

Douglas, Mary. 1967. 'If the Dogon.' *Cahiers d'Etudes Africaines* 7(4): 659–72.

Drucker-Brown, Suzan. 2000. 'Germaine Dieterlen and Meyer Fortes.' *The Cambridge Journal of Anthropology* 22(2): 50–59.

Dupaigne, Bernard. 2006. *Le scandale des arts premiers: La véritable histoire du musée du quai Branly*. Paris: Mille et une nuits.

———. 2017. *Histoire du Musée de l'Homme: De la naissance à la maturité (1880–1972)*. Paris: Sépia.

———. 2018. *Musée de l'Homme II, Guerres et Paix (1972–2015)*. Paris: Sépia.

Durkheim, Emile. 1898. 'La prohibition de l'inceste et ses origines.' *L'Année Sociologique* 1: 1–70.

Elwin, Verrier. 1947. *The Muria and their Ghotul*. Oxford: Oxford University Press.

Etienne, Pierre. 1975. 'Les interdictions de mariage chez les Baoulé.' *L'Homme* 15(3–4): 5–29.

Evans-Pritchard, E.E., and M. Fortes (eds). 1940). *African Political Systems*. Oxford: Oxford University Press.

Faure, Sonya, and Cécile Daumas. 2017. 'Disparition, Françoise Héritier, corps et âme.' *Libération*, 15 November. Retrieved 8 February 2019 from https://www.liberation.fr/debats/2017/11/15/francoise-heritier-corps-et-ame_1610348/.

Favret-Saada, Jeanne. 2008. 'Jeanne Favret-Saada.' In *Comment je suis devenu ethnologue*, ed. Anne Dhocquois. Paris: Le Cavalier bleu.

Gaillard, Gérald. 1989. 'Chronique de la recherche ethnologique dans son rapport au Centre National de la Recherche Scientifique 1925–1980.' *Cahiers pour l'Histoire du C.N.R.S.*3: 85–126.

———. 1990. *Cadres institutionnels et activités de l'ethnologie française entre 1950 et 1970*. Paris: CNRS. Retrieved from https://hal.arch ives-ouvertes.fr/hal-01245125.

———. (as Gaillard-Starzmann). 2006. 'Regarding the Front National.' In *Neo-Nationalism in Europe and Beyond: Perspectives from Social Anthropology*, ed. Andre Gingrich and Marcus Banks, 177–96. New York and Oxford: Berghahn.

———. 2017. 'Georges Balandier (1920–2016).' *Modern Africa* 5(1): 5–25.

———. 2018. 'Jacques Lombard (1926–2017): French Africanist of the Third Generation.' *Modern Africa* 5(2): 6–27.

Gardin, Jean-Claude. 1955. 'Problèmes de documentation.' *Diogène* 11: 107–24.

———. 1974. *Les analyses de discours*. Neuchâtel: Delachaux et Niestlé.

Gaudemar, Antoine de. 2009. 'Claude Lévi-Strauss, un déraciné chronique.' *Libération*, 3 November. Retrieved 8 February 2019 from https://next.liberation.fr/culture/2009/11/03/levi-strauss-un-derac ine-chronique_591675.

Geertz, Clifford. 1989. *Works and Lives: The Anthropologist as Author*. Cambridge: Polity Press.

Godelier, Maurice. 2004. *Métamorphoses de la parenté*. Paris: Fayard.

———. 2007. Lecture on 10 November 2007 as part of 'Forty Years of Research on Women and Gender series. Institut Emilie du Châtelet. Paris: National Museum of Natural History. Retrieved 11 November 2018 from https://www.youtube.com/watch?v=frouIjk9new.

Herrenschmidt, Olivier. 1966. *Le cycle de Lingal: essai d'*étude textuelle de mythologies*: Les mythologies des tribus de langue gondi (Inde Centrale)*. Paris: Ecole Pratique des Hautes Etudes.

———. 2014. 'Les commencements . . . et après.' *Journal des africanistes* 84(2): 222–29.

Hopkins, Keith. 1994. 'Le mariage frère-sœur en Égypte romaine.' In Épouser au plus proche*: Inceste, prohibitions et stratégies matrimoniales autour de la Méditerranée*, ed. Pierre Bonte, 79–95. Paris: Ecole des Hautes Etudes en Sciences Sociales.

Izard, Michel: see Izard [Héritier], Françoise. 1958a, 1958b, 1959, 1968a, 1968d.

———. 1966. 'Mission chez les Mossi du Yatenga.' *L'Homme* 6(1): 118–20.

———. 1968. 'Le second congrès international des africanistes (Dakar, 11–20 Décembre 1967).' *Notes et documents voltaïques* 1(2): 14–19.

———. 1970. 'Introduction à l'histoire des royaumes mossi.' PhD thesis published in 1970 as issues no. 12 and 13 of *Recherches voltaïques*.

———. 'Les archives orales d'un royaume africain: Recherches sur la formation du Yatenga.' Doctorat d'Etat, Université René Descartes-Paris V, 1980, 5 vols.

Izard, Michel, and Pierre Smith, eds. 1979. *La Fonction symbolique*. Paris: Gallimard.

Izard, Michel. 1982. 'L'anthropologie et les recherches en sciences sociales dans le tiers monde.' In *Les sciences de l'homme et de la société en France: Analyse et propositions pour une politique nouvelle*, ed. M. Godelier, 123–45. Paris: Ministère de la Recherche et de l'Industrie.

———. ed. 2004. *Lévi-Strauss, Cahier de l'Herne n° 82*. Paris-Lausanne: L'Herne.

Jamard, Jean-Luc, Emmanuel Terray, and Margarita Xanthakou, eds. 2000. *En Substances: Textes pour Françoise Héritier*. Paris: Fayard.

Jaulin, Robert, and Solange Pinton. 1973. *Gens du soi, gens de l'autre*, 10–18. Paris: Union générale d'éditions.

Kabore, Oger. 1992. 'Marcel Poussi-Le précurseur.' *Eurêka* n°3. Publication Trimestrielle du CNRST- Education et développement (Documents du Burkina Faso, October 1992, 20 p. Ouagadougou: Quarterly CNRST publication, October). Retrieved 23 March 2019 from http://www.nzdl.org/cgi-bin/library?e=d-00000-00---off-0tu lane--00-0----0-10-0---0---0direct-10---4-------0-0l--11-en-50---20 -about---00-0-1-00-0--4----0-0-11-10-0utfZz-8-10&cl=CL2.6.1 &d=HASH565353645e031e7700a7b2.5.2&x=1.

Kawada, Junzo. 2017. 'Trialogues pour Georges Balandier: Un Comtois serein et dynamique.' *Cahiers d'Etudes Africaines* 17(4): 1079–99.

Leach, Edmund. 1961a. 'Structural Contrasts between Symmetric and Asymmetric Marriage Systems: A Fallacy.' *Southwestern Journal of Anthropology* 20: 218–27.

———. [1951]1961b. 'The Structural Implications of Matrilateral Cross-Cousin Marriage.' *Rethinking Anthropology* 54–104. London, Athlone Press.

Lebrun, Jean. 2018. 'Interview by Johanna Bedeau: Notre guerre, les années sida.' Radio broadcast, 21 October, France-Culture (3/5). Retrieved 21 October 2018 from https://www.franceculture.fr/ emissions/a-voix-nue/jean-lebrun-35-notre-guerre-les-annees-sida.

Lévi-Strauss, Claude. 1955. 'Des Indiens et leur ethnographe.' *Les Temps Modernes* 116: 1–50.

———. 1956. 'The Family.' In *Man, Culture and Society*, ed. H.L. Shapiro, 261–85. Oxford University Press. [1983 French translation in *Le regard éloigné*, 90–9. Paris: Plon.]

———. 1958. *Anthropologie Structurale*. Paris: Plon.

———. 1959. 'Le problème des relations de parenté.' In *Système de parenté: entretiens interdisciplinaires sur les sociétés musulmane*s, 13–20. Paris: École des Haute Études, section des sciences économiques et sociales.

———. 1962. *La Pensée Sauvage*. Paris: Plon. [*Wild Thought*. A new Translation by Jeffrey Mehlman and John Leavitt. University of Chicago Press, 2021.]

———. 1965. 'The Future of Kinship Studies: The Huxley Memorial Lecture 1965.' In *Proceedings of the Royal Anthropological Institute of Great Britain and Ireland for 1965*, 13–22.

———. 1967. 'Foreword.' To the second edition of *Les structures élémentaires de la parenté* (1948). Paris: Mouton, xxiv–xxx. [A reissue was carried out in 2017 with a foreword by Emmanuel Désveaux and a bibliography previously absent. Paris: Maison des Sciences de l'Homme.]

———. 1970. *Mythologiques IV: L'Homme nu*. Paris: Plon. [English translation: *The Naked Man*. New York: Harper and Row, 1981.]

———. 1973a. *Anthropologie structurale II*. Paris: Plon.

———. 1973b. 'Réflexions sur l'atome de parenté.' *L'Homme* 13(3): 5–30.

———. 1983. *Le regard éloigné*. Paris: Plon. [English translation *The View from Afar*. Basic Books, 1985.]

———. 1997. 'Quei patenti cosìar caici.'*La Repubblica*, 24 December, 40–41. In 2004, the article was translated into French as 'Le Retour de l'oncle maternel. In *Lévi-Strauss, Cahier de L'Herne*, ed. Michel Izard, 37–40. Paris-Lausanne: L'Herne.

———. 2008[1996 and 2001]. 'La leçon de sagesse des vaches folles.' *La lettre du Collège de France*, 48–50. Retrieved 19 September 2018 from https://journals.openedition.org/lettre-cdf/226.

———. 2018a. *Roman Jakobson et Lévi-Strauss: Correspondance (1942–1982)*. Paris: Seuil.

———. 2018b. 'Lettre à Françoise Héritier du 5 avril 1994.' In *Françoise Héritier, Cahier de l'Herne n°124*, ed. S. D'Onofrio and E. Terray, 221–27. Lausanne-Paris: L'Herne.

Murdock, George Peter. [1949]1965. *Social Structure*. New York: Macmillan.

Murphy, Robert, and Leo Kasdan. 1959. 'The Structure of Parallel Cousin Marriage.' *American anthropologist* 61(1): 17–29.

Nahoum-Grappe, Véronique. 2018. 'Un jour, un cours.' In *Françoise Héritier, Cahier de l'Hernen° 124*, ed. S. D'Onofrio and E. Terray, 187–90. Lausanne-Paris: L'Herne.

Needham, Rodney. 1962. *Structure and Sentiment: A Test Case in Social Anthropology*. Chicago: Chicago University Press.

———. ed. 1970.*Rethinking Kinship and Marriage*. London: Tavistock.

Pairault, Claude. 2001. *Portrait d'un jésuite en anthropologue. Entretiens avec Jean Benoist*. Paris: Karthala.

Perrot, Michelle etal. 1986. 'Culture et pouvoir des femmes: essai d'historiographie.' *Annales* 41(2): 271–93. [Translated in the *Journal of Women's History* (1989) and in *Writing Women's History: International Perspectives* (1991).]

———. 2000. 'La présidence.' In *En Substances: Textes pour Françoise Héritier*, ed. J-L. Jamard et al., 537–47. Paris: Fayard.

Piault, Marc, ed. 1987. *Vers des sociétés pluriculturelles: Études comparatives et situation en France*. Paris: Éditions de l'Orstom [Retrieved from https://horizon.documentation.ird.fr/exl-doc/pleins_textes/divers4/23682.pdf.]

Radcliffe-Brown, Alfred Regis. [1940, 1952]1965. 'The Study of Kinship Systems: Presidential Address.' *The Journal of the Royal Anthropological Institute* 71(1/2): 1–18. [Reprinted in *Structure and Function in Primitive Society*. Glencoe: The Free Press, 49–70.]

Rouget, Gilbert. 2011. 'In Memoriam, Michel Cartry (1931–2008).' *Journal des Africanistes* 81(1): 149–50.

Schneider, David. 1976. 'The Meaning of Incest.' *Journal of the Polynesian Society: Incest Prohibitions in Micronesia and Polynesia*, ed. Judith Huntsman and M. McLean 85(2): 149–71.

———. 1984. *A Critique of the Study of Kinship*. University of Michigan Press.

Tahon, Marie-Blanche, ed. 2010.*Une Anthropologue dans la Cité: Autour de Françoise Héritier*. Québec: Athena.

Terray, Emmanuel. 1986. 'Sur l'exercice de la parenté.'*Annales* 41(2): 259–70.

———. 1987. 'Ouverture: Précision.' In *Vers des sociétés pluriculturelles: Études comparatives et situation en France*, ed. M. Piault, 39–42. Paris: Orstom.

Terray, Emmanuel, and Salvatore D'Onofrio, eds. 2018: see D'Onofrio, Salvatore, 2018.

Touraille, Priscille. 2008. *Hommes grands, femmes petites: une évolution coûteuse: Les régimes de genre comme force sélective de l'adaptation biologique*. Paris: MSH.

Vincent, Joan. 1990. *Anthropology and Politics: Visions, Traditions, and Trends*. Tucson: University Arizona.

Wehn-Damisch, Teri. 2008. *Françoise Héritier, la pensée de la différence*. Paris: film/France 5/Cinétévé/CNRS Images.

Xanthakou, Margarita. 2000: See Jamard, Jean-Luc, 2000.

INDEX

Soares, Mário, 86–87
sorcerers, 36, 43
Soustelle, Jacques, 4, 8, 119
Stahl, Paul-Henri, 100
Staude, Willem, 30
sterility, 58–59, 74, 78, 138–139. *See also* cold/hot (concept)
Stresser-Péan, Guy, 8
Sullerot, Evelyne, 58

Tabah, Léon, 98
Tahon, Marie-Blanche, 119
Taraud, Cristelle, 119
Tardits, Claude, 8, 44, 68, 73
Taylor, Anne-Christine, 110
Tazi, Nadia, 91
Terray, Emmanuel, 16, 39, 41, 67, 85, 107–109, 120, 123, 128–129
Thébaud, Françoise, 106
Thomas, Dylan, 125
Thomas, Louis-Vincent, 41, 68, 120
Thought, 21, 43–44, 51, 70, 84, 86, 116, 130, 132, 136, 139, 141–142, 158, 161
Touraille, Priscille, 120–121, 124
Tremblay, Pierre-André, 119

universities: Bordeaux, 10; Collège de France, 13, 15, 55, 68–125 passim, 147, 161; Ecole des Hautes Etudes en Sciences Sociales (EHESS), 62, 74, 81, 83, 109, 125; Ecole normale supérieure (ENS), 15, 23; Ecole Pratique des Hautes Études (EPHE), 6, 13–20 passim, 27–35

passim, 43, 62, 73, Florianópolis, 110; Institut d'Etudes Politique, 15, 112, 148; Mirail, 105; Mohammed V, 119; New School for Social Research in NewYork, 4; Ottawa, 119; Palermo, 74, 112; Provence, 105; Rio de Janeiro, 110; Paraná, 110; Paris, 110; São-Paulo, 111; Sorbonne, 3–4, 131, 161; Strasbourg, 4, 42; United Nations in Tokyo, 111, 118; Vincennes, 41

Verdier, Yvonne, 52
Vernant, Jean-Pierre, 74, 85
Verstraeten, Pierre, 69
Vidal, Catherine, 121, 124, 144–145
Veil, Simone, 42
Vincent, Joan, 3
violence, 61, 63, 69, 96, 106, 108, 111–112, 129–130, 145, 154
Vrignaud, Dominique, 98

Wehn-Damisch, 62, 91, 124, 131
Wenders, Wim, 125
White, Douglas, 92
Wiesel, Elie, 128

Xanthakou, Margarita, 109, 115

Yaméogo, Maurice, 19, 36
Yourcenar, Marguerite, 69

Zahan, Dominique, 30
Zonabend, Françoise, 5, 52, 96
Zuidema, Reiner Tom, 93